SEMANTIC ANALYSIS

SEMANTIC ANALYSIS

Paul Ziff

CORNELL UNIVERSITY PRESS

Ithaca and London

P
3 25
,2 5

First published 1960 by Cornell University Press.
Published in the United Kingdom by Cornell University Press Ltd., 2-4 Brook Street, London W1Y 1AA.

Fourth printing 1964
First printing, Cornell Paperbacks, 1967
Second printing 1978

International Standard Book Number (paper) 0-8014-9051-0
Printed in the United States of America

For Max Black

PREFACE

SOME years ago while working on a manuscript in aesthetics I thought it would be helpful to say at least roughly what the phrase 'good painting' means in English. And so I tried to say. But then I began to wonder whut had led me to say what I did, particularly in light of the fact that what I had said appeared to be contrary to re- ceived opinion. I then wrote what is essentially the concluding Part VI of this essay. But having done that, I was still troubled by ques- tions of confirmation: Why should anyone believe what I said? What made me think it was so? And so I worked back and back to the be- ginning of this essay.

What I have to say is of interest to me. I suppose it will be of some interest to some others. But I have never given serious thought to such matters. I have been seriously concerned with this: that what I say be so, or true, or right, or correct, and so forth. So I have tried not to say what is not so, or what is false, or not true, or untrue, or incorrect, and so forth. I do not believe that I have succeeded. I have found something wrong every time I have gone over this essay: the induction is depressing.

Although I have been concerned not to say what is not so, I have not been over concerned not to be misleading. I believe that if one writes precisely one is nowadays bound to mislead many. It seems that nowadays hardly anyone pays any attention to what a man says, only to what one thinks he means. But virtually no such exegesis, virtually no such interpretation, virtually no such construal, is called for here. If I say what is stupid, do not say "What he must have meant is such-and-such": I almost certainly meant what I said and if it was stupid then I was being stupid at the time whether I meant what I said or not. But since I believe that hardly any words have exact synonyms in English, I have tried to choose my words carefully. And since I believe that it is difficult to construct or to hit upon exactly synonymous constructions in English, I have tried to use words carefully. For example, the question I begin with is 'What does the word 'good' mean?': to ask this question is not the same as asking 'What is the meaning of the word 'good'?'. I have no objection to the latter question, but it is not the question I raised; neither is it the question I asked, in the rhetorical sense of 'asked' appropriate in an essay of this sort. Again, the question 'What meaning does the word 'good' have in English?' or what is different, 'What meaning does the word 'good' have?', is not the question that I raised. And of course I did not raise such questions as 'What is the sense of the word 'good'?', 'What is the significance of the word 'good'?', 'Is the word 'good' meaningful?'.

I am afraid that writing in this way makes demands on the reader. For it is an unfortunate fact that the clarity of the logical relations between the various things said in the course of an essay tends to vary inversely to the precision of what is said. Thus, for example, even though in the first paragraph of Section 2 the question evidently is 'What does the word 'good' mean?', in the second paragraph of that section I say I want to answer the question 'What does the word 'good' mean in English?': I expect the reader to see that a different question is now in question. I have not tried to explain why the question has been shifted, in part because I believe the reason why is obvious enough in context. But the main reason is that one simply cannot explain each shift, each qualification, and so forth, and still expect a reader to follow the argument. For example, I occasionally shift from one expression to another even though I do not think that the two expressions are synonymous if the fact that they are not synonymous makes no difference to the truth of what is said and to the point at issue. Thus on occasion I have said something using the word 'untrue' and then continued using the word 'false'.

Contrary to the general practice of philosophers concerned with questions of language, I have not begun by changing the subject. I am concerned with a natural spoken language, English, and not with a sign system, not with a code, not with a calculus. And contrary to the prevailing practice of philosophers, I adhere to or try to adhere to every distinction that speakers of my English dialect generally make in talking about or in saying something pertaining to words. It is often said that natural languages are horribly confused and so there is no sense in paying attention to such distinctions. I think that that is a silly thing to say. A natural language like American English has the form it has owing to the actions and reactions and interactions of millions of speakers over hundreds of years. In the mouths of these speakers the language has been modified, altered, varied, and endlessly refined, to serve the multitudinous purposes that any natural language serves. Philosophers who claim to find confusion in a natural language generally seem to me to introduce the confusion they claim to find.

It is necessary to say something about my use of quotation marks. I enclose an expression in single quotes when I wish to say something about the expression, as e.g. I am concerned with the word 'good'. I use punctuation marks within single quotes to indicate intonation contours; e.g. the utterance 'Can he go.' has an assertive contour despite the fact that the syntactic form of the utterance is that of an interrogative. Owing to this special use of punctuation marks some sentences in the text may seem to have extra punctuation; e.g. consider the utterance 'That is good.'. Here the punctuation mark within the single quotes indicates an intonation contour while the mark outside the quotes is the genuine punctuation for the sentence beginning with the word 'owing'. Punctuation marks within double quotes have no special significance. I enclose an expression in double quotes when it is either a genuine, an imagined, or a rhetorical quotation, when I wish to draw attention to an expression that I am using, or when I am using an expression both to say something about the expression and to say something about something else; e.g. we do not speak of something "meeting with our approval" except in a special sort of case.

Finally, I should like to point out that on occasion I employ certain types of metonyms. For example, I say I am concerned with the question 'What does the word 'good' mean?'. Strictly speaking, 'What does the word 'good' mean?' is not a question. It is not even an interrogative utterance for it is not an utterance at all. It is an inscription of a type that is associated in a certain way with an interrogative utterance. The question I am actually concerned with is one that could be asked by uttering the interrogative utterance associated with the inscription in some appropriate way and in some appropriate context of utterance. Consequently my remark that I am concerned with the question 'What does the word 'good' mean?' is metonymical.

I am indebted to many people, more than I can possibly mention here. In recent years I have profited from discussions with R. Firth, J. L. Austin, and H. D. Aiken. But I am chiefly indebted to N. Chomsky, H. Putnam, and I. H. Stadler for suggestions, criticisms, and corrections. I also wish to express my appreciation for a grant from the Rockefeller Foundation that enabled me to begin this essay.

PAUL ZIFF

The University of Pennsylvania
February 1960

CONTENTS

SEMANTIC ANALYSIS

Miracula sine doctrina nihil valent

I

LANGUAGE

1. What does the word 'good' mean? I want to answer this question not because the answer matters but because answering it does. This essay is a discussion of metatheoretic questions in the philosophy of language.

The word 'good' is not important. It is useful, not indispensable. One can say whatever one wants to say without using it. This would entail only loss of brevity: what can be said and what can be said briefly are not the same. It is not even difficult to say what 'good' means. Only 'true' in the trinity of "The True, The Good, and The Beautiful" offers difficulties because it is a metalinguistic term: 'true' and 'meaning' are hard words. But 'good' is a good example for the purposes of a methodological investigation: just about anything you like has been said ·about this word.

2. My question is not an old question asked by Heraclitus. It could not have been asked before 401 A.D., perhaps the birth century of the English language. In asking 'What does the word 'good' mean?' I am asking something about a certain word of English: Aristotle could not have asked this question.

I want to answer the question 'What does the word 'good' mean in English?'. To ask it is to begin at the beginning *in medias res:* there is nowhere else. But it is necessary to look around.

3. I am concerned with 'good' and that is to say a great deal. The word can be phonetically rendered as [gʊd]. The phonetic sequence [gʊd] may be uttered in the course of speaking various

languages, and, what is more, an utterance of it may constitute an utterance of some word other than the English word 'good'. Since I am not concerned with all utterances of the phonetic sequence [gʊd] but only those that constitute an utterance of the English word 'good', it is necessary to specify the relevant utterances.

Am I inventing problems for myself? One can say which utterances of [gʊd] are not relevant and which are, viz. those that constitute an utterance of the English word 'good'. To say "those that constitute an utterance of the English word 'good' " is to specify the relevant utterances in a way that one can understand. But it is not as simple as that.

The question can be shifted slightly: possibly the phonetic sequence [gʊd] is uttered in the course of speaking various languages. The relevant utterances of [gʊd] are primarily those uttered in utterances of the English language: which ones are they?

I would avoid generality if I could but I cannot and that I cannot will be clear but only very much later.

4.   Figuratively speaking, a language is determined by the memories, habits, dispositions, tendencies, and the like of its native speakers. It takes its locus in their collective larynx and ear. It is defined only by the utterances that can be uttered without deviation from certain regularities. Utterances that have been and are actually being uttered are tangents and of tangential importance: if everyone were silent or deaf for a moment English would not be a dead language.

Yet what can be said is not independent of what has been and is being said. What is meant by speaking of "utterances that can be uttered without deviation from certain regularities" will become clear later: we are *in medias res*.

5.   I shall not be concerned with the fact that many languages are written as well as spoken. Not all of the world's languages have or had or even will have an associated writing system. It is possible that by ignoring written language one may be led to a distorted conception of spoken language but it is unlikely.

There is at least one striking difference. The written sentence unlike the spoken utterance is an enduring element, the parts of which coexist simultaneously for a certain time: the written word is fixed fast, not held loosely in mind. (See 132 below.[1]) The greater stability and regularity of written as opposed to spoken language may stem from this fact; the existence of algebraic and logistic systems depends on it.

There are other differences between a spoken language and an associated written language but they are largely derivative from the difference noted. The use of words in Mallarmé's *Un coup de dés*, or in some of e. e. cummings' poems, can be found only in graphic systems. Such peculiarities do not matter: they are only variations on familiar themes, a combination of graphic and phonetic forms. The sequence of sentences constituting a lengthy novel is not likely to be matched by any sequence of utterances. Novels are not like poems characteristically read aloud. But stories are told, speeches made, lectures given: any linguistically interesting features of a long sequence of sentences (other than those dependent on memory) are likely to be found in the spoken language as well. A greater dialectal variation is found in spoken than in written English. But this is a difference in degree only: William Barnes wrote in the Dorset dialect and Faulkner writes in some American English dialect while Joyce, as it were, coined his own. And so on.

6. Consider a tentative set of native speakers where membership in the set is determined by reference to mutual intelligibility and to cultural and geographical factors. We could say that English utterances are primarily those uttered by such speakers. That would have its difficulties.

It is difficult to separate language and culture areas or to discriminate cultural features without attention to linguistic features. Presumably this can be done to an extent sufficient to enable us to isolate and then ignore American Indian groups to be found within the prescribed geographical limits of the language area in question. But the criterion of mutual intel-

---

[1] All cross references in the text are to sections.

ligibility leads to a more serious difficulty. A Yorkshireman and a man from Alabama count as native English speakers: some such pair would not understand one another. If we were to consider regions in Africa where Bantu is spoken, we could find villages w, x, y, all of which are classed as Bantu-speaking, while village z is not so classed, yet w speakers understand x speakers, who in turn understand y speakers, who in turn understand non-Bantu z speakers, but w speakers do not understand y speakers.

A further criterion could be introduced here, viz. that the speech of the various speakers exhibit common elements. The difficulties remain. There are important phonetic and syntactic variations throughout the language area we are concerned with. 'The children wull soon have noo pleäce vor to plaÿ in.' is an utterance of the Dorset dialect but not of New England American English.

These difficulties exist only if one supposes, which I do not, that speaking English is a definite and specifiable activity. Is 'wull' an English word? The phonetic sequence is frequently uttered in the course of speaking in the Dorset dialect, not in New England American English. If we say that 'I wull.' is an English utterance because it is an utterance of Dorset and 'Ahm goan.' (i.e. 'I'm going.') is an English utterance because it is an utterance of dialects in southeastern United States, we shall be describing a language that no one speaks: apart from special contexts, such a pair of utterances is not likely to be uttered by a single speaker.

7. Various moves are possible here. One wants to insist that both 'I wull.' and 'Ahm goan.' are in some sense utterances of one and the same language. Since we can hardly deny that such a pair of utterances is not likely to be uttered by any one speaker except in very special contexts, we should have to say that we are describing the language not of a single speaker but of several speakers. But this would not enable us to deny the fact that we should then be describing a language that no one person speaks: the language described would be spoken only

by that monster the average man who may have 2 and ⅔ children and ⁶⁄₇ of a cat.

The usual unprofitable move is to say we are concerned with "Standard English." Neither utterances of the Dorset dialect nor utterances of the dialects in southeastern United States are classed as "Standard English." What sort of utterances are?

Apparently such utterances as 'You was wrong.' and 'He don't believe it.' are not, in spite of the fact that they are uttered by millions of American speakers, in spite of the fact that the procedures of present-day descriptive (synchronic) linguistics indicate that 'was' and 'were' are morphemically identical in the environment 'You . . . wrong.', the differences between them being simply free variations owing to differences in dialect.

What is wrong with 'You was wrong.' is its style: to say this is to mark oneself a member of the masses. 'You was wrong.' is objectionable on what might be called "ritualistic" but not grammatical grounds. Every language has taboo expressions. Names, divine or otherwise, are frequently taboo: "Thou shalt not take the Lord's name in vain" and "I am he who is," while a Cree Indian will not utter his sister's name, out of respect he says. Certain expressions pertaining to excrement or to sexual functions are largely taboo in English. 'You was wrong.' is taboo for a certain class of speakers. Theologies, grammars, and philosophies have been erected on such bases.

"Standard English" appears to be what the "right" people speak or what one learns at a private school. I am not here concerned with it: it is impossible to give a nontrivial specification of anything to be so called. Consequently I am not concerned with what might be referred to as "the meaning of 'good' in Standard English." I have no objection to speaking of "proper English" or "Standard English" but not seriously in philosophy.

8. A natural language is sensibly thought of as a set of dialects where membership in the set is more or less vaguely determined on the basis of various family resemblances. To say that the relevant utterances of [gʊd] are primarily those uttered in utterances of the English language is then a loose way of saying

that the relevant utterances are primarily those uttered in the course of speaking any of the various English dialects.

To deal with the question 'What does the word 'good' mean in the English language?' it would be necessary either to give an answer that holds true for every English dialect or to deny that 'good' has a unique meaning in the English language. For it is conceivable that the word linguistically associated with the phonetic sequence [gʊd] in one English dialect has one meaning while the word linguistically associated with that sequence in another English dialect has another meaning. In either case, to deal with the question it would be necessary to consider every English dialect, in so far as any clear sense can be found for (or given to) the phrase 'every English dialect'.

This conclusion may seem somewhat skeptical. It is the vogue nowadays in philosophy to talk about what is not English, the chief charge of the current inquisition being "a misuse of English." But the difficulty of establishing such claims cannot sensibly be denied. If this is a skeptical position then skepticism is unavoidable.

9.   I shall not deal with the question 'What does the word 'good' mean in the English language?'. Once one has dealt with the question 'What does the word 'good' mean?' with respect to a particular English dialect, no new metatheoretic problems arise in extending the procedures employed to the various other English dialects. But for the same reason I shall not deal with the question 'What does the word 'good' mean in New England American English?'.

The problems that arise in attempting to specify English also arise in attempting to specify a particular dialect of English. Just as English is sensibly thought of as a set of dialects, so a particular dialect is sensibly thought of as a set of idiolects where an idiolect is the speech of a single person. To deal with the question 'What does the word 'good' mean in New England American English?' it would be necessary to consider every idiolect of the dialect in question, a tedious and, from a theoretical point of view, unprofitable task.

10. But I shall not consider the question 'What does the word 'good' mean in my idiolect?'. My reasons for not doing so are heuristic rather than theoretic. Despite the fact that concern with an idiolect has been criticised by certain linguists, there is in principle no reason not to be so concerned; for example it has been said:

'Idiolect' is the homogeneous object of description reduced to its logical extreme, and, in a sense, to absurdity. If we agree with de Saussure that the task of general linguistics is to describe all the linguistic systems of the world,[2] and if description could proceed only one idiolect at a time, then the task of structural linguistics would not only be inexhaustible (which might be sad but true), but its results would be trivial and hardly worth the effort.[3]

As against this, there is no reason to suppose that an idiolect is a "homogeneous object" (see 24 below). All that is guaranteed is that in describing an idiolect one is describing a language that at least one person speaks. The answer to the charge of triviality is to be found in de Saussure's own discussion. A language "is not a function of a speaking subject"; it is a "social product" that the individual reflects more or less passively.[4] An investigation of the relatively general features of a particular idiolect is inevitably an investigation of the relatively specific features of a particular dialect, and this in turn is an investigation of the specific features of a particular language.

There would be certain advantages in restricting attention here to a single idiolect. It might help dispel the widespread illusion that any useful and significant inquiry about language must be primarily statistical. That is not true. I speak a language and my language can sensibly be investigated without recourse to statistics. Statistical data derived from an investigation of an idiolect are not likely to be of much linguistic interest. The utterance 'Communication theoretic models of a natural language are wonderfully illuminating.' has never before

[2] F. de Saussure, *Cours de linguistique générale*, p. 20.
[3] U. Weinreich, "Is a Structural Dialectology Possible?" in *Linguistics Today*, p. 269.
[4] *Op. cit.*, p. 30.

been uttered by me. I am not likely to utter it again. That fact is of no linguistic significance. (See 27 below.)

I shall not be concerned exclusively with a single idiolect simply because there is no need to be that specific. Possibly there are important differences between the word linguistically associated with [gʊd] in one idiolect or in one dialect and that in another. It is also possible that there are not. So I shall talk in a general way and say that I am concerned with what the word 'good' means in English without specifying either a particular English dialect or idiolect. I shall be more specific only when there is need to be so. In so far as I am truthful and accurate, what I have to say will at the worst be true of at least one English idiolect, viz. my own.

That I shall proceed in this general way may seem perverse. It suggests that what I have to say will not be subject to disconfirmation. If I say " 'Good' means thus-and-thus in English" and it be objected "No, that is not so," then it seems to be open to me to say "That is what 'good' means in my idiolect and I ought to know." But that is not so. That I say " 'Good' means thus-and-thus in English" doesn't matter. That you reply "Yes, that is what I think too" doesn't matter either. We may both be right, and then again we may not. It is not enough merely to say that 'good' means thus-and-thus in English. What is wanted here is confirmation of some sort. Thus the means and the method of confirmation must be indicated.

Given that such-and-such are the facts about 'good' in the language or dialect or idiolect in question, then, on that basis, 'good' in that language or dialect or idiolect can be said to mean thus-and-thus. That such-and-such be the facts about 'good' depends on the language or dialect or idiolect in question. If it is my idiolect, I am perhaps apt to know the facts about it in a way that you are not. But if these are the facts about 'good' then that 'good' means thus-and-thus does not depend on and is not peculiar to the language or dialect or idiolect in question. The speaker of the idiolect is not in a privileged position here: one is not likely to be though one may be mistaken about the facts about 'good' in one's own idiolect. But that one appreciates these facts is another matter.

11.   Consider (some unspecified set of) native speakers of English. It might be said that the relevant utterances of [gʊd] are primarily those uttered in utterances uttered by such speakers. That will not do: not every utterance of [gʊd] by native English speakers can sensibly be said to constitute an utterance of the word 'good': [gʊd] is uttered in uttering 'Mr. Goodyear is here.'.

That the phonetic sequence [gʊd] uttered in uttering 'Mr. Goodyear is here.' cannot sensibly be said to constitute an utterance of the word 'good' is intuitively clear, but an intuition is not an argument. (I shall frequently appeal to what is intuitively clear, to my intuitions about various matters. I trust my intuitions: I do not ask you to trust them. My appeal to intuition need not be misunderstood. I may open a case on the grounds of intuition: I do not rest the case on the grounds of intuition. If I did so I would have no case. An intuition poses a question, not an answer. And an answer to the question renders an appeal to intuition superfluous.) There are procedures available that render the appeal to intuition superfluous in determining whether or not the word 'good' is uttered in uttering 'Mr. Goodyear is here.'.

The phonetic sequence [gʊd] uttered in uttering 'Mr. Goodyear is here.' need not be linguistically associated with 'good'. One way of seeing that is by seeing that the phonetic sequence does not constitute a distinct "morphemic segment" of that utterance according to at least one procedure of morphological analysis. It is uttered simply in the course of uttering the name 'Goodyear': it need not be ascribed an independent status. On the other hand, the phonetic sequence [gʊd] uttered in uttering 'The goodness of the man was apparent.' does constitute a distinct morphemic segment of that utterance according to at least one procedure of morphological analysis. This can be seen without attending to what (if anything) the elements in question may mean or without attending to what (if any) meaning the elements in question may have. The particular segment constituted by the phonetic sequence [gʊd] of the utterance 'The goodness of the man was apparent.' can be established as a distinct morphemic segment on the grounds of distribution, thus on the basis of the fact that various other distinct and contrasting phonetic sequences are uttered in precisely the same (linguistic) environment. Thus 'The goodness of the man was apparent.' can be matched with 'The ruthlessness of the man was apparent.', 'The gentleness of the man was apparent.', 'The sweetness of the man was apparent.', and so on. Since virtually no such matchings can be found in connection with the phonetic sequence [gʊd] uttered in uttering 'Mr. Goodyear is here.', [gʊd] need not be said to constitute a distinct morphemic segment of the utterance, in so far as one is concerned simply with questions of distribution.

That not every utterance of the phonetic sequence [gʊd] need be linguistically associated with 'good' indicates that a linguistic and in particular some type of morphological analysis of the utterances in question is called for. More significantly, this means that it is necessary to specify the utterances in some way. A linguistic analysis (of the kind indicated) can be performed only on a corpus of utterances, and so it is necessary to specify the relevant corpus.

12.   A person's speech can be analyzed in various ways and at various levels of analysis so as to yield elements of different types. At one level of analysis we find utterances, or in contrast with utterance parts, whole utterances. An utterance is here taken to be a stretch of a person's talk; a whole utterance is a stretch of a person's talk bounded by silence at both ends. Every utterance is constituted of certain linguistic elements. By the phrase 'linguistic elements' I mean to refer to the various constituents of a language according to various modes of analysis. Phonemes, morphemes, words, phrases, utterances, and the like are elements. Every utterance is constituted of at least two morphological elements.

Some utterances consist of a single word, e.g. 'Fire!', 'Perhaps.'. But every utterance, whether of one or more words, also has an intonation contour; (using italics or punctuation marks within quote marks to indicate the position of the stresses and changes in tone) 'No!', 'No?', '*That* is a good painting.', 'That *is* a good painting.', are different utterances. An intonation con-

tour evidently cannot be linguistically associated with any particular segment of an utterance and is thus a suprasegmental
morphological element. (The use of italics or punctuation marks
is perhaps a crude device for indicating intonation contours
since it fails to distinguish between tone and stress or between
primary stress, secondary stress, and so forth, but it will do
for my purposes. I do not want to exploit these distinctions: I
want to remind you of their existence.[5])

If no specific contour is indicated in the text, as in 'That is
a good painting.', or in 'a good apple', it is to be assumed that
the utterance or part of an utterance represented has any normal
contour consistent with the lack of specific indices; if no stops
are indicated, a contour of the sort associated with stops is
precluded, thus 'an apple good' is not to be construed as 'An
apple? Good!'.

Every utterance of more than one word is constituted of at
least three morphological elements, namely the words, the intonation contour, and the word order; 'That is a good painting.'
and 'Is that a good painting.' are different utterances.

13. 'That is a good painting.' is both a whole utterance and a
sentence. But not every whole utterance is a sentence; 'No.', 'If
you like.', 'John!', 'Yes.', are whole utterances but not sentences.
They are what are sometimes called "incomplete sentences."

Neither is every single sentence a single whole utterance. 'It
looks as if there is a glass on the table, if you look at it in the
right way.': this may be one sentence but it is nonetheless a
sequence of two whole utterances. (I can give no account of what
counts as a single sentence. But that will be of no importance:
the spoken whole utterance and not the written sentence is the
significant unit of analysis here.)

'It looks as if there is a glass on the table' and 'If you look at

---

[5] For more sophisticated methods of indicating intonation contours see
R. Wells, "The Pitch Phonemes of English," *Language*, XXI (1945), 27–39;
K. L. Pike, *The Intonation of American English*. But also see N. Chomsky,
M. Halle, and F. Lukoff, "On Accent and Juncture in English," *For
Roman Jakobson*, pp. 65–80.

it in the right way' are two whole utterances in that when uttered they, or relevantly similar utterances, are generally preceded and followed by silence. Although 'There is a glass on the table.' is a whole utterance, it has not been uttered here: the proper utterance part 'there is a glass on the table' differs in intonation contour from the whole utterance. But more significantly, 'it looks as if' is obviously a proper utterance part in that when it is uttered it is not likely to be preceded and followed by silence. Consequently we count it as a proper part of the utterance 'It looks as if there is a glass on the table' and therefore we cannot here count 'there is a glass on the table' as a single whole utterance. There is a slight difference in intonation contour between 'It looks as if there is a glass on the table,' and 'It looks as if there is a glass on the table.' but the difference is not marked enough to demand being taken into account here.

14.   The words 'utterance', 'sentence', 'word', and the like have what are called "type-token" ambiguities: 'A cow.' and 'A cow.' may be counted as either one or two utterances. We can say that 'A cow.' uttered at one time and 'A cow.' uttered at another time belong to one and the same utterance type, are two utterance tokens of the one utterance type. To talk about an utterance type is (on occasion) to discount certain differences between utterance tokens, differences deemed irrelevant, and treat them as one and the same. (But see 52 ff. below.) I shall not in general try to eliminate these ambiguities by explicitly stating which sense is intended. Sometimes both senses are intended, sometimes not. In general the context is sufficient to indicate what is meant. I shall be more specific only when there is need to be so: if everything had to be spelled out, nothing could be said.[6]

---

[6] There are problems in connection with type-token distinctions that I do not propose to discuss, e.g. 'A COW' and 'a cow' in one sense are and in one sense are not tokens of the same type. There are various ways of drawing type-token distinctions and different ways yield different senses of 'type' and 'token'.

15. A corpus of utterances can be analyzed at various levels so as to yield elements of different types. At the crudest level of analysis we find whole utterances. At the opposite extreme, at the level of syntax, we encounter such familiar elements as subjects, predicates, noun phrases.

I shall assume that some sort of syntactic analysis of the corpus we shall eventually be concerned with has been given and that the procedures whereby it is given are not in question. (The enormity of this fiction will become clear or clearer later.) More specifically, I shall assume an analysis of the corpus that yields imperative utterances, interrogative utterances, declarative utterances, and so on as elements as well as syntactic subjects, predicates, noun phrases, and so on.

16. At another level of analysis, so-called "morphological analysis," a corpus yields a set of elements called "morphemes." [7]

(It is necessary to say something here about the procedures of morphological analysis. For the sake of definiteness and concreteness, I shall give a very brief, rough, and very crude sketch of such matters. But I wish to insist, and that emphatically, that the metatheoretic statements made in the course of this essay are not based on and do not express or reveal or in any way indicate a commitment to any particular or specific form of linguistic analysis. I have been speaking of various levels of analysis. But I would not suggest that any type of linguistic analysis at a single level, thus an analysis restricted to elements of a single type, is likely to be altogether adequate to the purposes of such an analysis. I choose to give simple examples dealing with relatively simple questions of distribution simply because such examples are easy to provide, easy to understand, and obviously do not involve questions of meaning. But linguistic structure is deep as a well. There is reason to suppose that highly abstract procedures of analysis are called for, procedures that would involve a simultaneous consideration of various types

[7] For a detailed account of morphological analysis see Z. Harris, *Methods in Structural Linguistics;* E. A. Nida, *Morphology.*

of elements at different levels of analysis; I am inclined to suppose that such procedures would yield results in far greater accordance with one's basic intuitions about matters of linguistic structure.[8])

In so far as simple questions of distribution are concerned, a morphological analysis may be thought of as divided into two stages. First, a particular corpus of utterances is segmented so as to yield a set of morphemic segments; the utterance parts 'in', 'good', 'in-', '-ing', '-ed', '-er', and the like are morphemic segments. Roughly speaking, as indicated above, a particular segment, i.e. an utterance part, is established as a morphemic segment on the basis of matching (linguistic) environments; since we find that an utterance of 'good' can be paired off with utterances of 'new', 'old', etc., in the environment 'That is a . . . book.', this particular segment of the utterance 'That is a good book.' is a morphemic segment. (However, the segment 'to' of the utterance 'I want to go.' is also a morphemic segment even though this utterance of 'to' cannot be so paired off. That it is a morphemic segment may be established derivatively on the basis of the fact that 'I', 'want', and 'go' are morphemic segments.)

Secondly, certain elements, usually called "allomorphs" (but also called "morpheme alternants"), are associated with the morphemic segments yielded in the first stage of analysis. Allomorphs may be said to occur over the associated morphemic segments. Allomorphs are associated with and sets of allomorphs may be said to constitute single elements called "morphemes"; the prefixes 'in-' and 'im-' are both allomorphs of a single morpheme.[9] The plural morpheme includes such allomorphs as

[8] For similar views see Nida, *op. cit.*, pp. 2–3; N. Chomsky, *Syntactic Structures*, pp. 49–60.

[9] It must be noted that many linguists characterize morphemes in terms of meaning. Thus C. F. Hockett writes: *"Morphemes are the smallest individually meaningful elements in the utterances of a language"* (*A Course in Modern Linguistics*, p. 123). Oddly enough, Hockett somewhat later remarks: "Some morphemes . . . serve not directly as carriers of meanings, but only as markers of the structural relationships between other forms" (p. 153). For a characterization of morphemes without any appeal

'-s' (in 'books') and '-en' (in 'oxen'). The criteria for grouping allomorphs into sets are exceedingly complex and shall not be discussed here. But roughly speaking, allomorphs are grouped into sets in such a way as to yield a simple, compact, and in some sense illuminating account of the distribution of the morpheme in the corpus, i.e. its occurrence in various (linguistic) environments found in the corpus; both '-s' and '-en' are uttered in plural forms: 'Where are the cows?' and 'Where are the oxen?', not 'Where is the cows?' and not 'Where is the oxen?'.

A morphological analysis of a single utterance is possible only on the basis of or in connection with other utterances of a corpus. And this is true no matter what procedures of morphological analysis may be employed, no matter whether they be simple distributional procedures or highly abstract multilevel procedures. There is nothing internal to the utterance considered in isolation that will allow us to establish a particular segment of it as a morphemic segment. The importance of this point in the analysis of meaning can hardly be exaggerated. It follows that if we cannot establish that the word 'good' is uttered in the utterance 'That is a good painting.' without comparing that utterance with or relating it to other utterances in the corpus, we cannot establish that the word 'good' means such-and-such in that utterance without comparing the utterance with or relating it to other utterances on the basis of which or in connection with which the morphological identity of 'good' was established. (The precise significance of this point will be seen later.)

17. Let H^* be the set of utterances that have actually been uttered by native English speakers. We have no way of knowing

---

to meaning see Harris, *op. cit.*, pp. 20 ff. Since Harris' procedures of distributional analysis clearly do not involve questions of meaning, and since his procedures evidently do yield a morphological analysis of a corpus, they may be taken as a basis for the morphological statements made in the course of this essay. Whether or not such procedures are wholly adequate for the purposes of linguistic analysis is essentially irrelevant here, at least for the time being.

what the membership of H^* is. At best, we can know only some proper subset of H^*. (I am using the word 'proper' in its logical sense such that a is a proper part of b if and only if a is a part of b and b is not a part of a. I am not talking of correctness or propriety.)

Let H be the proper subset of H^* that we know of, i.e. the set of utterances or parts of utterances that we remember, or that we recall having been uttered, or that there are available records of, and so forth. (Much of what I have to say about or in connection with utterances strictly applies to utterances or parts of utterances but for the sake of brevity I shall frequently omit the qualification 'or parts of utterances'.)

H may be too limited for the purposes of morphological analysis. For example, I know that the utterance of [gʊd] in 'That is a good atomic pistol.' can be paired off with the utterance of a different phonetic sequence in precisely the same environment, for one can say without being ungrammatical 'That is a heavy atomic pistol.'. That such pairs can be found indicates that [gʊd] is a morphemic segment of the utterance in question, and this fact can eventually lead us to associate an element that we speak of and refer to as "the word 'good' " with this particular utterance of [gʊd]. But it is possible that the utterance 'That is a good atomic pistol.' be unique in the corpus H in that no phonetic sequence other than [gʊd] occurs in the environment 'That is a . . . atomic pistol.' and that there are no variants of the utterance: only 'that' occurs in the environment '. . . is a good atomic pistol.', only 'is' occurs in the environment 'That . . . a good atomic pistol.', and so on. Thus it might not be possible to establish on distributional grounds that [gʊd] is a morphemic segment of the utterance in question and is to be associated with 'good'.

Furthermore, I eventually want to talk about what 'good' means and not merely about what it meant. H may be too limited for that purpose. Even H^* may be too limited even to allow one to formulate an adequate account of what a word meant. H^* is constituted solely of utterances that happen to have been uttered. The persons who uttered the utterances of

H* did not utter all that they could have uttered without deviating from certain regularities to be found in or in connection with their language. Consequently many facets of a word's meaning may not be indicated in the corpus; 'faerie' occurs in Spenser's *Faerie Queene,* but neither that text nor the other recorded uses of the word are sufficient to enable one to say exactly what the word meant. *H** provides a rear view of the language, the traces it is leaving: we shall be wanting a better view.

18. One can elicit certain utterances from an informant that it would be natural for the informant to utter in certain situations: such elicited utterances constitute a natural extension of *H.* I shall refer to the set of utterances or parts of utterances composed of *H* together with their natural extensions as '*E*' (where the letter is intended to suggest but only suggest "English today").

Consider utterance (1):

(1) There is a purple gila monster on my lap blinking at me.

Here (1) is an utterance of *E* but perhaps not of *H.* How do I know that it is an utterance of *E?*

At this point it is necessary to betray a split personality for I must disentangle myself as an analyst concerned with the language linguistically associated with *H* from myself as a native speaker of the language linguistically associated with *H:* I am my own informant. As an analyst I can relate (1) to *H* by eliciting it from a native speaker. This means that "in effect, we try to provide a speaker with an environment in which he could say that utterance—if he ever would naturally say it—without extracting it from him if he wouldn't." [10] The environment is the linguistic and not the physical environment: gila monsters are nasty little beasts and there are no purple ones anyway. Furthermore, if we succeeded in eliciting (1) from a speaker in the appropriate physical environment, (1) would simply be an utterance of *H* (and not of *E* less *H*).

[10] Z. Harris, "Distributional Structure," in *Linguistics Today,* p. 41.

Since I am my own informant here, I have no serious problems about eliciting utterances from myself. I as an analyst know what I as a speaker would say naturally and what I would not. I must take care not to deceive myself but that is no problem for me or at any rate it does not trouble me. Thus as an analyst I can easily elicit (1) from myself as an informant. Therefore (1) is an utterance of E where E is a natural extension of H.

If I am asked "How do you know that you would naturally say (1)?", as an analyst I can only say that I elicited (1) from an informant. It appeared to come quite naturally, smoothly: I did not, as it were, extract it. Hence I see no reason not to accept it as a datum. One can usually check with other informants but conceivably in connection with some American Indian languages this might not in fact be possible. Since the utterance does not occur in corpus H there would still be the problem of eliciting it from these other informants should there happen to be any. But as a native speaker of the language linguistically associated with H, I need not answer such a question: I as informant do not claim to know that I would naturally say (1).

19.   That I am an adequate informant for the purposes of studying English may certainly be called into question. I have some doubts about the matter myself. I am a native speaker of English. But I am inclined to suppose that reflecting on the use of words tends to alter one's use of words. So it is possible that certain distinctions now to be found in my idiolect were not to be found prior to my preoccupation with the structure of language. Whether or not this is in fact the case I find difficult to say. But even if it is the case, I do not believe that it is of any great metatheoretic importance. For example, there is a distinction to be found in my idiolect between a word's having meaning in English and a word's having a meaning in English. Whether such a distinction was to be found prior to my linguistic studies I cannot say. I think it was but I can find no evidence to support that contention. Furthermore, I have been assured by other speakers of my dialect that no such distinction is to be found in their idiolects. (That they say on being queried that no

such distinction is to be found does not of course guarantee that no such distinction is to be found. But from what I have been able to observe, I am inclined to accept their contention as correct.) Consequently, the idiolects of such speakers may differ from mine in this particular respect. But that such speakers do not distinguish at all between having meaning in English and having a meaning in English does not indicate either that I did not or that I do not make such a distinction (and neither does it indicate that such a distinction cannot profitably be made). I believe that this much can be said: in so far as my idiolect tends to be somewhat idiosyncratic, my analyses of particular words are likely to be of less general interest to speakers of English. But this should not really interfere with or detract from the metatheoretic significance of this essay.

20. E is an indefinitely large but at most a finite corpus of utterances. Since both H^* and H are at most finite sets of utterances and since only a finite number of utterances will be elicited from an informant, E is at most a finite set. If we view a natural language extensionally in terms of the set of utterances composed of all the utterances that have been or ever will be uttered in the language regardless of whether they were uttered naturally or were in some way elicited, we can say that this set, call it 'E^*', is at most finite. Evidently E^* would be the ideal corpus to work with were it available. Consequently E can be thought of as an available sample of E^*.

21. A natural language could be said to constitute a (potentially) infinite set of utterances, for any such language allows of the formation of new utterances out of available elements; if u_i and u_j are utterances of the language, we can, perhaps, form the new utterance u_k, where u_k is a combination of u_i and u_j. Thus we could describe the (potentially) infinite set E^{**} where E^{**} is a projection of E^* on the basis of certain regularities present in E^*.

Whether a natural language, viewed extensionally, can sensibly be identified with a set like E^* is a nice question that need not concern us, for no matter what we say on that point it is perfectly clear that E^* would provide a more satisfactory basis for statements about the associated language than would E. Because E is at best a sample of E^*, and a sample whose adequacy it is virtually impossible to assess, any conclusions about a natural language on the basis of a set like E are at best merely probable.

For example, in determining what the word 'good' means I shall later consider more than one hundred utterances of E. On the basis of such a sample I shall say that 'good' means thus-and-thus. But there is no guarantee that I have not overlooked certain crucial cases which if I had attended to them might have considerably altered the whole picture. It has been said that 'This is good.' is synonymous with 'I approve of this: do so as well!': this is at least doubtful with respect to my idiolect. Such an utterance as 'This is good but I can't say that I approve of it.' is uttered without any apparent deviation in my idiolect, e.g. while sunning myself on the beach when I should be working.

That E is at best a sample of E^*, and a sample whose adequacy it is virtually impossible to assess, indicates that any conclusions about a natural language on the basis of a set like E are at best merely probable. But this fact is neither cause for alarm nor a basis for skepticism. Much may be said about a natural language on the basis of a set like E. It is true that further evidence about the language, when available, may lead us to revise some of our views. But the fact that our views may be subject to revision in no way indicates either that they are not likely to be correct or that they are not worth expressing.

22. We can conclude that the relevant utterances of the phonetic sequence [gʊd] are those that by means of a morphological analysis of the corpus E can be linguistically associated with an element that we identify and refer to as "the word 'good'." Each of the relevant utterances of [gʊd] can then be said to constitute an utterance of the word 'good'. This would appear to be the minimum specification of what is referred to in speaking of the word 'good' if what one says about or in connection

with the word is to admit of some sensible form of confirmation or disconfirmation.

I have not tried to say or even to indicate exactly what a word is. Possibly a word can be analyzed primarily in terms of equivalent morphemic segments and junctures as word boundaries. (But that in itself would hardly constitute an exact analysis of the word 'word'. A proper name is not, or is not in general classed, a word, but if 'word' were analyzed simply in terms of equivalent morphemic segments and junctures, 'James' should be classed a word.) The precise details of such an analysis need not concern us here. I have been using and I shall continue to use the word 'word' in an ordinary way. What matters here is the fact that, in so far as one is concerned with questions of confirmation or disconfirmation, even a minimum specification of what is referred to in speaking of the word 'good' can be given only by linguistically associating the word with a particular corpus of utterances.

23.   Since I am concerned with what the word 'good' means, I am concerned with a certain word that is uttered in certain utterances of E. Merely to identify the word, let alone determine what it means, it is necessary to discriminate between various utterances of E. This should be obvious once it is realized that E includes H where H is a set of utterances known to have been uttered. H includes utterly incoherent utterances, e.g. vocal noise occurring as a stretch of a person's talk preceded and followed by silence, the uttering of which can hardly be said to constitute a use of words. Furthermore, misuses of words occur: utterances exemplifying such misuses are included in H and so in E. Consequently it is necessary to sort the utterances of E into classes.

It may be said that E ought to be specified in such a way as to exclude misuses of words. Such a suggestion may sound attractive: in fact it is pointless. I may hear someone utter the utterance 'He shot the man inadvertently.'. I may know that on that occasion the utterance constituted a misuse of words. Possibly the speaker wanted to say 'He shot the man accidently.'.

But on what grounds can I exclude the utterance 'He shot the man inadvertently.' from the corpus *E?* "That it constituted a misuse of words": but how can I show that it constituted a misuse of words? My saying so doesn't make it so. I believe that the utterance 'He uttered a true sentence.' exemplifies a misuse of words but many philosophers would probably disagree with me. That the utterance 'He shot the man inadvertently.' did, in a certain case, constitute a misuse of words can be shown but it can be shown only on the basis of the data provided by the corpus (or a corpus like) *E.*

The corpus of utterances *E* is continually changing: our memories are short, records are lost, and we keep on talking. Furthermore, the various factors responsible for the utterance of utterances are continually changing. Even so, there are regularities to be found in or in connection with *E*. That *E* changes does not show that there are no regularities to be found. Suppose a tape of unknown but finite length had a series of numbers printed on it; only a short section of the tape is visible at any one time; thus at one moment we see the numbers *16, 18, 20, 22, 24;* later we see *56, 58, 60, 62:* we could then infer with some probability that the function describing the series is $+2$.

24.   There are regularities to be found in or in connection with *E* but they are to be found primarily in or in connection with a proper part of it: "The following regularity is found in English: adjectives precede the nouns they modify; thus 'a good apple' and 'a red house' occur but not 'an apple good' or 'a house purple'." That is not true of *E:* what I shall now say, viz. there is an apple good on my lap (and now have said), is included in *E*. 'An apple good' has just been uttered here.

(Since capitals are associated with an intonation contour, what has just been uttered here—assuming that all this is being read aloud—is not the utterance part 'An apple good' but rather the utterance part 'an apple good'. However, I propose to follow the usual convention for capital letters: the first letters of sentences, names, and representations of whole utterances or sentences, whether in quote marks or not, will be capitalized and, apart from special symbols, nothing else will.)

The utterance part 'an apple good' has just been uttered here. It has been uttered by way of an example. The statement of the regularity need not be construed as applying to such cases, which is to say that it is at best concerned with only a proper part of E.

Almost any statement of a regularity supposedly to be found in or in connection with the written language associated with E and not merely in some proper part of it can be shown to be false by appealing to *Finnegans Wake:* it is not an accident that such a work can be written and read and understood.

Again, it is possible that speakers of English will in the distant future put adjectives after nouns owing to some influence from the French. Thus the regularity noted, viz. that adjectives precede the nouns they modify, may be found only in a proper temporal part of E.

Even if E were defined with reference to a single speaker, it would still be true that linguistically interesting regularities are found only in or in connection with a proper part of E. Even the speech of a single speaker varies and that even throughout the course of a single day. I speak one way at home, another while at the university; when I talk with my cat an utterance of the form 'What can I do for you?' has one intonation contour, another when I talk with a student; and so on.

Again, it is more than likely that the majority of utterances actually uttered are ungrammatical. Confirmation of this is readily available. Record any unrehearsed conversation, discussion, lecture, or the like. Then examine the data. What one will find is this: utterances are larded with so-called "hesitation forms" such as 'ah', 'uh', 'well', 'now', 'so'; utterances are broken off, 'But I want . . .', 'Well, then I'll . . .'; utterances are started over again, 'Yes, I told him that I . . . ah . . . I suppose I shouldn't . . . ah . . . there's no need to mention, I mean . . . ah . . . you you see.'; and so on. (It is hard to hear the ungrammatical even when one is listening for it and this is like looking at the world as a two-dimensional expanse.)

I shall speak simply of regularities to be found in or in connection with E without prejudice to the question whether these are to be found only in or in connection with a proper part of E or which part of E they are to be found in or in connection with. I shall be more specific only when there is need to be so. Generally speaking, however, any regularity sufficiently interesting to warrant discussion here is to be found only in or in connection with a proper part of E.

25.   That a regularity is to be found only in or in connection with a proper part of E is not cause for alarm. On the contrary, only such regularities are likely to be of interest in syntactic and semantic studies.

The claim that a certain syntactic or semantic regularity is to be found in or in connection with E and not merely in or in connection with some proper part of E can generally be defeated by uttering an utterance that deviates from this regularity. The claim that 'the' is never uttered in the environment '. . . is in here.' can thus be defeated by saying as I now say: the is in here.

But not every claim about a regularity to be found in or in connection with E can be so defeated; whenever an utterance is uttered, there is a speaker to be found, there will be certain sound patterns, movements of the larynx, and so forth. Such regularities are matters of logic, of physiology, or physics, and the like: they are largely irrelevant to the problems of either syntax or semantics.

(If we view the uttering of an utterance by a speaker either in behavioristic terms as a response to prior stimulation or in communication theoretic terms as an output consequent upon a prior input, the fact that any relevant syntactic or semantic regularity does in fact admit of deviation can in part but only in part be expressed by saying that the relevant response is a conditioned response and the relevant output is one that is controlled by means of some sort of feedback. And this is a way of saying that language is essentially something learned. If one were forced to choose some one fact about language and say of it that it was the most important fact of all then it might be this: that one can generally in fact deviate from syntactic or semantic regularities.)

26. It has been said, "The relation between language and the world is conventional." There are ways of twisting this remark so that it turns true: as it stands, it is at best false.

'Conventional' sometimes indicates that which is customary: wearing a tie, saying 'How do you do?' when introduced to a person, shaking hands, and so forth are matters of convention, custom. That a speaker in using 'I' may be speaking of himself is not a matter of custom.

'Conventional' sometimes indicates that which is in some sense agreed upon; we can adopt the convention that in this essay 'thater' is to be employed as an exact synonym of 'that'. Perhaps we would then say, "The relations between 'thater' and the world are conventional." It does not follow that something of the same sort must be said about the word 'that'. The point here can be readily seen in connection with onomatopoeia. The word 'meow' stands in a relatively natural relation to a cat's meow in that the sounds made in uttering the word are somewhat similar to the sound of a cat meowing. Let 'woem' be an exact synonym of 'meow'; then perhaps any regularity pertaining to 'woem' and a cat's meow is conventional: it does not follow that the resemblance between an utterance of 'meow' and a cat's meow is conventional.

Onomatopoeia is of no great importance in language. I would not suggest otherwise. But the possibility of it indicates that not every semantic regularity can sensibly be characterized as "conventional." What is important and true about the thesis that "the relation between language and the world is conventional" is this: only those semantic regularities that can more or less felicitously be characterized as "conventional" are generally relevant in semantic studies. The only semantic regularities pertaining to 'meow' that are in general semantically relevant are those that pertain equally to 'woem'. If I say 'What's making that cat meow?' then whether I like it or not part of my utterance stands in a natural relation to a cat's meow, but this natural relation must generally be semantically irrelevant for generally (but not absolutely invariably) I could have asked the same question by asking 'What's making that cat woem?'. (In an appropriate context, e.g. one in which a cat is meowing loudly and plainly, there might well be a striking and semantically relevant difference between the utterance 'The cat is *meowing*.' and 'The cat is *woeming*.' for the stress on 'woeming' might be puzzling in a way that the stress on 'meowing' might not. See 56 below.)

27.   There are two fundamentally different types of regularities to be found in or in connection with *E:* these are what could be spoken of as "statistical" and "type" regularities. *E* is a corpus of utterance tokens. Certain regularities pertaining to the frequency of the occurrence of tokens can be noted in *E*. Tokens of the type 'the' occur more frequently than tokens of any other word type; the relative frequency of an occurrence of a token of the type 'the' followed by an occurrence of a token of the type 'man' is considerably greater than the relative frequency of an occurrence of a token of the type 'the' followed by an occurrence of a token of the type 'pterosaur'; the frequency of an occurrence of 'the' followed by 'is' is virtually nil; and so on. Any investigation of the regularities pertaining to the frequency of the occurrence of tokens in *E* will be essentially statistical. Such regularities are of little interest here. Utterance tokens of the type 'The cat is on the mat.' are uttered infrequently by speakers of the language associated with *E:* that is owing to the surprising fact that we have little occasion to say that. I shall not be concerned with statistical regularities here. (See 30 and 61 below.)

There are two types of type regularities to be found in or in connection with *E:* syntactic and semantic regularities (or more strictly speaking, syntactic semantic regularities and nonsyntactic semantic regularities; but see below).

A syntactic regularity is a regularity of some sort to be found in the corpus and pertaining exclusively to linguistic elements, to utterances or sets of utterances or to utterance parts or sets of utterance parts: that adjectives precede the nouns they modify is (presumably) a syntactic regularity. Syntactic regularities are the concern of the grammarian: I am not directly concerned with grammar here. The only syntactic regularities I am interested in here are ones that shed light on certain semantic regularities. (Thus I shall be much concerned with syntactic regularities.)

Semantic regularities are not simply regularities pertaining exclusively to linguistic elements: they include but are not restricted to such regularities. Semantic regularities are regularities of some sort to be found in connection with the corpus pertaining to both linguistic elements and other things, e.g. to utterances and situations, or to phrases and persons, as well as to utterances and utterances.

Strictly speaking, instead of speaking in terms of a contrast between syntactic and semantic regularities I should speak in terms of a contrast between syntactic semantic regularities and nonsyntactic semantic regularities. But there is no need to be that strict. So I shall speak more simply of syntactic and semantic regularities, where by 'semantic regularities' I shall unless otherwise indicated mean nonsyntactic semantic regularities. Later on we shall have occasion to notice if only briefly that syntactic regularities are after all semantic regularities.

(A similar terminological question arises in connection with the familiar distinction between the so-called "use" and "mention" of words. If I say 'Cats are edible.' then I am said to be "using" the word 'cats', whereas if I say ' 'Cats' has four letters.' then I am said to be "mentioning" the word: strictly speaking, I am using the word in each case. The difference is that in the former case I used the word 'cats' to say something about cats, whereas in the latter case I used the word 'cats' to say something about the word 'cats'.)

28. What a (nonsyntactic) semantic regularity is can be seen by considering one. Utterances of the type 'Pass the salt!' have been uttered almost always when there was salt present.

There are clues to the existence of a semantic regularity. A deviation from a semantic regularity can, as it were, be felt. Ordinarily I would be startled if on meeting someone on the street, he said to me 'Pass the salt!'. I would also be startled if he said 'A hydrogen bomb has just been exploded in Washington.': I would not be startled in the same way. One can feel the difference, or better, one can hear the difference.

One's own verbal behavior indicates the existence and is a partial cause of such a regularity. I never say 'Pass the salt!' when I either know or believe that there is no salt present unless I want to give an example, to startle people, or the like. Direct observations of other people's linguistic behavior are relevant but generally they are not of much use if one is already a fluent speaker of the language: in such a case such observations can at best serve to correct idiosyncrasies in one's own behavior.

The syntactic structure of an utterance frequently indicates the existence of a semantic regularity. The semantic regularity noted above is merely a special case of a more general regularity to be found in connection with such utterances as 'Close the window!', 'Open the door!', 'Stamp the letter!', 'Burn the house!', all of which have the form *verb + definite article + noun*, with an imperative contour.

One may remember that certain words, or phrases, or utterances, were uttered in certain situations. I recall various situations in which an utterance of the type 'Pass the salt!' has been uttered and in most such cases (all except ones in which philosophers or linguists were giving examples) there was salt present. Our memories provide some clues to the existence of semantic regularities but not the most important clues.

29.   In dealing with the question whether or not there are semantic regularities to be found in connection with E and H it is by the nature of the case impossible to establish anything solely by an appeal to records in the written language associated with H. We rarely have records of the situations in which the utterances of H were uttered. Even if we had them, if we had

only them we could do nothing with them here: records in *H* are not enough when we are concerned with regularities pertaining both to the records and to what is recorded.

The situations in which the utterances of *H* were uttered are in the past: they have left their traces in our memories but even more in our habits, tendencies, and so on and in the linguistic structure of our words, phrases, and utterances.

There are few words whose meaning we could be said to remember. I say 'I remember what 'attrahent' means.', having looked it up in a dictionary last week. I do not say 'I remember what 'perhaps', 'but', 'is', and 'table' mean.'. The words whose meaning one does on occasion speak of remembering are also the words whose meaning one forgets, technical words, words from a foreign language, and so on: not the everyday words of one's everyday discourse.

Memories provide some clues to the existence of semantic regularities but the importance of memory in that connection is easily exaggerated. Our awareness of semantic regularities obviates the need of remembering the situations in which our utterances are uttered; it facilitates the remembrance of such situations when such remembrance is called for. (It is easier to remember 'There is a purple gila monster on my lap.' than it is to remember 'Lap my is monster purple on there gila a.'.)

30. The word 'good' has been uttered in various utterances in sequence with other words. It has frequently been uttered in certain sequences, e.g. 'a good painting', 'some good books', 'a good red apple'. But some sequences are rare, e.g. 'a good despair', 'the good atrophied muscles', 'an apple good'. (These sequences have been uttered: I have used them as examples.)

No one can sensibly say that a particular short sequence of words has not been uttered. There is no way of knowing. The English language dates from 400 A.D. (not that a language has a beginning as a game has a beginning); since that time an enormous number of utterances have been uttered; an enormous number of them can be said to have been in the English language. But an infinitesimal proportion of them has been recorded. For all I know, the sequence 'an apple good' may have been uttered prior to my uttering it.

Whether the sequence 'an apple good' has been uttered before or not, there is something odd about it. (It would not sound so odd if it occurred in a poem: given a special enough context, nothing need sound odd in that context. Unlike 'an apple good', the phrase 'a good apple' would sound odd only in a special context.) 'An apple good' is odd but not because it has not been uttered before or has been uttered infrequently: as far as I know the utterance 'There is a purple gila monster on my lap.' has never been uttered before yet it is not odd in the way that 'an apple good' is odd. If I were to say, not by way of example but seriously, 'There is a purple gila monster on my lap.', what would be odd would be the situation, not the utterance. But if I were to say 'There is an apple good on my lap.', what would be odd would be the utterance (and perhaps the situation as well, though it is not clear what the situation can be supposed to be). Or again, 'There is a monster purple on a gila lap my.' is odd in a way that 'There is a purple gila monster on my lap.' is not, yet for all I know neither have ever been uttered before in the language.

31. 'There is an apple good on my lap.' is odd, in a way that 'There is a purple gila monster on my lap.' is not, owing to the fact that the former, and not the latter, utterance constitutes a deviation from certain regularities to be found in *E*. That the locution 'an apple good' sounds odd is simply a fact. One knows it simply by listening to it, in the way that one knows that a note is flat. It is not an accident that it sounds odd.

That it sounds odd is owing to the fact that we, the native speakers of the language, are aware of these regularities. That it can be made to sound less odd by thinking of 'criminal lawyer', 'house breaker', or bits of poetry, "But I in armes, and in atchieuments braue," is owing to the fact that we are also aware of certain other regularities to be found in *E*.

That a locution sounds odd is an excellent clue to the pres-

ence of certain regularities to be found in or in connection with
E. It is also a partial cause of (hence its excellence as a clue to)
such regularities for we do not, not even poets, make a practice
of saying things that sound odd to us.

32.   That 'an apple good' sounds odd is simply a fact. If it does
not sound odd to someone even though he is a native speaker
of the language then he has no ear for language. This is not
likely but it is possible. If such a locution really does not sound
odd to him then there is likely to be a difference between his
and our use of words. I should not be surprised to hear him say
'Here is an apple good.' in some situation in which we might say
'Here is a good apple.'.

But he might never say it. It is conceivable that he uses
words much as we do, that on occasion he says 'Here is a good
apple.' but virtually never 'Here is an apple good.' and even so
such an utterance does not sound odd to him. Assuming that
he is a native speaker, this would be somewhat curious but I see
no reason to deny that it could be so.

A person to whom an utterance like 'Here is an apple good.'
does not sound odd, even though he speaks in a normal way,
would lack an important clue to the existence of certain regularities in or in connection with *E*. In consequence, if he were
a linguist investigating the structure of *E* or a philosopher
concerned with what certain elements of *E* may mean, the
practical problem of discovering certain regularities would be
more difficult for him. But it could have no bearing on the
validity of his conclusions. The intuitions of a linguist or a
philosopher can be of enormous help in the discovery of regularities in a language but they are logically irrelevant to the
existence of such regularities. "It sounds odd to me" is not an
existence proof.

Consider the utterances 'What does that sentence mean?'
and 'What does the sentence 'It is raining.' mean?'. Both utterances are included in corpus *H* for I have heard both uttered.
But the latter utterance sounds odd to me. Furthermore, even
though the utterance 'What does 'Es regnet.' mean?' does not

sound odd to me, the utterance 'What does the sentence 'Es regnet.' mean?' does sound odd to me. Hence I suspect that these utterances that sound odd to me constitute deviations from certain regularities to be found in or in connection with E. I suspect this but it need not be so (though I believe it is so). To show that it is so it would be necessary to find and state the regularities that the utterances are thought to be deviations from. (See 159 below.)

Here one must take care not to confuse an analyst with an informant. If an utterance sounds odd to an informant that suggests that it will not be possible to elicit the utterance from the informant and consequently the utterance may have to be excluded from the corpus (if it is not already included in H). But what an informant says about an utterance need not be accepted at face value. An informant may say that a certain utterance sounds odd and even deny that he ever utters it and yet it may be possible by observation to determine that he does in fact utter it. Conversely, but less interestingly, an informant may maintain that he would in fact utter a certain utterance in the natural course of things and yet we may find that he never does utter such an utterance even in an environment or a context that seems appropriate; an informant may deny that he ever says 'overly cautious' and insist that he does say 'over cautious' but we may in fact find 'overly cautious' being uttered frequently while 'over cautious' is uttered only in special contexts, e.g. a situation in which he is being queried about his language. The converse case is less interesting in that, in so far as a sane and sensible informant honestly maintains that he would in fact utter a certain utterance in the natural course of things, the utterance will have to be included in the corpus.

That an utterance is or is not included in the corpus does not show that it either does or does not constitute a deviation from certain regularities to be found in or in connection with the corpus.

33. Oddities may occur owing to a deviation from either a syntactic or a semantic regularity. Oddity, or a certain degree

of oddity, at the level of syntax corresponds to a certain degree of ungrammaticalness. The words 'ungrammatical', 'grammatical', offer a slight difficulty here. For although they are not over liable to misinterpretation, in everyday discourse 'ungrammatical' is a term of criticism and not every deviation from a syntactic regularity either is or need be the subject of criticism. *Finnegans Wake* exemplifies many deviations from syntactic regularities but only a pedant would characterize *Finnegan* as "ungrammatical" and he would be misusing the word. However, just as it would be odd to speak of any deviation whatsoever from a syntactic regularity as "ungrammatical," so it would be odd to speak of any such deviation as "odd." Some are and some are not. There would be no sense in, as it were, stretching the word 'odd' in order to avoid stretching 'ungrammatical'.

There is no obvious word for speaking of deviations from semantic regularities. Neither 'meaningless' nor 'senseless' will do at all. First, they are primarily terms having a critical import: not every deviation from a semantic regularity either is or need be the subject of criticism. It is neither meaningless nor senseless to call a female cat 'Charlie' yet such a use of the name constitutes a deviation from a semantic regularity. Secondly, what 'meaning' and 'sense' mean is one of the things I must discuss. To use the cognate terms 'meaningless' and 'senseless' in speaking of deviations from semantic regularities could only serve to confuse matters (and exemplify a misuse of the terms).

There is no obvious word for speaking of deviations from syntactic or semantic regularities but there is an obvious phrase and I shall use it, viz. 'deviations from regularities'. Thus I shall say that an utterance like 'The is here.' constitutes a deviation from a regularity, or for short I shall say that it is a deviant utterance or that the utterance is deviant. I shall also say that an utterance like 'The is here.' is odd for it is odd and it is odd primarily because it constitutes such a marked deviation from a syntactic regularity. On the other hand, I shall not say that an utterance like 'The sentence 'Caesar crossed the Rubicon.' is true.' is odd even though such an utterance does I believe constitute a deviation from a regularity to be found in the language. Thus I shall say that an utterance like 'The sentence 'Caesar crossed the Rubicon.' is true.' is a deviant utterance or that the utterance is deviant.

I shall be talking a great deal about what can or cannot be said without deviating from regularities to be found in or in connection with the language. For the sake of brevity I shall sometimes omit the qualifying clause 'without deviating from regularities to be found in or in connection with the language' after the words 'can' or 'cannot'. Thus I shall sometimes say "One cannot say such-and-such" where of course I mean that one cannot say this without deviating from regularities to be found in or in connection with the language. The qualifying clause will be omitted only in cases in which the utterance constitutes a relatively extreme deviation from regularities to be found in or in connection with the language. One can say almost anything one likes but not always without deviating from syntactic or semantic regularities—almost anything one likes, for some things are phonetically difficult.

APPENDIX TO I

34. I am concerned with regularities: I am not concerned with rules. Rules have virtually nothing to do with speaking or understanding a natural language.

Philosophers are apt to have the following picture of language. Speaking a language is a matter of engaging in a certain activity, an activity in accordance with certain rules. If the rules of the language are violated (or infringed, or broken, etc.) the aim of language, viz. communication, cannot save *per accidens* be achieved. Rules are laid down in the teaching of language and they are appealed to in the course of criticizing a person's linguistic performance.

The picture admits of variation, of elaboration, but I shall not probe deeper into these mysteries. Such a picture of language can produce, can be the product of, nothing but confusion. An appeal to rules in the course of discussing the regularities to be found in a natural language is as irrelevant as an appeal to the laws of Massachusetts while discussing the laws of motion.

It is possible to misuse words, or to use them correctly or incorrectly; e.g. philosophers who speak of "the rules of language" (or of "moral rules") are I believe misusing the word 'rule'. But I do not think they are breaking any rules. It is possible to misuse a screwdriver, to use it correctly or incorrectly: are there rules for using screwdrivers? This too would be an odd use of the word.

If there were "rules of language" then presumably such rules would be laid down in the course of teaching the language. This is another confusion: one is not taught one's native language, one learns it. In our culture a child is not taught to speak at school: he can speak before he goes to school. If he cannot, he is not likely to be taught much at school. If he can speak before he goes to school, who taught him to speak? The parent who teaches his child an occasional word may think he is teaching his child to speak. But a normal person during the early part of his life learns a thousand words a year, more than three words a day on the average. Who teaches him these words? There are other reasons for supposing that parental instruction must be irrelevant. There are children whose parents are aliens, who cannot speak the local language. Such children learn to speak the local language as well as the children of natives. Who teaches these children? Children learn from one another: they rarely if ever teach one another. The children of aliens learn to speak the language: presumably they listen to, observe, and perhaps imitate native speakers of the language; no doubt they use or try to use the words of the language; what else they do is far from clear; how it is that they do learn the language is not known.[11]

[11] Although philosophers nowadays are prone to ask "How would you teach a child to use the word . . . ?" the sensible reply would seem to be "I don't know." This aspect of *Kindersprache* is a difficult and not a

There are so-called "rules of grammar" which children are taught at school. While at school an infringement of these rules carries with it the sanction of low grades. Apart from school matters such rules are associated with certain social taboos (see 7 above). Generally speaking, such "rules of grammar" are laid down to inhibit the speakers of the language from speaking in a way they in fact speak. There are millions of speakers of American English who say 'You was wrong.', 'He don't believe it.', and the like; in so doing they violate "rules of grammar." The proper reply to this is the equally colloquial 'So what?' for nothing (linguistically significant) follows.

A deviation from the regularities to be found in or in connection with a language may on occasion interfere with communication. But the importance of communication is usually exaggerated. 'How do you do?', 'I had a pleasant time.', 'You're a hypocrite!', 'Come if you like.', 'She had the smile of an angel committing a sin.', are utterances of English having practically nothing to do with communication. If it were not possible to say nothing at length, diplomacy between nations or individuals would be impossible and cocktail parties could not be given.

> My heart in hiding
> Stirred for a bird,—the achieve of, the mastery of the thing!

The regularities found in or in connection with a language are not sources of constraint.

A rule is easily confused with a regularity. This may be one reason why rules have been thought to be of some importance in the use of language. By first confusing 'George regularly walks to school.' with 'As a rule, George walks to school.' and then confusing that with 'The rule is that George walks to

---

fruitful subject for philosophical speculation. See W. F. Leopold, *Speech Development of a Bilingual Child.* Leopold writes: "It is one of the purposes of this study to show that casual references to child-language, usually delivered with naive confidence, cannot be trusted. The processes of the acquisition of the speaking faculty, fruitful as their study is for general linguistics, are anything but simple and obvious" (III, 120).

school.', one can easily arrive at the view that rules have a significant part to play in language.

That George regularly walks to school may simply be an observable fact. I do not know George; neither do I know anything about him other than this: each morning I see him leave his house and walk to school. I say 'George regularly walks to school.'. But I may hesitate to say 'As a rule, George walks to school.'. That would suggest that it is, as it were, George's policy to walk to school. Consider the difference between saying 'The train is regularly two minutes late.' and 'As a rule, the train is two minutes late.': again, there is the suggestion in the latter case that that the train be two minutes late is as it were in accordance with some policy or plan. The shift from 'regularly' to 'as a rule' is barely noticeable, one must listen carefully, in cases where policies or plans may be in question. It is more noticeable when questions of policies or planning are or are likely to be precluded. That the train be two minutes late is not likely to be the policy of the railroad but that it be two minutes late may be a factor some one counts on, that fits in with some plan or policy. But one does not pass as easily from 'George regularly beats his wife.' to 'As a rule, George beats his wife.'. Again, however, if we think of George beating his wife at tennis, not taking a strap to her, the shift is not difficult: it is sound policy to have George as a partner at tennis rather than his wife. But one can hardly pass from 'George regularly rapes his wife.' to 'As a rule, George rapes his wife.'. Now consider a case in which a policy or planning of some sort is almost certain to be in question: 'George regularly avoids doubled pawns.'. Here one can almost hear 'As a rule, George avoids doubled pawns.'. (Yet even here if you listen you can hear the difference.) Rules connect with plans or policies in a way that regularities do not.

The main source of the confusion is most likely this: rules are of metatheoretic importance in the description of syntactic and semantic structures. A particular syntactic or semantic system, constituted of special symbols, axioms, formation and transformation rules, and so on may be offered as a (more or less) adequate projection of a particular natural language. Some of the rules of the syntactic or semantic system will then correspond (more or less) to regularities in the corresponding natural language. To argue that therefore there must be rules in the natural language is like arguing that roads must be red if they correspond to red lines on a map.

A man chooses certain numbers, say, 18, 73, 21, 4, at random and then paints them on his forehead. "If you want to do as he does, paint the numbers 18, 73, 21, 4, on your forehead": then I am not doing what he does.

II

SEMANTIC ANALYSIS

35. The word 'mean' and its cognates are difficult to analyze and pose many problems. I would avoid both the words and the problems if I could. But if I did so I should have to cease asking 'What does the word 'good' mean?' and I want to ask and to say what it means. If there were an available synonym the case would be otherwise. But there isn't. So there is nothing for it.

One difficulty with the word is that it occurs in a great variety of linguistic environments and has many cognate and related forms. Owing to the welter of terminology it is necessary to say something at once, if only tentatively and for the time being, by way of specifying the relevant locutions. For the time being I shall speak or try to speak in an ordinary way. It is possible that I shall not succeed for it is far from clear what such a way is. If anyone objects that the way I use certain words is not the way he does, I can only say that I am trying to avoid idiosyncrasies but we may use these words in different ways. Even so, I trust that I shall be understood.

36. I want to ask and to answer the question 'What does the word 'good' mean?'. To do this I must know, in some sense at least, what the word 'mean' means. Otherwise I do not understand what I am asking. I think I do know what 'mean' means. But it is difficult to say and anyway even if I said it, why should you believe me? So there is a difficulty here.

It is necessary to proceed by indirection. It is difficult to say what the word 'mean' means but it is not difficult to stake out, as it were, certain fields, to focus attention on certain areas of investigation.

The word 'good' has meaning in English, thus the word is one of the elements of E that have meaning in English. Which elements of E have meaning in English?

37. Since E is a corpus of utterances, it can be analyzed at various levels so as to yield elements of various types. Thus E may be said to be constituted of whole utterances, clauses, phrases, words, nouns, verbs, roots and affixes, and so forth. But in particular, E can be analyzed so as to yield a set of morphological elements. It is convenient here for the purposes of exposition to think of morphological analysis as a definite procedure yielding a unique result.[1] Thus we may suppose that the corpus E is analyzed and that the analysis yields a specific set of morphological elements.

In considering the elements of E that presumably have meaning in English it will not be necessary here to consider more than a proper subset of the set of morphological elements of E. Let M be the set of elements of E that presumably have meaning in English. Then, without a doubt, a great many words, prefixes, suffixes, and the like are members of M. I do not believe that this can reasonably be questioned. No doubt a great many phrases are also members of M. But it is far from clear what one is to say either about whole utterances or about the elements of syntactic structure. It is of course necessary to understand the syntactic structure of an utterance if one is fully to understand the utterance. So one might say that the structure of an utterance has a certain significance. But this does not necessarily mean that the structure must have meaning.

---

[1] That a morphological analysis has a unique result may be something of a fiction. See Yuen Ren Chao, "The Non-Uniqueness of Phomenic Solutions of Phonetic Systems," *Bulletin of the Institute of History and Philology*, IV (1934), 363–397. Whether or not this is so is irrelevant here for the time being.

Since I am here primarily concerned with the meaning of words, and only tangentially concerned with the significance of utterances, I propose simply not to consider the question of structural meaning.

38. Not only does it seem reasonable to suppose that M, the set of elements of E that presumably have meaning in English, certainly includes a very large subset of the set of morphological elements of E but it is, I believe, quite clear that it includes only a proper subset of that set.

The set of elements yielded by the procedures of morphological analysis cannot, strictly speaking, be wholly included in the set of elements of E that have meaning in English. Consider the word 'to' in the utterance 'I want to go through Istanbul.'. Intuitively speaking, I am inclined to suppose that 'to' in that utterance does not have meaning. Notice that it has no contrasts in the language; e.g. consider the second 'to' in 'I want to go to Istanbul.': unlike the first 'to', the second 'to' contrasts with 'by', 'through', 'near'.

39. If someone says "The word 'to' in the utterance 'I want to go through Istanbul.' does have meaning" I have, at this point, no way of proving him wrong. I propose to give an account of meaning that will account for the fact, or what I take to be a fact, that 'to' in that utterance does not have meaning. If you like, that 'to' in that utterance does not have meaning is simply an intuition of mine about meaning and I propose to give an account of meaning that will account for my intuitions about the matter. On the basis of that account I can account for the fact that 'to' in the utterance in question does not have meaning.

If my theory neatly fits what seems to be the facts then I am inclined to accept what seem to be the facts as in fact the facts about the matter. I do not see any other way to proceed. (*Miracula sine doctrina nihil valent.*)

40. So intuitively speaking, the word 'to', unlike the word 'through', in the utterance 'I want to go through Istanbul.'

does not have meaning. What is the relevant difference between the two?

The utterance 'I want to go through Istanbul.' provides a peculiar environment for the word 'to'. The environment 'I want . . . go through Istanbul.' is closed to all elements of E other than (or not including) 'to'. But this is to say that the utterance of 'to' in the environment 'I want . . . go through Istanbul.', unlike the utterance of 'through' in the environment 'I want to go . . . Istanbul.', is simply in accordance with syntactic and virtually only syntactic regularities. Unless 'to', either alone or in combination with other elements, were uttered in the environment 'I want . . . go through Istanbul.', the resultant whole utterance would constitute a deviation from syntactic regularities to be found in the language. This is not true of the utterance of 'through' in the environment 'I want to go . . . Istanbul.'.

Consequently I am inclined to suppose that meaning is essentially a matter of nonsyntactic semantic regularities. This is not to say that meaning is simply a matter of such regularities but it does seem reasonable to suppose that an element's having meaning in the language can be explicated primarily in terms of the nonsyntactic semantic regularities to be found pertaining (directly or indirectly) to the element.

41.　As evidence in support of this contention I offer, for what they are worth, the following facts. Compare the first and second 'do' in 'Please do not do it!'. That 'do' is uttered in the environment 'Please . . . not do it!' is simply in accordance with the syntactic regularities to be found in E. No significant nonsyntactic semantic regularities can be found pertaining to 'do' when uttered in that environment. But that is not the case with respect to the utterance of 'do' in the environment 'Please do not . . . it!'. Notice that there 'do' contrasts with 'forget', 'break'.

Consequently, if my contention about meaning is correct then the first 'do' in 'Please do not do it!', unlike the second 'do', does not have meaning. This is testified to by the fact that generally the first 'do' in 'Please do not do it!', unlike the second 'do', will not admit of being stressed. Thus 'Please *do* not do it!' unlike 'Please do not *do* it!' is somewhat odd. Again, notice that the same is true of 'to' and 'through' in 'I want to go through Istanbul.'. There is nothing odd about 'I want to go *through* Istanbul.' but 'I want *to* go through Istanbul.' is generally quite odd. And this should not be surprising: if an element does not have meaning in an utterance, stressing the element is not likely to be, and indeed can hardly be, significant.

(There is a case, however, in which the 'to' in question will bear a stress. If I say 'I want to go through Istanbul.' and someone says 'You want not to go through Istanbul?', I may reply 'I want *to* go through Istanbul.'. An explanation of this is not hard to find. If I say 'I want him to go.' and someone says 'You want them to go?', I may reply 'I want *him* to go.', stressing the word after the verb for that was the point at which the utterance was misunderstood. But if I say 'I want to go through Istanbul.' and someone says 'You want not to go through Istanbul.', the confusion is owing to the insertion of 'not' after the verb. Thus in reply one is likely to stress whatever occurs over the segment immediately after the verb. Thus not 'to' but the stress it bears is significant in 'I want *to* go through Istanbul.': the stress contrasts with 'not' in the previous utterance.)

42.   I am inclined to suppose, for the reasons given, that meaning is essentially (though not necessarily simply) a matter of (nonsyntactic) semantic regularities. Consequently, if an element of E has meaning in English then there must be semantic regularities pertaining (either directly or indirectly) to the element. The problem of finding such regularities can seem complex. To make it seem so no more is needed than to consider the number of elements of E that obviously have meaning in English.

The set of morphological elements of E that presumably have meaning in English is obviously a finite set. Since there are about 400,000 (relatively distinct) words in E and since a considerable number of these constitute combinations of morphological elements—e.g. the four words 'form', 'disform', 'conform', and 'disconform', are combinations of the three elements 'form', 'con-', and 'dis-'—the members of the set number considerably less than 400,000.

Let m_i be a morphological element that is a member of M, thus a morphological element of E that presumably has meaning in English. The problem then is to find semantic regularities pertaining (either directly or indirectly) to m_i.

43. Confronted with this complexity, various moves are possible and as in theology every logically possible unprofitable move seems to have been made at one time or another. One move is to suppose at once that one has no business in supposing that 'of', '-er', 'tiger', and the like can all be said to have meaning in English in the same sense of 'meaning' (or possibly in the same meaning of 'meaning'). So one might say that 'of' has meaning in one sense of 'meaning', 'tiger' has meaning in another sense of 'meaning', '-er' has meaning in still another sense, and so on. A further move would be to say that 'of' has one meaning in one utterance, another in another utterance, and so on. So 'meaning', 'of', and so on would require plural dictionary entries.

There is no point in multiplying dictionary entries beyond necessity. (That is the point of Occam's eraser.)

44. The element m_i, a morphological element of E that presumably has meaning in English, is essentially a product of some sort of morphological analysis of the corpus E. If there are semantic regularities pertaining to m_i then there must be semantic regularities pertaining to the utterances in which m_i occurs, utterances on the basis of which or in connection with which it is possible to establish the morphological identity of m_i, viz. syntactically nondeviant whole utterances of E containing an occurrence of m_i.

The problem of finding regularities pertaining to m_i then has two distinct parts which need not be confounded though they cannot be separated. First, there is the problem of finding tentative semantic regularities pertaining to the syntactically nondeviant whole utterances of E. Secondly, having found tentative regularities pertaining to the syntactically nondeviant whole utterances of E in which m_i occurs, there is then the problem of tentatively attributing something about the regularities to the occurrence of m_i in the utterances; e.g. suppose one finds that if the utterance 'Look at that swine!' is uttered then generally there is a swine present in the context of utterance: one could not attribute the regularity to the occurrence of 'at' in the utterance. In each case the solution of each problem can be given only tentatively at first since each has to be adjusted in the light of the other. (See 170 ff. below.)

That there are semantic regularities pertaining to elements of E can hardly be denied. Consequently I propose (later) to consider certain types of semantic regularities pertaining to the syntactically nondeviant whole utterances of E before attempting to discern the relevant regularities pertaining to the morphological elements of E that have meaning in English, viz. single words, affixes, and the like.

45. Let $u_1, u_2, \ldots$ be syntactically nondeviant whole utterance types of E. The first problem then is to find semantic regularities pertaining to u_i. To speak of semantic regularities pertaining to the syntactically nondeviant whole utterance types of E presupposes at least a minimal syntactic analysis of E for it presupposes that some discrimination is made between the utterances of E.

This is why it will not do to say as is sometimes said that one must answer questions about meaning in doing grammar. On the contrary; only in so far as a syntactic analysis is given is it possible to raise a question about meaning. We must be able to identify u_i if we are to ask 'What are the regularities pertaining to u_i?'. Type regularities presuppose a type.

But this is not to deny that there is some give and take here. Knowing what a man wants to say may enable us to make out what he says. Suppose a lisping slave whose master is Castor is asked who his master is. The slave might utter what we would in certain situations take to be 'Mat the cat the.'. But in the given situation the utterance he uttered need constitute only a slight deviation from a syntactic regularity: it could be construed as essentially an idiolectal form of 'Master Castor.'. Again, knowing what the man may be wanting to say facilitates the construal of 'Th-the cat is on th-th-th-th-m-m-m-mat.' as an idiolectal form of 'The cat is on the mat.', a form characteristically associated with a certain type of speech defect, viz. stuttering.

Generally speaking, although various semantic factors may guide us in construing a particular utterance, how we construe the utterance, what we take it to be, depends primarily on syntactic matters. A man who utters what we would in certain situations take to be the word 'alligator' could in a given situation be taken to be uttering a dialectal form of 'I'll *get* her.'. But a man who clearly utters the utterance 'There is an alligator crawling across the ceiling.' with a characteristic English intonation would probably be taken by speakers of his dialect to be saying just that no matter what the situation was.

46.   The first problem is to find semantic regularities pertaining to u_i. But I am concerned not only to find such regularities but to state them in English. Thus I am concerned for the moment to make metalinguistic statements in English about syntactically nondeviant whole utterance types of E. Later I shall make metalinguistic statements in English about specific morphological elements of E. Generally speaking, a metalinguistic statement of a regularity pertaining to u_i will have the form 'If u_i is uttered then generally such-and-such.'; e.g. 'If 'Hello!' is uttered then generally one person is greeting one or more others.'. Later I shall be concerned with metalinguistic statements of the forms 'If u_i is uttered then, in a standard case, such-and-such.', 'The element m_i has associated with it such-and-such.', and so on.

The metalinguistic statement 'If 'Hello!' is uttered then generally one person is greeting one or more others.' is a statement of a nonsyntactic semantic regularity. In particular it is a statement of a correlation between two types of events, viz. a speaker of the language associated with E uttering an utterance token of the type in question and one person greeting one or more others. But not every statement of a semantic regularity is a statement of a correlation between two types of events. 'If 'Pass the salt!' is uttered then generally salt is present.' does not state a correlation between two types of events: it is rather a statement of a correlation between a type of event and a type of state of affairs. And of course there are metalinguistic statements of indefinitely many other types.

47. It is more than convenient to have some one way of talking about semantic relations of various types, whether they be correlations between types of events, or a type of event and a type of state of affairs, or a type of word and a type of thing, or a word and a thing, and so forth. Fortunately there is no difficulty here.

The statement of a regularity such as 'If 'Hello!' is uttered then generally one person is greeting one or more others.' can be construed as a statement to the effect that a pairing of the utterances (whole or part) 'Hello!' and 'one person is greeting one or more others' is in accordance with a semantic regularity to be found in connection with the corpus E. Thus a dictionary, which provides semantic information, is nonetheless constituted essentially of pairings of utterance parts with utterances (whole or part). More generally, instead of saying 'If u_i is uttered then such-and-such.', or 'The element m_i has associated with it such-and-such.', etc., letting w be a variable for expressions that enter into metalinguistic statements, we can speak of a pairing of w_i with u_i or of a pairing of w_i with m_i. We can then say that such a pairing is in accordance with regularities to be found in connection with the corpus, or that such a pairing is an instance of (what I shall later call) a "projection" from regularities to be found in connection with the corpus, or that such a pairing is made on the basis of such-and-such regularities, or projections, or extrapolations, and so forth. I propose to adopt this way of talking here whenever it is convenient to do so.

48.   It is possible to make and so it is necessary to avoid uninformative metalinguistic statements; e.g. it is altogether uninformative to say that w_i may be paired with u_i if $w_i = u_i$.

It should be noted, however, that a statement like ' 'Cape Town' is the name of Cape Town.' is not uninformative. The metalinguistic statement ' 'Cape Town' is the name of Cape Town.' is informative in that one learns that 'Cape Town' is a name. Thus what one learns is not that 'Cape Town' may be paired with 'Cape Town' but rather that 'a name' may be paired with 'Cape Town' on the basis both of syntactic regularities and of (what I shall later call) a "nominative" relation.

Again, a statement like 'If 'It is raining.' is uttered then generally it is raining.' is not altogether uninformative, no matter whether it be true or false. For notice that one could not say 'If 'The book.' is uttered then generally the book.'. Thus the former statement provides certain syntactic information, which in turn yields certain semantic information, about the utterance 'It is raining.'. What one learns here is that 'It is raining.' may have paired with it 'a declarative-speech act' (to be explained later). Consequently, to be told 'If 'It is raining.' is uttered then generally it is raining.' is not simply to be told that 'It is raining.' may be paired with 'It is raining.' which would be altogether uninformative.

49.   Whether or not and to what degree a metalinguistic statement that w_i may be paired with u_i is informative depends (at least to a certain extent) on the degree of distributional similarity between the elements of w_i and u_i.

Any two utterance types have certain similarities and certain dissimilarities. Generally speaking, any two utterance types are similar in that each is constituted of ordered morphological elements and each has a certain contour. Any two utterance types are two and not one in that they have either different morphemic constitutions, or a different order, or different contours;

e.g., 'Is he gone?' and 'Most of the time.' have totally different morphemic constitutions; 'The cat is on the mat.' and 'The hat is on the mat.' have markedly similar morphemic constitutions.

Similarity in morphemic constitution, order, or contour, are three factors that provide a measure of the morphological similarity and dissimilarity of two utterance types. Another measure, and the relevant one here, can be stated in terms of the distribution of the different elements. By 'the distribution of an element in E' I mean the sum of the linguistic environments of E in which the element occurs; e.g. 'cat' and 'dog' have similar distributions in E in a way that 'cat' and 'hat' do not. Either 'cat' or 'dog' but not 'hat' occurs in the environment 'The . . . has hurt its paw.'. (Generally speaking, one can say that the "information-content" of an element is inversely proportional to the size of its distribution; thus a hesitation form such as 'uh' that occurs virtually anywhere and everywhere conveys virtually no information. See 109 below.)

The avoidance of uninformative metalinguistic statements is in accordance with what I shall call "the principle of information," a principle governing the semantic analysis of a corpus. In its most general form the principle of information is that the degree to which a metalinguistic statement that w_i may be paired with u_i (or that w_i may be paired with m_i) is informative varies inversely with the degree of distributional similarity between the elements of w_i and u_i (or m_i). (This should not be surprising: since the information-content of an element is inversely proportional to the size of its distribution, a maximal difference in distribution between the elements of w_i and u_i (or m_i) will correspond to maximal information-content of the metalinguistic statement that such a pairing may be made.)

The principle of information imposes a condition on the metalinguistic statements of pairings made in our semantic analysis of a corpus. The principle would be satisfied automatically if the statements were bilinguistic; e.g. ' 'Je suis en retard.' means much the same as 'I am late.'.'. But since I am concerned with the problem of stating a semantic analysis of E in the (written) language associated with E, it is necessary to attend to and make sure that the metalinguistic statements of pairings to be made accord with the principle of information.

50.   That a pairing of w_i with u_i is in accordance with the non-syntactic semantic regularities to be found in connection with E is a statement form that is open to confirmation or disconfirmation. To make a statement of that form is to make a statement that is confirmable or disconfirmable primarily though not exclusively on the basis of what one finds when one looks not simply to the corpus E but, to speak loosely and vaguely for the moment, to the world at large.

It has been said that the world is everything that is the case. Against this it has been said that the world is the totality of objects, not facts. We are not here concerned with metaphysical issues: the course of a man's life (Anglo-Saxon 'weorold'), or even more narrowly, the course of a child's life, is all that need concern a person engaged in the semantic analysis of a language. The world that matters for my purpose or our purpose is my world or our world, the one in which we learn to use and do use words, in which we speak a language. So the world we are concerned with is a remarkably limited four-dimensional spatio-temporal continuum: it need spread no further than thirty-odd years in the northern hemisphere. It need not spread that far: there is no reason why seven years in a room or even a cell would not do. If the cell were well equipped with suitable furnishings, food, and so on, and suitable means for affecting the behavior of the child, the child could learn a language in such a "world." So we could assume that our world is limited to the interior of a well-equipped cell.

"Such an assumption would lead to difficulties in connection with statements about the distant in space or time." That is true. But the difficulties are there: I am not inventing them. To assume at the outset of a semantic analysis of a corpus that our world is an infinite four-dimensional continuum is simply to refuse to face issues; it is to behave like a metaphysical ostrich. Logically speaking, it makes no difference whether we assume that our world has a seven-year or a twenty-five-cosmic-year span: so long as we fix a spatiotemporal limit there will always be the problem of dealing with statements about something beyond the limit; if we limit our world temporally to seven years then we must deal with statements like 'Eight years ago there was an earthquake.'.

51. Although it is necessary to look to the world (to speak loosely and vaguely again for a moment) in attempting to confirm or disconfirm metalinguistic statements about semantic regularities, it is not necessary to make any strong assumptions about what is to be found. If we say 'If 'Hello!' is uttered then generally one person is greeting one or more others.' what we are saying could be said by saying that one type of event is correlated with another type of event, or that an utterance type is correlated with a type of situation, and so forth. Talk about a type and in particular a type of situation, or event, or state of affairs, and so forth may be objected to in some quarters as a form of so-called "Platonism." It is held that such talk indicates that one has made an "ontological commitment," that one believes that as well as cats and cows and chairs "There are situations."

I do not wish to enter into these issues and there is no need to do so. The locution 'ontological commitment' is not one I have any use for, and neither do I care to ask or to answer the curious question "What is there?" I say 'There are chairs in the room.' and if someone wants to say 'Therefore there are chairs.' tout court, it sounds odd to me, like a proper utterance part, not a whole utterance. It is as though one had run out of breath. I do not say 'There are chairs.' tout court any more than I say 'There are situations.' tout court. But I see no reason not to say 'There are different types of situations that we shall have to consider.'.

Nothing of any consequence follows from this. The fact that one can say 'If 'Hello!' is uttered then generally one person is greeting one or more others.' instead of saying ' 'Hello!' is correlated with a type of situation in which one person is greeting one or more others.' shows that one has two ways of saying much the same thing. It does not show anything else. If this is ontology then ontology is a mouthful of air.

52. Not only "Platonistic" locutions but even seeming "Platonistic" locutions can be avoided here. By speaking of a pairing of w_i with u_i all talk of types of situations, events, states of affairs, and the like can be dispensed with. And though it would be inconvenient to do so, we could avoid speaking of utterance types.

First it may be worth noting that an utterance type may be "abstract" in what appears to be a fairly literal sense of the word 'abstract'. Certain utterance types are direct abstractions from utterance tokens, the method of abstraction being to discount certain differences between tokens, differences that are deemed irrelevant for the purposes of semantic analysis. Thus types can be generated from tokens by certain operations on tokens.

Not all utterance types are direct abstractions from utterance tokens. A novel utterance type such as 'There is a purple gila monster on my lap blinking at me.' is not a direct abstraction from utterance tokens of the type. Relatively few such utterance tokens have been uttered. Furthermore, one can easily specify an utterance type, no token of which may have ever been uttered; e.g. if one numbers the items in a dictionary, one can then refer to the utterance type constituted by items *72, 59,* and *83,* in that order with an assertive contour. Thus it is possible to generate utterance types from word types by certain operations on word types.

53. All statements about utterance types that will be made in the course of the analysis of E given in this essay will be reducible in one way or another to statements either about utterance tokens or word tokens. Thus a statement about the utterance type 'I have a live gila monster on my back.' is reducible to a statement about (either utterance or word) tokens even though, as far as I know, few such utterance tokens have ever been uttered.

With respect to the utterances actually found in the corpus E, the utterance type u_i to which an utterance token t_i belongs can be defined in terms of operations on utterance tokens. More specifically, we can identify the type with a set of utterance tokens and then define the set in terms of the responses of an informant. Thus: letting t_1, t_2, . . . be utterance tokens of E, t_i is a member of u_i; for $j \neq i$, t_j is a member of u_i if and only if the informant would (or if you like, does) discount differences between t_j and t_i and count(s) them as the same utterance and t_j's being a member of u_i is in accordance with theoretic considerations. The need for the proviso that the assignment of t_j to u_i be in accordance with theoretic considerations can be seen as follows. Although being the same as is a transitive relation, being counted as the same as is not a transitive relation. This can pose problems. For example, if the informant says that t_j is the same as t_i and that t_k is the same as t_i, he has committed himself to saying that t_j is the same as t_k. But of course from the fact that the informant counts t_j as the same as t_i, and t_k as the same as t_i, it does not follow that he counts t_j as the same as t_k. Consequently the preceding definition without the proviso would lead to contradiction if the informant were not infallible. To avoid this difficulty it is necessary to add the very strong proviso so that if the informant proves fallible, in the sense indicated, whether or not the problematic tokens are members of the set can then be decided on theoretic grounds, e.g. on the basis of considerations of simplicity, the power of the resultant syntax, and the like.

With respect to utterance types not actually exemplified in the corpus, utterance types can be defined in terms of operations on word types and then word types can be defined in terms of the responses of an informant with respect to word tokens as above. By means of this double procedure we can allow for and distinguish between utterance types of which there are or of which there are no utterance tokens. On the other hand, no allowance has been made for word types of which there are no tokens. If we were concerned to allow for the fact that a language may allow for the construction of word types as well as utterance types, we should have to define constructed word types with respect to some particular set of nonconstructed word types initially found in the corpus.

54.   The problem of determining what semantic regularities (if any) pertain to a particular utterance type is exceedingly complex. Both so-called "observational" and "theoretic" considerations are involved. But to begin with, one notes that an utterance token t_i is uttered at a certain spatiotemporal position. From that position one looks about to see what can be said. In attempting to discover semantic regularities the problem is, and it is essential to remember that it is, one of passing from the utterance in question to something else and not vice versa. Thus the question is: if we know that the utterance in question is uttered then what? The question is not: if what then we know that the utterance in question is uttered?

It may be pleasant (or unpleasant depending on one's taste) to suppose that one can predict what utterance(s) if any a given person will utter in a given situation but this pleasant fiction cannot be taken seriously here. It is common practice today to speak of the uttering of an utterance in behavioristic terms as the response of an organism to certain stimuli. That it is in fact impossible (today) to specify the relevant stimuli is usually glossed over as a gross consideration that must not be allowed to interfere with the flights of scientific fancy.

The sterility of a stimulus-response model of a natural language can be seen in this: if we specify the stimulus, we cannot specify the responses; if we specify the response, we cannot specify the stimuli. And this is to say that in terms of stimulus and response we can say virtually nothing of either syntactic or semantic relevance.

55.   Given that we know that t_i is uttered at a certain spatiotemporal position then what? There will be all sorts of things to be noted but not all of these can be relevant in a semantic analysis of a corpus.

The uttering of an utterance is a physical event that produces divers causal effects. No doubt the uttering of an utterance is itself an effect of some cause. But just as it is virtually impossible (today) to say in general what effected the uttering of an utterance so it is virtually impossible (today) to say in general what effects the uttering of an utterance has or will have. Nonetheless, in particular cases one can on occasion see and say what effects are produced by the uttering of a given utterance. Consider the following case of psychosomatic symbolism:

An intelligent, thirty-two-year-old woman, who had previously been treated in various medical clinics for a chronic illness vaguely diagnosed as an "endocrine dyscrasia" or "anorexia nervosa," was referred to the Clinics because of persisting vomiting and severe cachexia. The terms in which the patient described her complaints were of immediate symbolic significance: i.e. she stated that for the preceding five years all references to sex had become literally "distasteful" and "disgusting" and that her "inability to stomach" men caused her actually to vomit in their presence. So pervasive was this spread of cognate somatic symbolism that even if she merely heard the telephone ring she became nauseated over the remote possibility that some man was calling her for a "date"; similarly, reading or hearing the word "date" or even seeing the fruit by that name produced abdominal discomforts.[2]

Even if we restricted our attention to the idiolect of the woman referred to, the regularity pertaining to the word 'date' and abdominal discomforts would be of no relevance in a semantic analysis of her idiolect.

In denying that the regularity pertaining to the word 'date' and abdominal discomforts is semantically relevant I do not mean to be denying that the regularity is semantic nor that it is of some relevance to someone, e.g. to a psychiatrist. I want to say only that it is irrelevant in a semantic analysis of the idiolect in question. It will not do to confuse a semantic analysis of a corpus with a psychiatric study of the corpus no matter how intriguing the latter may be.

56. The regularity pertaining to the word 'date' and abdominal discomforts is irrelevant in a semantic analysis of the idiolect in question. The only regularities relevant in a semantic analysis of a corpus are those semantic regularities that bear

[2] J. H. Masserman, *Principles of Dynamic Psychiatry* (Philadelphia: W. B. Saunders Co., 1946), pp. 159–160. Printed by permission.

on questions about what words mean, about learning and knowing what words mean, about using or misusing words, about understanding what is said, and the like. Regularities that do not bear on such questions as these may be semantic but they are irrelevant in the semantic analysis of a corpus.

Roughly speaking, if one finds out with respect to the woman in question that if she hears the word 'date' uttered then generally she experiences abdominal discomforts one has found out nothing whatever about her language or dialect or idiolect. Notice that if the regularity were semantically relevant one could not learn to speak her language in the way one normally learns to speak a language: one cannot learn to respond to the word 'date' by having abdominal discomforts (which is not to say that one cannot be conditioned in such a way that reading or hearing the word 'date' would produce abdominal discomforts).

57. If the woman in question generally experiences abdominal discomforts whenever she hears the word 'date' one can say 'The word 'date' evidently means something to her.'. This suggests that the regularity pertaining to the word 'date' and abdominal discomforts does bear on questions of meaning and hence is not irrelevant in a semantic analysis of the woman's idiolect. But this would be something of a confusion. It is not necessary to confuse a word's having meaning in the woman's idiolect with a word's meaning something to the woman. Only the former is relevant here.

On the basis of contemporary psychoanalytic theory one could infer that the word 'date' has something to do with sexual matters with respect to the woman in question, but exactly what the connection is is in no way indicated by the stated regularity. Possibly it has something to do with the fact that the word 'date' has meaning in the woman's idiolect (as indeed in this case it does) but it need not. Suppose George has a similar neurotic response to the German word 'Wohlgefallen', which response had been induced by the viewing of a primal scene at an early age while at the same time hearing the word 'Wohlgefallen' repeated over and over. Even if we suppose that George does not understand a single word of German, we can say 'The word 'Wohlgefallen' means something to George.' just as we can say 'The word 'date' means something to the woman.'. But it does not follow that we are entitled to say 'The word 'Wohlgefallen' has meaning in George's idiolect.' and neither does it follow from the case presented that we are entitled to say 'The word 'date' has meaning in the woman's idiolect.'. The word 'date' may mean something to the woman, even so it need not have meaning in her idiolect or dialect or language. (Compare 'The scratch on the table means something to George.' with the somewhat odd 'The scratch on the table has meaning.'.)

58. That a metalinguistic statement of a pairing must accord with the principle of information is one obvious condition of the significance of such a statement. But what I shall call "the principle of conventionality" is of greater metatheoretic importance: it provides a necessary condition of the relevance of a regularity in the semantic analysis of a corpus.

Generally speaking, the principle comes to this: a necessary but not a sufficient condition of a regularity being semantically relevant in the analysis of a corpus is that the speakers of the language associated with the corpus can deviate from the regularity at will. And since in general the only clear test of what the speakers of the language can do is what they in fact do, to establish that the regularity satisfies this necessary condition of semantic relevance it is generally necessary to find or to elicit instances of deviation. (See 25 above.)

The importance of the principle of conventionality can be seen in the fact that it rules out associations, psychosomatic correlations, physiological correlations, and the like.

59. The principle of conventionality may seem peculiar. It seems to demand that something go wrong for it does require that there be a real possibility of deviation from the relevant regularities. But suppose that 'Hello!' were never uttered except when one person was greeting one or more others: "Surely we would not then want to say that the regularity pertaining to

'Hello!' and one person greeting one or more others was semantically irrelevant"—no, for then we could not say it. By hypothesis 'Hello!' is never uttered except when one person is greeting
one or more others. But I may say ' 'Hello!' is uttered when one
person is greeting one or more others.' and no one need be
greeting anyone.

One need not confuse a deviation from a regularity with
something going wrong. 'Hello!' is in fact relevantly connected
with one person greeting one or more others but in saying this
I have just deviated from the regularity: nothing has gone
wrong.

60.   The principle of conventionality serves to mark off some
semantic regularities as irrelevant in the semantic analysis of a
corpus. But there are still other semantic regularities that, intuitively speaking, one feels to be irrelevant in the semantic
analysis of a corpus and which must be dealt with in some other
way.

Consider the utterance type 'Scott is the author of *Waverley*.'.
As far as I can recall, in the course of my life tokens of this
particular utterance type have been uttered only in the course of
a philosophical discussion. If one hears someone utter the
utterance, it is highly likely that that person is in the midst
of a philosophical discussion. Again, tokens of the type 'The
cat is on the mat.' are in fact uttered primarily in the course
of grammatical discussions, rarely in connection with some feline
on some mat.

Here one wants to say that it is only an accident that tokens
of the type 'The cat is on the mat.' loom large in grammatical
discussion. The regularity is not semantically relevant. In contrast, a regularity pertaining to 'The cat is on the mat.' and
some feline being on some mat would be semantically relevant.
This is what one wants to say. But on what grounds?

Again suppose that both w_i and w_j can be paired with u_i.
It may then seem that both pairings must be semantically relevant. But we may want to say something to the effect that only
the pairing of w_i with u_i is significant for the speakers of the

language associated with E, that the pairing of w_j with u_i is, as it were, an accident. 'A certain male is behaving in a certain way' can perhaps be paired with 'He is angry.'. But 'the adrenal glands of a certain male are secreting noradrenalin' may also be paired with 'He is angry.'. One wants to say that the latter pairing is perhaps psychologically interesting but semantically irrelevant. To put it crudely, when one says 'He is angry.' one may be talking about his behavior but one is not likely to be talking about his adrenals.

(Here one is confronted with at least an aspect of what is technically spoken of by philosophers as "the problem of the analytic and the synthetic." A philosopher may want to say that 'If he is angry then he is behaving in a certain way.' may possibly be an "analytic" statement but 'If he is angry then his adrenal glands are secreting noradrenalin.' can only be a "synthetic" statement. And the problem is: how is one to tell whether a given statement is "analytic" or "synthetic"?)

61. I have so far been concerned primarily with metalinguistic statements of nonsyntactic semantic regularities of the form 'If u_i is uttered then generally . . . .'. If a distinction of the sort indicated above can in fact be made, as in fact it can, it follows that such a statement form cannot be employed to state a relevant regularity pertaining to such utterances as 'The cat is on the mat.', 'Scott is the author of *Waverley*.'. The reason is simply that it is false to say that if 'The cat is on the mat.' is uttered then generally some feline is on some mat. On the contrary, if 'The cat is on the mat.' is uttered then generally a philosophico-grammatical discussion is under way. The irrelevance of the latter statement is what underlies the irrelevance of statistical inquiries to questions of syntax or semantics.

But the point here is not merely that the statement form in question cannot be employed to state a relevant regularity pertaining to 'The cat is on the mat.': it is rather that there is no relevant regularity to state. And this is true of all sorts of utterances. Consider the utterance type 'I have been holding a live and venomous Russell's viper in my bare hands for the last half hour.': it is not unlikely that no token of this type has ever been uttered before. But if so it would be somewhat absurd to speak of a regularity pertaining to this utterance. And the same can be said in connection with any relatively novel utterance type.

62. If 'The cat is on the mat.' is uttered then generally a philosophicogrammatical discussion is under way. But if 'The cat is on the mat.' is uttered in accordance with certain regularities to be found in connection with E then some feline is on some mat. Another way of saying this is to say that if 'The cat is on the mat.' is uttered then, in a standard case, some feline is on some mat.

Metalinguistic statements such as these are not statements of regularities though they are related to and ultimately based on statements of regularities. They are rather what I shall call statements of "projections." It is important not to confuse statements of projections with statements of regularities in so far as one is concerned with questions of confirmation or disconfirmation. The statement of a projection that if 'The cat is on the mat.' is uttered then, in a standard case, some feline is on some mat is not shown to be false by pointing out either that the utterance is rarely uttered or that when it is uttered neither a feline nor a mat is likely to be found.

63. Consider the two utterance types 'The cat is on the mat.' and 'The dog is on the mat.'. Tokens of the former type loom large in grammatical discussions but not tokens of the latter type. Yet the two utterances have a marked structural similarity, differing only with respect to the words 'cat' and 'dog', which have markedly similar distributions in E.

What is at issue here is a question of simplicity, and something more. The expression w_k may in fact, on the basis of observed regularities, be paired with u_i. But suppose that there is an utterance u_j that is markedly similar in structure to u_i and such that on the basis of observed regularities u_j has w_j paired with it. Further suppose that there is a w_i such that w_i is structurally similar to w_j and such that the structural similarity between w_i and w_j can readily be construed as a reflection of the structural similarity between u_i and u_j, whereas what structural similarity there is between w_k and w_j can hardly be so construed. Then it is simpler to pair w_i rather than w_k with u_i.

Thus if 'a philosophicogrammatical discussion is under way' is paired with 'The cat is on the mat.' whereas 'some canine is on some mat' is paired with 'The dog is on the mat.', what structural similarity there is between 'a philosophicogrammatical discussion is under way' and 'some canine is on some mat' can hardly be construed as a reflection of the structural similarity between 'The cat is on the mat.' and 'The dog is on the mat.'. Consequently it may be (and in this case is) simpler to construe 'The cat is on the mat.' as having paired with it 'some feline is on some mat'.

64.   What I have just been speaking of in terms of simplicity could and will be spoken of as "the principle of composition." In a general form, the principle of composition is absolutely essential to anything that we are prepared to call a natural language, a language that can be spoken and understood in the way any natural language can in fact be spoken or understood.

How is it that one can understand what is said if what is said has not been said before? Any language whatever allows for the utterance of new utterances both by the reiteration of old ones and by the formation of new ones out of combinations of old elements. Hence any natural language whatever allows for the utterance of both novel utterance tokens and novel utterance types. If a new utterance is uttered and if the utterance is not then and there to be given an arbitrary explication, that one is able to understand what is said in or by uttering the utterance must in some way at least be partially owing to one's familiarity with the syntactic structure of the utterance.

To deny the principle of composition would, I am inclined to suppose, be utterly absurd. Either the new utterance is arbitrarily explicated then and there or the explication is at least partially predetermined by the syntactic structure of the utterance. If every new utterance had then and there to be arbitrarily explicated, the corpus of utterances would not even resemble a language. It would not even be a mere aggregate of names. For one would not be able to use one of the "names" twice without a further arbitrary fiat; e.g. if w_i is paired with t_i by arbitrary fiat then if every and any form of the principle of composition is to be avoided, given an utterance of t_j, another token of the same utterance type, a further fiat would be required to pair w_i with t_j. For if one were to argue that w_i must be paired with t_j in virtue of the fiat pairing w_i with t_i, the only basis for the argument would be the similarity of syntactic structure between t_i and t_j in virtue of which both are classed as utterance tokens of the same utterance type. But to argue on the basis of similarity of syntactic structure is to appeal to the principle of composition.

65.   Unfortunately I find it impossible to state the principle of composition in a precise and explicit form. Roughly speaking, it is a principle to the effect that the relevant similarity between distinct semantic correlates of u_i and u_j be a reflection of the relevant similarity between the two utterances. Since the regularities in question are here being construed in terms of a pairing of utterances (whole or part), what is in question in each case are linguistic similarities. In a relatively precise but hardly explicit form the principle requires that the structural similarity between w_i and w_j be a reflection of the structural similarity between u_i and u_j, where w_i and w_j are what I shall call "exclusive" correlates of u_i and u_j respectively (see below). But part of the difficulty here is that I cannot spell out what is included under the heading "structural similarities and dissimilarities."

What is wanted and what is lacking here is a complete and adequate grammar. It is to be presumed that such a grammar would provide us with a measure of structural similarity. But in default of such a grammar one is forced to talk in a more or less vague way. One thing, however, is fairly clear; viz. not only is distributional similarity not sufficient but morphological similarity is not sufficient either. Morphological similarity may be taken to be a special case of structural similarity but nothing more. This can be seen in the case of utterances that are ambiguous out of context; e.g. 'Polishing machines can be a nuisance.': here either the act of polishing machines or a certain kind of machine, viz. a polisher, may be in question.[3] But this means that in certain contexts w_i is paired with u_i whereas in other contexts w_j is paired with u_i. If the principle of composition were stated in terms simply of morphological similarity since u_i is morphologically identical with u_i, the principle would fail to hold in this case. It is fairly clear, however, that the utterance 'Polishing machines can be a nuisance.' can be construed as having alternative structures, the ambiguity being resolved in context. Thus in one context 'polishing' is classed a verb whereas in another it is classed an adjective. (And the same may be said in connection with 'Visiting relatives can be boring.', 'Biting dogs can cause trouble.', and the like.)

There is a further complication along these lines that must be noted. That u_i and u_j are structurally similar while w_i and w_j are structurally dissimilar need not in itself establish that a pairing of w_i with u_i and of w_j with u_j constitutes a deviation from the principle of composition. 'Some feline' may be paired with 'The cat is on the mat.' while 'some feline is on some mat' may be paired with 'His cat is on the mat.'. Here the structural similarity between 'The cat is on the mat.' and 'His cat is on the mat.' is not reflected in a structural similarity between 'some feline' and 'some feline is on some mat'. But the conflict with the principle of composition is only apparent.

In the case in question, w_i and w_j are not exclusive correlates of u_i and u_j. I shall say that w_i and w_j are exclusive correlates of u_i and u_j if and only if not both w_i and w_j may be paired with both u_i and u_j. (Consequently no two correlates of one utterance are exclusive.) If the condition that w_i and w_j be exclusive in the sense indicated were ignored, virtually any pairing would automatically conflict with the principle. For suppose 'some feline is on some mat' is paired with 'Some cat is on some mat.'.

[3] I am indebted to N. Chomsky for this type of example.

We can then say that 'some feline' is also paired with 'Some cat is on some mat.'. Thus both w_i and w_j are here paired with u_i. Since u_i cannot here be construed as having alternative structures, and since w_i and w_j are structurally dissimilar, it follows that the structural identity of u_i with itself is not reflected in its semantic correlates. But there is no conflict with the principle of composition here owing to the fact that w_i and w_j are not exclusive correlates of u_i.

66.   Although I cannot spell out what is to be included under the heading "structural similarities," it may help to consider certain prima-facie objections to the principle of composition. The principle is that the structural similarity between exclusive correlates of u_i and u_j be a reflection of the structural similarity between u_i and u_j. It may seem as though cases of homophony or homonymy or multiple meanings would cause difficulty. But that is not the case.

Consider the utterance 'Look at the division!': out of context the utterance is ambiguous for the division in question may be either an arithmetic result or an army group. Consequently on different occasions the utterance will have different semantic correlates. But there is no conflict with the principle of composition here owing to the fact that 'division' can be construed as having alternative distributions in the corpus. If we list the total distribution of 'division' in the corpus it can be divided into two proper overlapping subsets of occurrences. This can be seen as follows. Let 'onisivid' be an exact synonym of 'division' in 'Do the division again!' and let 'noisivid' be an exact synonym of 'division' in 'The division is marching.'. Then the sum of the distributions of 'onisivid' and 'noisivid' will be virtually identical with the distribution of 'division'. Cases of homophony and homonymy can be handled in exactly the same way.

Again, suppose that 'rehtorb' is an exact synonym of 'brother' and consider the utterances 'He is my brother.' and 'He is my rehtorb.'. In such a case it seems quite clear that w_i could be paired with 'He is my brother.' if and only if it were paired with 'He is my rehtorb.'; thus both utterances would have one and the same utterance part paired with them. It might seem that the pairings would then fail to accord with the principle of composition. But that is not the case and that for two quite different reasons.

Even on the hypothesis that 'brother' and 'rehtorb' are exact synonyms it does not follow that 'brother' and 'rehtorb' have exactly the same distribution in E. On the contrary, 'rehtorb' but not 'brother' could be uttered without oddity in the environment 'I know he is your brother but is he your . . . ?'. Consequently there is a slight distributional dissimilarity between 'He is my brother.' and 'He is my rehtorb.'. In so far as the semantic regularity pertaining to 'He is my brother.' is the same as that pertaining to 'He is my rehtorb.' the similarity between the regularities pertaining to each utterance cannot be a function of the distributional dissimilarity between the two utterances.

But one cannot argue here that on the grounds of composition 'He is my brother.' and 'He is my rehtorb.' must be paired with different utterance parts owing to the distributional differences between 'rehtorb' and 'brother'. Although there is a distributional difference between 'rehtorb' and 'brother' and hence a distributional dissimilarity between 'He is my brother.' and 'He is my rehtorb.', it is nonetheless perfectly clear that according to any sensible criterion of structural identity the two utterances cannot fail to be structurally identical, "brother" and "rehtorb" can only be free variants of one and the same morpheme. Consequently that w_i be paired with 'He is my brother.' if and only if it be paired with 'He is my rehtorb.' is not contrary to but wholly in accordance with the principle of composition.

67. There is, however, a much more important reason why the preceding case does not support any objection against the principle of composition. Even if 'He is my brother.' and 'He is my rehtorb.' were structurally dissimilar, the principle of composition does not preclude pairing one and the same utter-

ance (or utterance part) with structurally dissimilar utterances. For if that were the case the principles of information and composition would tend to conflict automatically to such an extent that every informative pairing would violate the principle of composition. This can be seen as follows.

Suppose that the metalinguistic statement 'w_i may be paired with u_i.' conforms to the principle of information to such a degree that w_i and u_i are not only distributionally dissimilar but structurally dissimilar as well. We can then say uninformatively that w_i may be paired with u_j. This will be so in cases in which $w_i = u_j$. Thus if 'some canine is on some mat' is paired with 'The dog is on the mat.' then it is also possible to pair 'some canine is on some mat' with 'some canine is on some mat'. It then follows that w_i is paired with both u_i and u_j where u_i and u_j are, relative to any "comparison" of w_i with w_i, structurally dissimilar.

The principle of composition does not preclude pairing similar utterances with dissimilar utterances: it does preclude distinct pairings of dissimilar utterances with similar utterances. Hence the direction of the pairing is important. It is important to remember that the problem here is to provide a semantic analysis of the utterances and of the morphological elements of the corpus E. Thus the problem is: given u_i, what is there to say about it? Alternatively, the problem is: given u_i, what can be paired with it? Or still again, given u_i, what can be paired with it by way of providing an analysis of u_i? An analysis has a certain direction. Thus one may pair 'male sibling' with 'brother' by way of providing an analysis of 'brother'. But one could not sensibly pair 'brother' with 'male sibling' by way of providing an analysis of 'male sibling'. At best, such a pairing might be said to provide a "synthesis" of 'male sibling'.

68.   On the basis of both (the principles of) composition and conventionality universal regularities can be ignored.

Suppose it were the case that every utterance of E could have paired with it 'a swine is present'; e.g. this would occur if there were a taboo in the community of speakers sufficiently strong to deter them from speaking in the absence of a swine. Such a regularity would be anthropologically relevant in a study of the speakers of the language associated with E but it would be semantically irrelevant in connection with the corpus E. That an utterance is uttered by the speakers of the language only in the presence of a swine is primarily a fact about the uttering of an utterance by the speakers of the language associated with E: it is only derivatively a fact about the utterance uttered.

Generally speaking, a regularity pertaining to an utterance type u_i is semantically relevant only if there is an utterance type u_j such that the regularity pertaining to u_i does not pertain equally to u_j. This is simply to say that only those regularities pertaining to the utterances of E that enable us to discriminate semantically between the utterances of E are semantically relevant.

69. For any given utterance type u_i, a pairing of w_i with u_i may be made solely on the basis of composition. If a pairing is made solely on the basis of composition, as for example any pairing of anything with 'There is a purple gila monster on my lap staring at me.' is likely to be then the pairing is an instance of what I have called a projection. The principle of composition is an important projective device in a natural language. Only in terms of projection can the distant in space or time be dealt with.

But every projection must have a base and in particular must in general be based (directly or indirectly) on regularities. If w_k is paired with u_k solely on the basis of composition then there must be a u_i such that w_i is paired with u_i and not solely on the basis of composition and such that the structural similarity between w_k and w_i is a reflection of the structural similarity between u_k and u_i; e.g. 'some feline is on some mat' may be paired with 'The cat is on the mat.'. But this pairing is made on the basis of composition by appealing to the pairing of 'some canine is on some mat' with 'The dog is on the mat.'. If this latter pairing is itself made solely on the basis of composition then an appeal must be made to the pairing of, say, 'some canine is on some chair' with 'The dog is on the chair.', and so on.

70. Since statements of projections are based primarily on statements of regularities it is clear that the latter are of fundamental importance here. One might suppose that ideally a metalinguistic statement of a semantic regularity would be based simply and solely on what has been observed. But nothing ever really is and anyway a relevant metalinguistic statement of a semantic regularity need not be so based.

Let t_1, t_2, . . . be syntactically nondeviant whole utterance tokens of the syntactically nondeviant whole utterance type u_i. Suppose that on the basis of observation w_i can be paired with t_1 . . . t_n. It may then seem that w_i must be paired with u_i, the utterance type. But that does not follow at all. "If w_i were paired with every token of the type u_i then w_i would necessarily be paired with the type: to talk of a type is primarily a way of discounting differences between tokens"—but what sense is there here in talking of "every token of the type"? One can count the tokens of the type 'The dog is on the chair.' and sooner or later one stops. No matter when one stops one is never entitled to say 'These are all the tokens of the type.', not *tout court*. In talking of tokens of a type one is talking of an indeterminate number of elements. Hence the fact that w_i is paired with t_1 . . . t_n does not require one to say that w_i is paired with u_i.

71. One notes that an utterance token t_i is uttered at a certain spatiotemporal position. From that position one looks about to see what can be said to be paired with t_i. Eventually one formulates the hypothesis that w_i is paired with t_i, being guided in the formulation of this hypothesis by considerations of conventionality and composition as well as all sorts of other factors, e.g. the striking characteristics of the immediate situation or the behavior of the speakers. One may then find that w_i may be paired with t_j . . . t_n. And then one may formulate the further hypothesis that w_i is paired with u_i. In some extremely simple cases something of this sort may actually happen.

Unfortunately, it is (today at least) impossible to say what actually happens even in the simplest case. It is not that it is difficult to assign a value to the parameters in question but rather that the parameters are unknown. In the case of a roulette ball, if we knew the exact impetus of the ball, the wheel, the force of the air currents, the amount of friction, and so forth, we could perhaps predict where the ball would come to rest. We know what sort of information is required. But in the case of finding a semantic correlate of an utterance no reasonably effective procedure can be described.[4] The principles of conventionality and composition are not procedural principles but critical principles whose function is to evaluate the analysis a semanticist has hit upon in the course of his semantic studies.

One can of course say the obvious: thus it may be necessary to consider anything you can mention. (But see Part III below, in particular 138.)

72. Perhaps the foremost problem in attempting to determine what semantic regularity pertains to a given utterance type is that of allowing for the possibility of deviation from the regularity.

We may find that w_i can be paired with t_i but w_j is paired with $t_j \ldots t_n$. Here in so far as the immediate data of observation are concerned it may seem that we must say that w_j is paired with u_i and that the utterance of t_i must constitute a deviation from this regularity. Thus it may seem that on the basis of the immediate data of observation we are forced to conclude that the speaker in uttering t_i was either making a mistake, or confused, or lying, or joking, or the like. But that does not follow at all. Even if we restricted ourselves to the immediate data of observation an alternative conclusion is open to us, viz. that u_i has paired with it the disjunction of w_i and w_j.

The problem here is not significantly different from the traditional problem of finding the "intension" of a term by con-

---

[4] This is not to deny that various maxims to guide linguists in the field can be stated. Thus Nida, *op. cit.*, pp. 175–177, lists twenty-five steps in a monolingual field procedure: "1. Approach with a smile," "2. Talk," etc.

sidering its "extension." In order to discover the intension of
a term it is necessary to examine not its purported extension but
its actual or correct extension; e.g. if one attempts to grasp
the intension of the term 'cups' and mistakenly takes the extension of the term to include such things as cans and pots, then
one will fail to grasp the correct intension. On the other hand
it seems that one cannot differentiate between the purported
extension and the actual or correct extension except on the basis
of the intension of the term. Thus it seems that in order to discover the intension of a term one must first know it, which is
absurd. Contemporary enjoiners to examine the use of a term
to find out what it means are open to the same objection. Misuses of words occur. One cannot find out what a word means by
examining its actual usage unless one can recognize misuses
and deviant uses. But how is one to recognize a misuse? or a
deviant use?

73.   One simple and generally inadequate way of dealing with
this problem is to appeal to supposedly privileged cases, e.g.
to the usage of certain speakers of the language or to a dictionary. Such procedures are open to a fairly obvious objection,
in fact precisely the same objection that can be leveled against
equally simple theories of measurement in which it is maintained that whether or not a particular meter rod has altered in
length is to be determined on the basis of a comparison with the
standard meter rod in Paris. The objection is that it is of course
possible that the rod in Paris has altered in length; it is perfectly possible that a dictionary be mistaken.

The main entry for the word 'inspect' in the *Shorter Oxford
English Dictionary* is: "1. *trans.* To look carefully into." The
dictionary is clearly mistaken. Despite the dictionary one has
no assurance that an inspector will do his job properly. He may
inspect something carelessly, which is not to say 'He looked
carefully carelessly into it.'. Inspecting is not a matter of looking carefully or into but of looking, as it were, with a certain
care in mind, viz. looking with a view to whether or not certain
standards are met, or certain conditions are satisfied, etc.

74. Whether or not the meter rod in Paris has altered in length can be determined by first considering recorded and remembered measurements. Since the distance between cities, the heights of famous buildings, the lengths of certain rooms, ships, and automobiles, are all recorded, it will be possible to determine whether or not there is a discrepancy to be accounted for. Secondly, assuming that there is a discrepancy of some sort, precisely how it is accounted for depends on broad questions of physical theory. It is necessary to consider the likelihood of a change having taken place in the length of the meter rod, in the topography, in the size of ships, the likelihood of records having been altered or having been initially inaccurate, and so on. But whether one account is more likely than another depends on the physical theory and on the available data.

Given the present state of physical theory, and assuming that the likelihood of the recorded measurements' having been either initially inaccurate or altered is so slight as to warrant being discounted here, and given that a change has occurred, we should be forced to attribute the change to the meter rod rather than to the topography. But this is not to say that if our physical theory were different from what it is at present even so we could not conclude that the change was a change in the topography and not in the meter rod. To insist that under no conditions could the change be held to be a change in the topography would be to dogmatize about science: it would constitute an absurd attempt to impose artificial and à priori limits to the development of physical theory.

75. The problem of determining what semantic regularity pertains to a given utterance type is much the same but not exactly the same as the problem of determining the length of a given rod. There is a complication in the semantic case owing to the fact that talk about words occasionally leads to an alteration in the use of words.

At present the *Shorter Oxford English Dictionary* is simply mistaken with respect to the word 'inspect'. But that dictionary is frequently appealed to as an authoritative work on the English language. Consequently speakers of English frequently alter their use of words in accordance with the entries in the dictionary. Should this occur in connection with the word 'inspect' then in time the dictionary would prove to be correct. Since I am here concerned exclusively with synchronic linguistic matters such complications as these can and will be ignored.

76.　In determining whether or not a supposed meter rod has altered in length it is necessary to consider the likelihood of an alteration having occurred here rather than there. Just so in determining which utterances constitute deviations from regularities it is necessary to consider the likelihood of a deviation having occurred.

If one sees a man heating a metal meter rod there will generally be no problem whether or not that rod rather than another is actually one meter in length. Just so if in the course of reciting a poem someone utters the utterance 'Look at that swine!' there is generally no problem about whether the utterance constitutes a deviation from a regularity.

If I say 'Let us suppose . . .', 'Once upon a time . . .', 'I dreamt that . . .', I indicate that some regularities found in connection with the utterances of E may not be found in connection with the ensuing utterances. Such preambles as 'let us suppose', 'once upon a time', and 'I dreamt that' signalize (what may be signalized by the context alone without recourse to explicit linguistic forms) certain fairly regular variations on the predominant regularities in the language: they are standard variations on English themes. ("Assume that 4 is a prime: if so, . . ."—"But it isn't a prime!" to which one can only say "You don't understand.")

Any utterance whatever may be uttered as a quotation, or in a grammatical or philosophical discussion, or in the course of a story, poem, novel, or play. Both 'Look at that swine!' and 'God's in his heaven.' may be uttered in the course of reciting a poem. But the former utterance type, unlike the latter, may nonetheless have 'a swine is present in the context of utterance' significantly and relevantly paired with it. If one were to discount the pairing on the grounds that a token of the type could perfectly well be uttered in the course of a poetry reading (and has in fact been uttered here in the course of a philosophy discussion) given in the absence of a swine, one would in effect be discounting all regularities whatever pertaining to the utterances of *E*.

77. Perhaps it is in this sense and for this reason that poetry and the poetic use of words are sometimes said to be "parasitic" on the nonpoetic use of words. 'Look at that swine!' and 'God's in his heaven.' differ in significance but the difference cannot be established in the poetic context.

But this is not to say that the results of a semantic analysis of a language are irrelevant to the poetic use of words in that language. On the contrary, some such results can serve to explicate such a use. (See 187 below.)

78. It is (or is becoming) common practice today among philosophers concerned with the meaning of words to appeal to and to consider the use of words in so-called "ordinary language" (as though one spoke either French or German or "Ordinary"). The point of such an appeal is presumably to avoid contexts of utterance in which deviations from semantic regularities are likely to occur. Although the spirit of such an appeal may be somewhat sensible, the letter of it is not.

Presumably by 'ordinary language' is meant something like everyday discourse. But first, if one is concerned to explicate technical terms of philosophy, or of sailing, or of chemistry, it is useless to consider everyday discourse since such terms are hardly likely to occur in such discourse. Secondly, it is perfectly obvious that deviations from regularities occur in everyday discourse. If one is asked what one thinks of Professor Dimwit one may reply 'Oh he's a bright fellow, yes, very bright.' making it perfectly clear that one thinks the man is a fool. Irony is one form of deviation from a semantic regularity, a familiar variation on English themes: it frequently occurs in everyday discourse, when speaking "Ordinary." Or again, there may be unwitting deviations from regularities. Someone points to a plastic cup and says 'That is glass.': this is likely to be not a new use of the word 'glass' but a simple mistake.

There is no privileged context of utterance.

79.   The problem and the solution of the problem of determining what semantic regularity pertains to a given utterance type, of determining whether or not a deviation has occurred, can be seen (though not adequately stated) in all of its complexity in connection with an utterance from a foreign language, e.g. 'Nitastutin.', an utterance of Cree.

One can begin by observing various speakers of Cree uttering the utterance on various occasions. This of course presupposes that one has enough grasp of the phonology and morphology of the language to enable one to identify various utterance tokens as tokens of the type. Somewhere along the way one may expect to see either a hat or something that the speakers of the language take to be a hat. This means that it may be necessary to consider not only the context of utterance but both the remote and proximate spatiotemporal vicinity of that context. Perhaps there was a hat around, or perhaps there is a hat at a distance. It may also be necessary to consider the behavior of the speakers and hearers both before, during, and after the moment of utterance. What the investigator takes to be a hat may in fact be employed as a chamber pot. Thus it will be necessary to appreciate the situation, both to size up the context of utterance and to understand the behavior of the speakers and hearers to a certain extent. Thus it will be necessary to have some idea of the beliefs, attitudes, etc., of the speakers of the language. But to have an adequate idea of such matters it will of course be necessary to understand the language. This means that at first only a tentative account of a semantic regularity pertaining to 'Nitastutin.' can be given. Here as everywhere there is an interaction between observational and theoretic considerations. Still further complications arise owing to the fact that any conclusions about 'Nitastutin.' may have to be adjusted in the light of conclusions about 'Kitastutin.', 'Utastutin.', and the like.

Were it not for the fact that we can and do translate foreign languages one could be tempted to suppose that it is impossible. Just so, a physiological account of exactly what occurs when one walks can make one wonder. But even so, sooner or later one can pair 'my hat' with 'Nitastutin.'.

80.   That we can translate or learn foreign languages is simply a fact. It could be otherwise. There could be a foreign language that we could neither translate nor learn. Even with world enough and time it might prove to be impossible for us to discover the relevant semantic regularities pertaining to the utterances of that language.

To put the matter in another way, I can see no reason to suppose that there could not be a language spoken by creatures from outer space that we could neither translate nor learn even though such creatures could learn and translate our language. Very simply, the reason is that there might be contrasts in their world that we do not find and are incapable of finding in our own. To be able to speak and to understand English one must have (either natural or artificial) sensory organs capable of making contrasts between 'bin', 'din', 'fin', 'gin', 'kin', etc., and between a bin, a din, a fin, gin, kin, etc.

III

CONDITIONS

81. That there are semantic regularities or projections pertaining to virtually all syntactically nondeviant whole utterances of E is in one sense a trivial truth in that syntactic regularities are a species of semantic regularities (see 27 above). But there is another sense in which it is both true and not at all trivial. This can be seen by considering what I shall call "state regularities" and "state projections."

State regularities or projections are found in connection with virtually all syntactically nondeviant whole utterances of E. State regularities take the following form: given that a syntactically nondeviant whole utterance of E is uttered then generally certain conditions are satisfied. State projections have virtually the same form except that if the relevant utterance is uttered then not generally but in a standard case certain conditions are satisfied. In the former case, that the conditions are in fact satisfied must be confirmable in our relatively limited four dimensional world.

82. In uttering an utterance of E a speaker is performing various speech acts. In uttering an utterance in some appropriate situation and in some appropriate way one is doing something. One may be doing various relatively distinct and different things, such things as referring, asserting, stating, ordering, commanding. Uttering an utterance is doing something, is itself an act, and to say that u_i and u_j are different utter-

ances is to distinguish between the act of uttering u_i and the act of uttering u_j.

To refer, or to assert, or to state is in each case to perform a certain act. Furthermore, in so far as the performance of the act necessitates the uttering of an utterance the act may be classed a speech act.

83.   A given speech act can be performed under certain conditions and not others.

If one does something one does so under certain conditions and not others. In order for one to do whatever it is one is doing certain conditions must be satisfied. To swim one requires a quantity of fluid sufficient to immerse oneself in. Just so, certain conditions must be satisfied if one is to issue an order; e.g. one must be in a position of authority or there must be a second person subordinate to the first.

If a certain speech act is performed certain conditions must be satisfied and thus a certain state of affairs may obtain in our remarkably limited four-dimensional world (hence the appellation "state regularities"). It should be noted that conditions are fundamental here. The state of affairs in question is that characterizable in terms of the satisfaction of the conditions in question, viz. those conditions that must be satisfied in order for the performance of the speech act in question to take place. For example, if someone utters the utterance 'Hello!' then generally he is performing the act of greeting. In order to perform such an act a certain state of affairs must obtain in the context of utterance. More specifically, certain conditions must be satisfied; there must be someone present in a position to be greeted; e.g. a corpse won't do.

This indicates that the problem of finding tentative semantic regularities pertaining to utterances of E can be dealt with in two stages. First, it is necessary to find connections between the act of uttering u_i and the performance of certain other speech acts. Secondly, it is then necessary to discover the conditions under which the speech acts connected with u_i in the first stage of analysis can be performed.

84. Virtually every syntactically nondeviant whole utterance of E is connected with a certain set of speech acts. Think of an utterance of E as an extremely limited musical instrument and of the various speech acts as so many tunes that may be played on the instrument: that will give some idea of the plurality involved.

If I utter 'I waited for you.' then depending on the context I may be making a statement, or giving an explanation, or offering a reason, or making an accusation, or making a complaint, or quoting, or reciting a poem, or telling a story, and so forth. (Each of these is a speech act in that the performance of each act necessitates the uttering of an utterance.) Again, if I utter 'Shut the door!' then depending on the context I may be issuing an order, or giving a command, or making a request, or quoting, or reciting a poem, or telling a story, etc. Again, if I utter 'Hello!' then depending on the context I may be greeting someone, or quoting, or reciting a poem, or telling a story, and so forth.

85. Even though virtually every syntactically nondeviant whole utterance of E is connected with a certain set of speech acts, not every member of such a set is relevant in a semantic analysis of the utterance in question. More specifically, any utterance of E may on occasion be connected with the act of talking about the use of words. Consequently the fact that a given utterance is on occasion so connected tells one nothing about the given utterance. More generally, consider the set of speech acts constituted by the intersection of the sets of speech acts generally connected with the utterances of E. Then every member of that set is semantically irrelevant in the semantic analysis of E. (See 68 above.)

86. The number of speech acts that can be performed by the speakers of the language associated with E is considerably greater than the number of utterances of E (which number is itself indeterminate). This should be obvious. The act of uttering u_i is distinct from the act of uttering u_j if u_i and u_j are distinct, and in uttering u_i one may be performing various speech

acts; e.g. in uttering 'George is coming to visit.' one is not only uttering that utterance but one may be referring, stating, replying, etc.

87. Kinds of speech acts need not be confused with kinds of utterances.

An assertion is not a kind of utterance but a kind of speech act; to make an assertion and to give a description is to perform two different speech acts: in performing either act one may employ a declarative utterance. A declarative utterance is a kind of utterance and it can be employed in the performance of many different or distinct speech acts. Just so, an imperative is a kind of utterance and it can be employed in the performance of many different or distinct speech acts: giving a command, issuing an order, making a request, and so forth.

88. Different syntactic kinds of utterances are connected with different kinds of speech acts. An imperative like 'Shut the door!' is connected with ordering, commanding, requesting, etc., but not with asserting, stating, describing, etc. Again, an interrogative like 'Is the door shut?' is connected with asking, inquiring, etc., but not with asserting, commanding, describing, ordering, etc.

The syntactic structure of E thus provides a way of grouping large numbers of speech acts into certain classes. We can introduce generic terms for speaking of the sets of speech acts generally connected with different syntactic kinds of utterances such as imperatives, interrogatives, declaratives, etc. So we can speak of "imperative-acts," "interrogative-acts," "declarative-acts," etc.

89. In addition to the speech acts connected with different syntactic kinds of utterances, speech acts connected with so-called "response utterances" are worth considering here for it is perfectly clear that if such utterances are to be uttered without deviating from regularities to be found in connection with the language then certain conditions must be satisfied.

We can distinguish between what are called "situational

utterances" and "response utterances." [1] Certain utterances are characteristically uttered only in response to other utterances: 'No.', 'I don't believe it.', 'There are *no* books on the shelves.', 'I see what you mean.'. The clearest examples of response utterances are what might mistakenly appear to be proper parts of utterances: 'Yes.', 'Over there.', 'On the table.', '*This* book.', 'This *book*.'. (Notice that '*This* book.' could be an answer to 'Which?' while 'This *book*.' could be an answer to 'What?'.)

In contrast with response utterances, a situational utterance is one that is generally employed to initiate a discourse, conversation: 'How do you do?', 'I want to tell you something.', 'Do you have any books?'.

90. An important proper subset of response utterances is constituted by utterances of the set of so-called "response signals." Response signals play a prominent role in everyday discourse. If a speaker is speaking at some length, during the time the speaker is speaking the hearer will be signaling that he is paying attention. Thus the hearer will be nodding his head, or gesturing, or grimacing, or uttering such utterances as 'Yes.', 'I see.', 'Oh!', 'Well.', 'That's right.', 'Ha!', 'Quite.', 'Hmn.'. (Confirmation of the importance of response signals in everyday discourse is easily found in connection with telephone conversations. In such a context all response signals are easily blocked by placing one's hand over the mouthpiece: such a move will almost inevitably draw a query like 'Are you there?'.)

A large proper subset of response utterance parts is constituted by utterance parts in which so-called "anaphoric substitutes" occur without their antecedent forms. 'He' is an anaphoric substitute in 'Ask that policeman, and he will tell you.', and its antecedent form is 'that policeman'. A substitute that implies that a certain expression has recently been uttered is an anaphoric substitute and the recently uttered replaced form is the antecedent.[2] If an anaphoric substitute is uttered in

---

[1] See C. C. Fries, *The Structure of English,* pp. 29 ff.
[2] See L. Bloomfield, *Language,* pp. 249–266.

an utterance part without its antecedent form, e.g. 'Where is he?', then either an utterance part containing the antecedent form has recently been uttered or certain nonverbal substitutes have been employed; e.g. one says 'What does he want?' nodding in the direction of the man at the door, or one says 'How much are they?' pointing at the apples on the stand.

91. Suppose one enters a room, looks in a certain direction, and then says 'No, there is no cat on the mat.'. One can say this (without deviating from a semantic regularity) only if the situation has been structured in a certain way: there must be a mat, there must have been some question raised whether or not a cat was on the mat, and so forth.

(I use the word 'structure' in a relatively free and general way. Any set of elements may be said to have a structure in so far as its members are interrelated in certain ways over and above being members of the same set. If the elements of the set are interrelated with respect to certain linguistic features, the set may be said to have a linguistic structure; if they are interrelated with respect to certain physical features, the set may be said to have a physical structure; and so on.)

That a response utterance can be uttered without deviation only if a previous utterance has actually been uttered is of no real significance. The significant difference between a response utterance like 'No, there is no cat on the mat.' and a situational utterance like 'Will you see if there is a cat on the mat?' is that the former obviously can be uttered only in a structured situation whereas the latter utterance obviously partially structures the situation in which it is uttered.

92. But the difference is only a matter of degree of obviousness. A situational utterance can be uttered without deviation only in a situation having the appropriate structure. If we are walking on the desert and out of the blue I say to you 'Will you see if the cat is on the mat?' it would most likely be odd.

It need not be: there is no necessity here. We could structure the scene in such a way as to avoid a degree of deviation suffi-

cient to warrant saying that the utterance was odd, e.g. a discussion on the previous day about a missing cat, about a certain mat.

Either a situational utterance or a response utterance can be
uttered (without deviation) only in a situation having an appropriate structure and both partially structure the situation. If I
reply by saying 'No, there is no cat on the mat.' it would be odd
for you then to ask 'Are there any cats on the mat?': the question is precluded by my reply. Again, this is not to say that
there could not be a situation in which such a sequence of
utterances is uttered without a degree of deviation sufficient to
warrant saying that the second utterance is odd or deviant.

There is a difference of degree here: response utterances
obviously depend on the structure of the situation while situational utterances obviously (partially) structure the situations
in which they are uttered. (They do so by invoking the conditions
associated with the utterance.)

93.   Historically speaking, in so far as they have been concerned with language philosophers have tended to focus their
attention on two particular kinds of declarative-speech act: referring and making a true statement. Thus two types of semantic relationship have received considerable attention, that between an utterance part and its so-called "referent" and that
between a whole utterance and so-called "truth conditions,"
sometimes hypostasized as "a fact."

Owing to their unduly narrow focus philosophers have failed
to realize that what is fundamental here are conditions, not
referents and not truth conditions and not even the satisfaction
of conditions but simply conditions. 'Hello!' has no referent.
It cannot be associated with truth conditions. Neither can 'Why
is it so hard to see what's what?'.

The act of referring is of particular interest here in that it
seems to offer a way of avoiding consideration of conditions in
favor of spatiotemporal entities. Somehow it has seemed simpler
to associate words with things rather than with conditions. But
restricting one's attention simply to spatiotemporal referents is

not a fruitful approach to semantic analysis. Referring is only one among many speech acts.

94. I said previously (in 15 above) that I would assume that a syntactic analysis of E has been given and that the procedures whereby it is given are not in question. Thus I shall assume that the syntax of E has been formulated and that we are free to speak of proper names, nouns, demonstratives, subjects, predicates, and the like. Generally speaking, and in the clearest sort of case, in referring one utters an utterance in subject-predicate form, the expression employed to refer being uttered as grammatical subject. Furthermore, the utterance must be uttered in some appropriate context of utterance and in some appropriate way.

By 'the context of utterance' I mean that portion of space-time that takes its locus from the utterance token, i.e. the spatiotemporal vicinity of the utterance token. (But different utterances provide different radii: the context of utterance for 'Look at that star!' may be measured in light years while the context of utterance for 'Look at my finger!' may be measured in feet. This is a relatively vague notion that neither can nor need be pinned down.)

But merely uttering an utterance in subject-predicate form in some appropriate context is not sufficient to ensure that one is referring. If I am asked who wrote the *Faerie Queene* and I reply somewhat verbosely (and that it is verbose is significant) 'Spenser is the author of the *Faerie Queene.*' I am not referring: I am identifying the author of the *Faerie Queene.* Whether a person is referring or identifying is not always clear from the syntactic form of the utterance uttered. If I say 'George is coming to visit.' I am likely to be referring but I may well be identifying. If I had been asked 'Will you be seeing George?' and I replied 'George is coming to visit.' I would have been referring and not identifying. But if I had been asked 'Who is coming to visit?' and I replied somewhat verbosely 'George is coming to visit.', or more naturally 'George.', I would have been identifying the person who is coming to visit. On the other hand, if I say

'The person who is coming to visit is a bore.' I am clearly referring to the person who is coming to visit.

That one is not referring but simply identifying in replying 'George.' to the query 'Who is coming to visit?' is indicated by the following considerations. To suppose that one is referring in uttering 'George.' (in an appropriate way and in an appropriate context) would be to suppose that one could refer to George without saying anything about him. And this seems somehow repugnant.[3] (If we suppose that the individual variables of quantification theory serve as the carriers of reference, to suppose that one could refer *simpliciter* would be to suppose that an expression of the form '(Ex) $[x]$' was a well-formed formula, which it obviously is not.) Notice that it will not do to suppose that 'George.', when uttered in response to 'Who is coming to visit?', is a simple ellipsis for 'George is coming to visit.'; in that case it would be more reasonable to suppose that 'George.' is an ellipsis for 'The one who is coming to visit is George.': the elision of nominals is a customary feature of response utterances, e.g. as in 'Where is it?'—'On the table.'.

95.   If one utters 'Spenser lived in Ireland,' one may be referring to Spenser. But in saying 'Spenser's poetry is worth reading.' one is likely to be referring to Spenser's poetry, not to Spenser. Here in referring to Spenser's poetry one is also doing something somewhat different, viz. making a reference to Spenser. Again, in saying 'Spenser lived in Ireland.' one may have referred to Spenser and made a reference to Ireland.

That there is a reference to Spenser in 'Spenser's poetry is worth reading.' can be seen in the fact that from 'Spenser's poetry is worth reading.' one can infer 'Spenser wrote certain poetry.' and here 'Spenser' may be used to refer to Spenser.

96.   It is impossible to refer without referring to something or someone (or some things or certain ones, etc.). But this is not to deny that one can refer to that which does not and never did exist.

[3] I am indebted to T. Patton for this point.

If one says 'Pegasus was captured by Bellerophon.' one is likely to be referring to Pegasus: Pegasus never existed. This indicates that referring is like pointing, not like pointing at a duck: one can point even if there is nothing to point at but one cannot point at a duck if there is no duck to be pointed at. To say that one cannot refer without referring to something or someone (or some things, etc.) is thus like saying one cannot point without pointing in some direction or other.

If I say 'I referred to Pegasus.' I indicate that I did something. But doing what I did did not involve a relation between myself and the nonexistent Pegasus. That is simply a silly way of talking that makes for a mystery where there is none. 'I spoke to George.', unlike 'I referred to Pegasus.', does indicate that I did something that involved a relation between myself and George. Thus the name 'George' occurs as the indirect substantival object of the verb 'spoke'. But the name 'Pegasus' need not be thought of as the indirect object of the verb 're-ferred' in that way. The more sensible thing would be to think of 'Pegasus' as, say, a special form of an indirect adverbial object modifying the verb 'referred'.

Just as one can point to the east or point to a duck, so one can refer to Pegasus or refer to Lord Nelson. In either case, what one does, as it were, is to indicate certain conditions. The conditions indicated in referring or in making a reference are said to be a "referent." The so-called "referent" of a so-called "referring expression" is best thought of as the hypostatization of a set of conditions. What I mean by this will become clearer as we go along.

97.   Proper names are obvious and familiar examples of utter-ance parts frequently employed to refer or to make a reference to something or someone. Proper names are an important topic in the philosophy of language but only because their importance has been exaggerated by both philosophers and grammarians. They are of relatively limited theoretic importance in the speaking and understanding of a language.

Various metalinguistic expressions of English, e.g. 'synonym', 'synonymous', 'homonym', 'metonym', 'common name', tend to reinforce the common misconception of the theoretic importance of proper names. But these expressions are the products, as it were, of an extremely naïve analysis of language, not one to be taken seriously.

98.   The word 'word' is sometimes used in an extended way that allows one to speak of any and all proper names as words; e.g. a use that allows one to say 'Edmund Spenser' is a phrase composed of the two words 'Edmund' and 'Spenser'. Ordinarily one speaks of 'Edmund Spenser' as a name, or as a proper name, not as a phrase. It is the proper name of the author of the *Faerie Queene* and it, the proper name, may be used to refer to him.

One may not know a single word of Chinese and yet know of Hsieh Ho. 'Hsieh Ho' is a Chinese proper name: is it a word or phrase in English? It would be odd to say so. If I say 'Are you familiar with Hsieh Ho's views on art?' I am speaking English: I am not speaking a combination of English and Chinese. Yet if 'Hsieh' and 'Ho' are words then they can only be words in Chinese and so I must be mistaken in supposing that I do not know a single word of Chinese and I must speak a combination of Chinese and English, which is absurd.

It is essential to distinguish between names and proper names in *E*. Proper names are generally not words even though a name in *E* that is not a proper name is a word. For example, the word 'agaranthus' is the name but not the proper name of a type of plant. Thus if something is a proper name, it is a name in *E*, but the converse need not hold. 'Rose' in 'Rose is here.' is a proper name but 'rose' in 'A rose.' is only a name, not a proper name.

It is an unfortunate accident that both 'rose' in 'A rose.' and 'Rose' in 'Rose is here.' are spoken of as names. For that suggests that much the same kind of semantic regularity is to be found in connection with 'rose' and 'Rose' and that is not so. Such a use of 'name' may make for good poetry but it makes for bad philosophy.

99.   Not only are proper names generally not words and most

words not proper names, neither proper names nor words are (generally) either signs or symbols.

The student in logic asked to symbolize 'All men are mortal.' cannot properly reply that it is already symbolized. Jesus on the cross may be a symbol of something but 'on', 'the', and 'cross' are words, not symbols, whereas 'Jesus on the cross' is a phrase, not a symbol. Notice that unlike 'How do you pronounce the word that is spelt 'a', 'n', 'i', 's', 'o', 't', 'r', 'o', 'p', 'y'?', the utterance 'How do you pronounce the symbol that is spelt 'a', 'n', 'i', 's', 'o', 't', 'r', 'o', 'p', 'y'?' is odd. One spells words, not symbols. Again, 'I don't like the sound of that symbol.' is curious in a way that 'I don't like the sound of that word.' is not. If something is a symbol it is a symbol of something or it is a symbol for something: the word 'the' is not a word "of" something (other than English) and it is not a word "for" something. And so on. There is, in short, no good reason to suppose that words are either signs or symbols and every reason not to suppose that.

(In the written language associated with *E*, the plus sign '+' is a sign, not a word, and the word 'plus' is a word, not a sign. That it is essential to distinguish 'plus' from '+' is indicated by the fact that '+' cannot substitute for the affix '-plus' in 'He was nonplussed.', 'There was a surplus.'.)

100. The word 'name' has been used in a curious way by philosophers and logicians in speaking of sentences, utterances. 'That is a good painting.' is a sentence. It is also an utterance. More precisely, ' 'That is a good painting.' ' is a representation of both a sentence and an utterance. But ' 'That is a good painting.' ' is sometimes said to be the "name" of a sentence. I object to this way of speaking. It makes for a mystery where there is none. If it is a name, it may be a name in the way 'rose' in 'A rose.' is a name but not in the way 'Rose' in 'Rose is here.' is a name. For if it is a proper name, it is odd that I know what it is the name of without being told. 'Witchgren' is a proper name. It is the proper name of . . . . You cannot complete that sentence.

A picture is a picture of a certain house because of a close correlation between the parts of the picture and certain visual features of the house. A picture of the house is correlated with visual features of the house. A blueprint of the same house is correlated with structural features of the house. Either the blueprint or the picture could be said to be a representation of the house.

' 'That is a good painting.' ' is a representation of the sentence 'That is a good painting.' because of the close correlation between the parts of the inscription printed here and the parts of the sentence that it represents. Analogously, ' 'that' ' is not the name but the representation of the word 'that'.

' 'That is a good painting.' ' is a relatively crude representation of an utterance. The relation between the printed matter and an utterance is like the relation between a musical score and the sounds that occur on an occasion of the performance of the music. It may be odd to speak of a score as a representation of the music: it would be odder to speak of it as a proper name.

Consider statement (1):

(1)   The world will end with a bang.

Since (1), or 'The world will end with a bang.', is here taken to be a statement, '(1)' is here being used as the (temporary) proper name of a statement, not as a representation. '(1)' is a proper name and not a representation owing (in part) to the fact that there can be no correlation between the parts of '(1)' and that which it is a name of: statements have no parts (in the relevant sense).

But ' 'The world will end with a bang.' ' is not the proper name of a statement. It is a representation of an utterance, the uttering of which in an appropiate way and in an appropriate situation would constitute the making of the statement that the world will end with a bang. ' 'The world will end with a bang.' ' stands in a similarity relation to the utterance represented. Hence the relation is somewhat akin to that found in metaphoric uses of words. But the relation between ' 'The world will end with a bang.' ' and the statement made by uttering the represented utterance in an appropriate way and in an appropriate situation is rather akin to that found in metonymic uses of words.[4]

Consequently, we could say that ' 'That the world will end with a bang.' ' is a representation of an utterance token, and a metonym of an utterance type and of a statement, or an assertion, etc. (whereas ' 'The world will end with a bang?' ' is a metonym of a question, etc.).

101. A speaker of the language associated with E looks at the cat on the mat and says 'Witchgren is on the mat.'. A state regularity (or projection) is to be found in connection with this utterance; viz. if the utterance is uttered then generally (or in a standard case) there is something named 'Witchgren' on some mat. Consequently the utterance can be associated with certain conditions. But it is also possible to say something quite different in connection with this utterance. We can ignore the fact that we can associate the utterance with certain conditions and instead consider only the fact that owing to the nature of the conditions the utterance can be related to a particular spatiotemporal entity.

The picture I wish to suggest here is this: we look at the language and we look at the world and we look back and forth. We find various occurrences of 'Witchgren is on the mat.' in E and we find that these utterances of the utterance can be related to a particular spatiotemporal entity, viz. Witchgren. The relation is a many-one relation. There is a relation between the utterance in E and a particular spatiotemporal entity. This is an instance of what I shall call a "nominative relation."

If a nominative relation is found in connection with an utterance of E then, generally speaking, a proper name occurs in that utterance. Thus generally speaking, a fairly reliable indication of the occurrence of a proper name in an utterance is

[4] See R. Jakobson, "Two Aspects of Language and Two Types of Aphasic Disturbance," pt. II of R. Jakobson and M. Halle, *Fundamentals of Language;* in particular, see "The Metaphoric and Metonymic Poles," ch. v.

that there be a many-one relation between the utterance and a particular spatiotemporal entity. (See 120 below.) This is not a necessary condition. 'I shall do a picture of Pegasus.' cannot be related to a particular spatiotemporal entity yet the proper name 'Pegasus' occurs in that utterance. And 'Smith' is a proper name yet it cannot be related to one and only one particular spatiotemporal entity.

102.   That the utterance 'Witchgren is on the mat.' can be related to a particular spatiotemporal entity is one thing, that the relation be attributable to the fact that the proper name 'Witchgren' occurs in the utterance is another. But the problem of attribution (see 44 above) is easily solved in connection with proper names.

Consider the following set of utterances:

'Witchgren is on the mat.'
'Witchgren was on the mat.'
'Witchgren was by the mat.'
'Witchgren was by a mat.'
'Witchgren was by a table.'
'Was Witchgren by a table?'
'He is on the mat.'

Precisely one and the same entity can be found in relation to all except the last of the utterances listed. All of the others can be related to one and the same particular spatiotemporal entity, viz. Witchgren. The relation is not attributable to the morphemes 'is', 'on', 'th-', '-e', and 'mat', and neither is it attributable to the word order or to the intonation contour. This is shown by the fact that tokens of the utterance type 'He is on the mat.' cannot generally be related to one and the same spatiotemporal entity.

Further evidence in support of this thesis is found in the fact that members of what I shall call the "distributive set" for the proper name 'Witchgren' in E can generally be related to one and the same spatiotemporal entity. By 'the distributive set for an element of E' I mean the set of utterances of E in which the element occurs. Thus the utterances in which 'Witch-gren' occurs can generally be related to one and the same spatiotemporal entity.

103. I shall say that Witchgren is the spatiotemporal referent (hereafter abbreviated to 'st-referent') of the proper name 'Witchgren'. (This is a relatively trivial statement of a semantic relation but of course I am not here concerned to say something particularly informative about the particular name 'Witch-gren'.) Thus the proper name 'Witchgren' names a particular spatiotemporal entity, its st-referent, viz. Witchgren. But not all names have an st-referent: 'Pegasus' does not.

Nothing qualifies as an st-referent unless it be spatiotemporal. It need not be an entity but it must be spatiotemporal. But I cannot pin down the precise way the phrase 'st-referent' is being used here. I am sure that 'Witchgren' has an st-referent. I am sure that 'Pegasus' does not. I am not at all sure about 'Arabia'. What matters is its spatiotemporal location and I am not sure that Arabia has one. Can Arabia be located in space time? Then 'Arabia' has an st-referent. But if Arabia was some sort of political organization then 'Arabia' does not have an st-referent. It is not that having an st-referent is essentially a relation between linguistic elements and either things or persons. On the contrary, the phrase 'the great San Francisco fire' has an st-referent for the st-referent can be located in space time. But the phrase 'the reign of Elizabeth I' cannot be related to anything having a spatiotemporal location for although we can date it we cannot locate it in space (or so I am inclined to suppose).

Possibly what I am saying here suggests a "metaphysical view," viz. that to be is to be spatiotemporal. I would not suggest it. I am not here concerned with "metaphysical views." I am concerned only to make clear how I am using the expression 'st-referent'. A many-one relation can be found between a linguistic element and something spatiotemporal; in particular, such a relation can be found between 'Witchgren' and Witchgren for we find that the speakers of the language associated with E relate the proper name 'Witchgren' to Witchgren the cat, a spatiotemporal entity. I say ' 'Witchgren' names Witchgren.'. No such relation can be found between 'the square of 2' and the number 4 because the number 4 is not something spatiotemporal. Hence, as I am using the expression 'st-referent', the phrase 'the square of 2' does not have an st-referent. I would not deny that there is a relation between 'the square of 2' and the number 4. But the relation is not of the same sort as the relation between 'Witchgren' and Witchgren. The latter relation is clearly a relation between a linguistic element and an obvious element of the world, viz. something spatiotemporal. Whatever the relation between 'the square of 2' and 4 may be, it is not the same as that between 'Witchgren' and Witchgren.

104.   That one and the same st-referent can generally be found in connection with utterances of the distributive set for 'Witchgren' in E is something of an ideal: it must not be taken too seriously.

I say 'He is the elder son of O'Shaughnessy.'. Which O'Shaughnessy? 'Patrick O'Shaughnessy.'. Which Patrick O'Shaughnessy? 'Patrick Michael O'Shaughnessy.' and on occasion even this is not enough.

Although we have been told that Scott is the author of *Waverley* there are at least eight notable Scotts and thousands of others listed in telephone directories. An ordinary name in E, e.g. 'Smith', 'Jones', 'Edward', does not in fact refer in E to a particular spatiotemporal entity. But this is in fact true of practically all names in E. It may be true of any name in E: any name may tarnish in time and become common.

105.   A speaker of the language associated with E says 'Witchgren is on the mat.' pointing to Witchgren as he says it. He points and one must be able to pass from his finger to that which is pointed at. I throw a cat a piece of meat. It does not see where the meat fell. I point to the meat: the cat smells my finger. The speaker points and unlike a cat I do not look at his finger. What do I look at?

There is a distance between his finger tip and that which he is pointing at. But it is not a distance that can be closed up. It would not help if he put his finger on the cat. On the contrary: it would make it worse. What is he pointing to? A hair on the cat's back? A type of dust?

That a proper name can be learned simply by following a finger is a myth. (We might call it "the myth of the pure ostensive definition.")

106. I believe that it is not possible to state a simple strong generalization about proper names. One can only say what is so for the most part and that must be qualified. For the most part then, proper names are not said to have meaning in English or to have a meaning in English. But certain proper names are said to mean something to someone and certain proper names are said to have a meaning. It may seem as though I am drawing excessively subtle distinctions here but I do not think so. I am for the moment simply trying to speak in an ordinary way.

First, it may seem curious to say that a certain proper name has a meaning and yet deny that it have a meaning in English. But there is nothing curious about this at all. The name 'Theophilus' is a proper name and it is said to have a meaning for it means lover of god. But that it has a meaning is owing to a fact about the Greek language, not about English. The proper name is formed from two Greek words that have meaning in Greek. In this sense it is possible that my cat's proper name, 'Charlie', has a meaning but I do not know what it is. On the other hand, the proper name 'Witchgren' does not, in this sense, have a meaning. I simply invented the name (for a real cat).

Secondly, whether or not a proper name means something to someone depends on the person, his experiences. The proper name 'Charlie' means something to me for it is the name of my cat but the proper name 'Charles Garrington' means practically (but not absolutely) nothing to me. Even though 'Charlie' means something to me, it does not have meaning in (my) English (idiolect) and it does not have a meaning in (my) English (idiolect). If I say 'Charlie is hungry.' I may mean my cat is hungry but that is not to say that for me 'Charlie' means the same as 'my cat'. (And to say 'For me, 'my cat' means the same as 'Charlie'.' would be an appropriate but nonliteral way of talking.)

So I do not want to deny that certain proper names may be said to mean something to someone or to have a meaning but I want to deny that proper names are, for the most part, said to have meaning in English or to have a meaning in English.

107.   Even though I want to deny that proper names are, for the most part, said to have meaning in English or to have a meaning in English, given what I take to be the way speakers of the language associated with E apparently use the word 'connotation', I want to say that proper names do for the most part if not invariably have a connotation.

If we are to say that a proper name has a connotation, why not say that it has meaning in English? For the time being, for this reason: not merely that we do not say so though that is relevant but that a proper name connotes what is, as it were, noted with the name by the hearer. It is not what the name means, neither is it what is meant by speakers of the language. It need not in any way connect with what speakers of the language mean. Given the way speakers of the language associated with E apparently use the word 'connotation' and cognate terms, one can say that a proper name connotes something primarily to the hearer. A speaker may say 'I mean . . .' but it would, or so I am inclined to suppose, be odd for the speaker to say 'I connote . . .'.

To talk about what is meant by a certain element is to talk from a speaker's point of view. Notice that to ask 'What is meant by the word 'good'?' is not at all the same as asking 'What does the word 'good' mean?'. The former but not the latter question lends itself to rephrasal as 'What does a speaker mean in using the word 'good'?' (this rather than 'What does a speaker mean by using the word 'good'?'). Thus one says 'The word 'inspect' means to look with a view to determining whether certain standards are met.', which is not to say 'To look with a view to determining whether certain standards are met is meant by the word 'inspect'.'. The passive voice of 'mean' clearly indicates that a speaker is in question.

To talk about what is meant by a certain element is to talk from a speaker's point of view. To talk about what is connoted by the element is talk from a hearer's point of view. But to talk about what an element means is, as it were, to be in between speakers and hearers. So we must take care to distinguish between what a speaker means, what an element means, and what an element connotes.

Both what a speaker means and what an element connotes to a hearer admit of enormous latitude. To confuse either with what the element means could only lead to utter confusion. If I say 'I'll meet you at my office.' I may mean that I'll meet you at Hunt Hall. But this is not to say that 'I'll meet you at my office.' means the same as 'I'll meet you at Hunt Hall.' nor that 'my office' is synonymous with 'Hunt Hall'. Again, for you, the word 'office' may have all sorts of connotations that would lead you to look for something other than the customary academic hovel; so you may look for and expect a secretary and business machines: that is not what the word 'office' means.

108.   The proper name 'Witchgren' in E can be related to a particular st-referent, but not merely that: it can be related to a particular st-referent that is named 'Witchgren'. 'Witchgren' is a proper name. This name was invented in order to have a name for a particular cat. If the name is not (or is) unique that is an accident. If it conveys any information that, too, is an accident so far as my intentions were concerned.

But the utterance part 'Witchgren' is not completely uninformative. The part has the style of a proper name in E. (It is not a word of E though there are words of E like it, e.g. 'witchen', 'witchetty'.) On hearing 'Witchgren' I would take it to be a proper name. This means that as a hearer I would take it to be related to the sort of entity that proper names in E are in fact related to, e.g. a person, an animal, a place, a body of water, something that is in some way single, one. We do not name water: we name a body of water.

One would not take 'Witchgren' to be related to something constituted of a particular leaf on a tree in Egypt and a particular rock in the Missouri. Something having such a constitution does not receive a proper name in E. It would be odd to give it a proper name. (Of course this has on occasion been done: that does not make it less odd.) It would be odd to speak of an "entity" having such a constitution. There are regularities to be found in connection with the word 'entity': an entity is also something having some sort of unity, that is one.

Few utterance parts seem as uninformative as 'Witchgren'. One hears the proper names 'Paula', 'Jane', 'Julia', and one knows at once that females are in question. 'Paula wants his own book.' would be odd. 'Paula and John are to be married.' is ambiguous out of context: 'Paula and Jane are to be married.' is not.

But the proper name 'Witchgren' in E does have a connotation: one can say what it connotes only by considering the distribution of the name in the corpus.

109.   Since every morphological element of E is identified by means of some sort of analysis of the corpus, every morphological element of E has a nonnull distributive set in E. The connotation of a morphological element of E is the set of similarities generally noted by the hearers of the language associated with E between the semantic regularities pertaining to the utterances of its distributive set.

An occurrence of 'Witchgren' in an utterance of E may on one occasion be related to, say, a small grey kitten. Another occurrence of 'Witchgren' in another utterance of E may on a later occasion be related to a large grey tomcat. Hence 'Witchgren' in E may connote tomcat but not small or large tomcat.

Frequently a more explicit and detailed statement can be made of what a proper name in E connotes. We may find that not only one and the same st-referent is generally found in connection with the distributive set for the name in E but that the st-referent of the name stands in certain constant relations. Thus 'The Empire State Building' connotes at least

New York City skyscraper. Generally speaking, the connotation of a proper name in E is a certain subset of the set of invariant characteristics (relational or otherwise) of its referent (spatio-temporal or otherwise).

But not any similarity will do. Generally speaking, the lower bound of the set of similarities constituting the connotation of an element of E is the set of similarities between the semantic regularities pertaining to the utterances of the distributive set for the element. Thus the lower bound for the set of similarities constituting the connotation of the proper name 'Witchgren' in E is the set of invariant characteristics of its st-referent. But not every such invariant characteristic can be said to enter into its connotation; e.g. one invariant characteristic of the referent of 'Witchgren', viz. Witchgren, is that of being a mammal. It seems absurd to say that 'Witchgren' connotes mammal. This indicates that an upper bound on the set of similarities is called for.

Generally speaking, the upper bound of the set of similarities constituting the connotation of an element of E is determined by what the hearers of the language associated with E take note of in connection with an utterance of the element in utterances of E. This is clearly not a precise notion. There is no way of pinning it down.

Consequently I propose to dispense with all talk of "connotation" and introduce in its stead the more precise notion of the "information-content" of an element of E. The information-content of an element is stated in terms of a semantic distribution formula.

110.   The proper name 'Witchgren' is a single morpheme in E. Consider the utterance 'Witchgren is on the mat.'. Here the name occurs in the environment '. . . is on the mat.' and it constitutes an environment for 'is on the mat.'; i.e. this latter expression can occur in the environment 'Witchgren . . .'.

Not every expression of E occurs in the environment 'Witchgren . . .', e.g. 'are on the mat.' does not and neither does 'are happy.'. Neither of these expressions are combined with

'Witchgren . . .'. Thus in filling the blank in 'Witchgren . . .'
we attend to syntactic features governing the combination of
one element of E with another. I shall refer to such features
as "combinative features."

111.   A speaker of the language associated with E says 'Witchgren is on the mat.'. Here the combinative features indicated
by '. . . is on the mat.' appear to tell us at once that a single
entity is being referred to. This would be a fallacious inference
suggested by an ill-chosen grammatical terminology.

It is usually said that 'is' is the third person singular present
indicative form of the verb 'to be'. This is a remarkably in-
felicitous characterization. Consider the utterance 'Curry is
difficult to prepare properly.': here 'is' has nothing to do with
a person, either third or otherwise; curry is not a single
"entity" or a "single" anything; nothing is indicated about
the present.

Rather than saying that 'is' is a singular form of the verb,
it would be more sensible to say it is the "implural" form.
The nouns of E can, for the most part, be roughly sorted into
two large classes: "count nouns" and "mass nouns." Count
nouns, as the word 'count' suggests, do contrast with respect
to singular and plural: 'a bean' vs. 'beans'. A bean is a single
entity. But mass nouns do not so contrast: 'rice' is a mass noun
and we do not (generally) speak of 'a rice' vs. 'rices'. 'Chicken'
in E is used both as a count noun, 'A chicken is running around
in the yard.', and as a mass noun, 'Chicken will be served.'.
Unlike a mass noun, a count noun cannot occur as a syntactic
subject: we cannot say 'Book is on the table.'. Instead, it is
necessary to employ a morphological construction: 'A book is
on the table.' or 'Books are on the table.' (i.e. 'book' + '-s').

The combinative features indicated by '. . . is on the mat.'
tell us at once that what is in question satisfies the condition of
being implural. But that this implural feature of our world is
a single entity is another matter.

Owing to the indications provided by combinative features
in ordinary discourse one may know what is said without

actually hearing the entire utterance; e.g. one may catch only
'. . . en is on the mat.' yet one would, in many cases, know
exactly what was said. One could go wrong: '[The p]en is on
the mat.'. But one could not be altogether wrong: without
hearing it, one knows that an implural term preceded 'is'.
Consequently, if one catches only 'Witchgren . . . on the mat.'
with a sufficiently short time span filling the gap, one knows
exactly what was said. Were it not for such so-called "redun-
dancies" ordinary discourse would be vastly more difficult to
follow than it is. Thus 'I have eight books for you.' and 'I have
a book for you.' are not easily confused, even in a loose style of
speech. 'I have aih books for you.' will not collapse into 'I have
a book for you.' owing to the "redundant" affix '-s'.

112.   To say that the morpheme 'Witchgren' in E is an implural term is to formulate, in a convenient way, an enormous
amount of data. We can see not only that 'Witchgren are on
the mat.' does not occur but that 'Witchgren eat.' and 'Witchgren run.' do not occur either. We thus indicate in a phrase
that 'Witchgren' occurs in such environments as '. . . runs.'
and '. . . is hungry.' but not in such environments as '. . .
run.' and '. . . are hungry.'. Thus to say that the element is an
implural term is (partially) to formulate the distribution of the
element in E.

If we consider the environments in which the morpheme
'Witchgren' occurs in E we find that it occurs in 'The cat . . .
is on the mat.' but not in '. . . wants to go to the cinema.',
'. . . needs a new dress.', '. . . is doing sums.'. How can we
formulate the distribution of 'Witchgren' in E with respect to
its occurrence or nonoccurrence in such environments as these?
In the previous case, where the problem was to formulate the
distribution of 'Witchgren' with respect to its occurrence in
such environments as '. . . runs.', '. . . is hungry.', we had a
general phrase available, viz. 'an implural term'. No such general phrase is available here. Yet it is perfectly clear why
'Witchgren' does not occur in such an environment as '. . . is
doing sums.': the reason is simply that it is the name of a cat.

We can, in consequence, formulate not only the data formulated in saying that 'Witchgren' is an implural term but also the data with respect to the occurrence or nonoccurrence of 'Witchgren' in the environments noted above by saying that the morpheme 'Witchgren' in E is the name of a cat. Since we find that the morpheme 'Witchgren' in E occurs in '. . . licking his paw.' but not in '. . . licking her paw.', or '. . . wants her dinner.', we can say that it is the name of a tomcat. So 'Witchgren' in E has the information-content of being a tomcat.

113.　Possibly a still more explicit and detailed statement can be made of the information-content of 'Witchgren' in E. This will depend on the particular utterances in the corpus; e.g. if we find that 'Witchgren' occurs in such environments as '. . . wants his dinner.', '. . . is looking for food.', '. . . is hungry.', we may formulate the hypothesis that 'Witchgren' in E has not merely the information-content of being a tomcat but of being a hungry tomcat. On the other hand, if we find that 'Witchgren' also occurs in such environments as '. . . has just eaten.', '. . . is well fed.', '. . . is not hungry now.', that would serve to refute the hypothesis.

But suppose we find that 'Witchgren' occurs in such environments as '. . . has hurt his tail.', '. . . moved his tail.', but never in '. . . has no tail.': are we to say that 'Witchgren' in E has the information-content of being a tomcat with a tail? Given the assumption that the distributive set for 'Witchgren' in E does not include such utterances as 'Witchgren has lost his tail.' and '. . . has no tail.', and that an appreciably large subset of the distributive set for 'Witchgren' in E is encompassed under the formula, then it does follow that 'Witchgren' in E has the information-content of being a tomcat with a tail. But if this were so it would follow that one had not elicited the utterance 'Witchgren has no tail.' from an informant. It is possible that even if we had attempted to do so we might not have succeeded in eliciting such an utterance from an informant owing either to the fact that it struck him as odd or that it struck him as obviously false and he simply refuses to consider obvious falsehoods. Both 'I saw a purple cow.' and 'I saw a married bachelor.' might evoke the same response from an informant, viz. 'That's ridiculous!', and we might not succeed in eliciting either from him. But all that matters here is the corpus we are working with.

114.   Here one can see that one cannot account for the failure of the substitutivity of certain elements in certain linguistic environments and in certain contexts simply by appealing to the information-content of the elements involved. Suppose the cat in question not only is named 'Witchgren' but is called 'Grenwitch'. Then we may discover to our surprise that Witchgren and Grenwitch are one and the same cat. Even so, 'Witchgren and Witchgren are one and the same cat.' is odd in a way that 'Witchgren and Grenwitch are one and the same cat.' is not odd. Yet 'Witchgren' and 'Grenwitch' have the same st-referent and may have the same information-content, viz. that of being a tomcat.

One might try to explain the fact that 'Witchgren' cannot be substituted without oddity for 'Grenwitch' in 'Witchgren and Grenwitch are one and the same cat.' by appealing to a difference in sense. Thus 'Witchgren' and 'Grenwitch' might be said to have different senses. Such a theory would confound sound and sense.

A sufficient condition for the avoidance of oddity in the environment '. . . and . . . are one and the same cat.' is that the blanks be filled by tokens of different phonetic types. If 'Dash' and 'Dot-dot-dot' are two names for one and the same cat then 'Dash and Dot-dot-dot are one and the same cat.' is not odd while 'Dash and Dash are one and the same cat.' and 'Dot-dot-dot and Dot-dot-dot are one and the same cat.' are odd. There is no need to invent a difference in sense to account for a difference in sound. (See 166 ff. below.)

115.   To switch back for a moment to the vaguer notion of a connotation, the explanation of the fact that an element of E may connote such different things to different people should now be obvious. The corpus E has an indefinite and varying

constitution. A given hearer will be familiar with only a proper subset of the distributive set for a given element of E. The connotation of the element for him will depend (in part) on the particular subset of its distributive set that he is familiar with. Furthermore, a given hearer familiar with only a proper subset of the distributive set for an element of E will take note only of a proper subset of the set of similarities between the semantic regularities pertaining to that proper subset of the utterances of the distributive set for the element in E that he is familiar with.

It should not be surprising then that enormous variations are to be found in what a given element of E connotes to various hearers.

116.   'Witchgren' is the proper name of a particular cat. But the relation between the name and the cat is not one that can be gleaned from an examination of either the name or the cat. Examining certain occurrences of the morpheme 'Witchgren' in E may lead one to suppose that the morpheme is the proper name of a tomcat but there is no way of telling precisely which cat is in question until one has observed people using 'Witchgren', until one has acquired information about Witchgren. More simply, the proper name 'Witchgren' does not lead one to the cat Witchgren. Knowing that 'Witchgren' in E has the information-content of being a tomcat is not enough. The proper name was introduced into the language, into E, and it was related to the particular st-referent. Baptismal rites occurred.

The striking difference between a proper name like 'Witchgren' and a "name," or better a common noun, like 'tiger' in virtue of which only the latter can be said to have meaning in English (where meaning is of course not merely a·matter of connotation) is this: if there are two animals in a cage and one is a tiger, a perfect specimen of a tiger, and the other animal is virtually indistinguishable from it, then the second animal is a tiger. But if there are two animals in a cage and one is Witchgren and the other animal is virtually indistinguishable from it, it does not follow that the second animal is Witchgren. The two animals have been individuated in virtue of Witchgren's baptismal rites. (And that is the difference between "names" like 'rose' and 'Rose'.)

The picture I wish to suggest here (as in 101 above) is this: we look at the language and we look at the world and we look back and forth and so relate 'Witchgren' to Witchgren. But this picture is now in sharper focus. One relates occurrences of 'Witchgren' in E to a particular st-referent (not so simply) in this way: through both extralinguistic means, e.g. observation, and intralinguistic means, e.g. information. Another way of saying this is: it may not be enough simply to have a speaker of the language associated with E point to Witchgren and say 'That is Witchgren.' for one may not know what to look at. It is for this reason that "the pure ostensive definition" is a myth. The frame of reference may have to be narrowed, Witchgren may have to be framed. The information-content of 'Witchgren' in E provides just such a frame. But given the appropriate frame of reference, it is still necessary to pick out this and not that spatiotemporal entity. If Glywellyn is another tomcat as much like Witchgren as you like, and if 'Witchgren' and 'Glywellyn' have the same information-content, what individuates Witchgren from Glywellyn need be nothing other than the act of ostension, pointing to Witchgren and saying 'That is Witchgren.'.

117. Certain proper names in E can be directly related to their st-referents, but not all. 'Théophile Gautier' has an st-referent but we cannot directly relate 'Théophile Gautier' to anything. Gautier is dead and gone: he no longer exists. In such cases it is necessary either to pair off 'Théophile Gautier' with other referring expressions in E, thus to attend to and to consider acts of identification, or to determine the information-content of the name by considering its distribution in the corpus. In either case one proceeds intra-linguistically.

We find that 'Théophile Gautier' may have paired with it 'the author of *Émaux et camées*', 'the author of *Le Capitaine*

Fracasse', and that it is uttered in such environments as '. . paraded the boulevards of Paris in a burnoose.', '. . . influenced Baudelaire.', '. . .'s house was filled with animals.'. There is more to be said. Theoretically speaking, there is no end to what can be said.

"A name introduced via description is nothing but an abbreviated description": this misses the point of a name. Abbreviation is beside the point (and the name has not been introduced simply by means of descriptive phrases). A name is a fixed point in a turning world. Descriptions change. Some of our information about Gautier may prove to be erroneous: the name is not tied to all of the reports, accounts, descriptions, etc., given in connection with Gautier. If all such reports, accounts, etc., should prove to be erroneous, we would (most likely) then no longer have any use for the name.

Certain things are likely to undo a name. George is not what he was. At one time he was two feet high, then three feet high, and now almost six feet high. Now he is flesh and bones: soon he will cease to exist. Even death does not undo a name in *E*. But lesser things are likely to. Were he to change in extraordinary ways, e.g. change sex, it is likely that his name would change from 'George' to 'Georgina'. Only the unexpected miracle matters.

This should not be surprising. The information-content of a name is (in part) a function of its distributive set. Death will produce only a relatively slight change in the distributive set of a proper name in *E*: a change in sex would produce a profound change. Gautier is dead, he no longer exists, yet we say 'Gautier is the author of *Émaux et camées.*'. (There is no present tense in *E*, only the past and the "nonpast" or the "impast.")

There are (at least) two ways of defining a circle: one draws the circle for someone; one shows someone Witchgren on the mat (and so proceeds extralinguistically). Or one draws tangents; one tells someone something in connection with Gautier (and so proceeds intralinguistically). A potentially infinite number of tangents can be drawn to a circle: there is, theoretically speaking, no end to what can be said in connection with

Gautier. Any number of tangents can be erased and the circle can still be made out: erase them all and the circle vanishes, and so with Gautier and what is said in connection with him.

118.   That 'Théophile Gautier' can be paired off with 'the author of *Émaux et camées*' does not guarantee that 'Théophile Gautier' can then indirectly be related to its st-referent. 'Pegasus' can be paired off with 'the winged creature captured by Bellerophon' but 'the winged creature captured by Bellerophon' cannot be related to an st-referent. Pegasus is a creature of myth. Here by (actually) drawing imaginary tangents we define an imaginary circle. But not any tangent will do: Pegasus is not the creature slain by Hercules.

There can be no question of directly relating 'Théophile Gautier' to its st-referent but neither can there be any question of directly relating 'the author of *Émaux et camées*' to its st-referent. The st-referent in question no longer exists. Whatever connection is established between 'the author of *Émaux et camées*' and its st-referent can be established only on the basis of composition. The principle of composition is the main projective device whereby the narrow spatiotemporal limits of our world are transcended.

119.   Certain relations and regularities are often found in connection with utterances in which demonstratives occur.

Consider the following sequence of utterances: 'This is a beautiful book. *This* one here? Yes, this is really well done.'. (I imagine the first utterance of 'this' to be accompanied with a nod in the direction of the book, the second and third utterances with pointing gestures.) We can imagine hundreds of speakers all of whom point to the book and say 'This is an extraordinary book.'—a book on display in a museum would do. A certain relation is found here in connection with 'this': we find utterances of 'this' related to a particular st-referent, viz. the book pointed at by the speakers. The relation is a many-one relation. 'This' is here related to a particular st-referent.

But it would not be true to say ' 'This' in E is related to a particular st-referent, viz. a particular book.': one may say 'This is a good one.' pointing to a painting, not the book in question. What 'this' is related to depends on the situation in which the word is used. A certain set of utterances of 'this' in E can be split up into various subsets each of which is related to a particular st-referent. The relation is then a complex one involving a plurality of many-one relations. This is an instance of the sort of regularity that I shall call a "material regularity."

To distinguish the nominative relation found in connection with 'Witchgren' from the material regularity found in connection with 'this', I say that the proper name in E refers to a particular st-referent whereas the demonstrative in E refers to a demonstratively determined member of a set of st-referents.

120.   Generally speaking, only a name, or a phrase involving the use of a name, in E refers to a particular referent (spatio-temporal or otherwise). Virtually all other elements of E that refer refer to a member (or members) of a set of referents. (But see below for an important qualification.)

Suppose no names were available. One says 'The blond girl has a spinsterish look.': the phrase 'the blond girl' here refers to a particular referent, viz. the blond girl, whoever she may be. But it would not be true to say 'The phrase 'the blond girl' in E refers to this particular girl, whoever she may be.': the phrase here so refers but on another occasion this same phrase may be used to refer to a different girl (or not to refer at all). By using the phrase 'the blond girl' one can refer to a particular girl but one can achieve a definite reference only in the appropriate situation. One is in a room with the blond girl, a brunette, and another person. One remarks, 'The blond girl has a spinsterish look.' to the other person nearby and nods in the direction of the two girls who are at the other end of the room. If there were two blond girls present, both at the other end of the room, one would have to employ either a different or a more elaborate descriptive phrase or do more than nod in the appropriate direction. Thus instead of 'the blond girl' one might say 'the tall blond girl' or 'the tall blond girl in the corner' or 'the tall blond girl in the corner to the left' and so on, depending always and relying always on the situation.

"The reference of the phrase 'the blond girl' may be situationally determined but the reference of the phrase 'the first prime after 10' is not, for the first prime after 10 is 11 and nothing but 11": this would be a double confusion. One says 'With respect to the series, 1, 3, 4, 6, 7, 9, 10, 12, 13, 15, 16, etc., the first prime after 10 is 13.': here the reference of the phrase is, as it were, situationally determined and the referent is 13, not 11. More significantly, it is not clear what one should say about '10': isn't it a name? Hence it is not surprising that the phrase 'the square of 2' has a unique referent, viz. 4.

A state of total independence from the situational factor determining the reference of a word or phrase not involving the use of a name can in general be approached only asymptotically: we locate a circle by drawing tangents. Apart from one very special type of case, to achieve total independence a proper name is needed. (But not any proper name will do: see 104 above.)

There is, however, one special type of case that must be noted. It is obvious that the phrase 'the first man to run the four-minute mile' does not have a unique reference, e.g. a judge at a track event says to the contestants 'The first man to run the four-minute mile will receive the trophy.'. Consequently the reference of the phrase is situationally determined. But one can relate the utterance to the widest possible context and so insure the uniqueness of the reference. And this is done by employing such expressions as 'anywhere', 'at anytime', 'in the world'. Thus the phrase 'the first man to run the four-minute mile anywhere and at anytime' has a unique reference.

121.   Nominative relations are actually found in connection with few proper names in *E*. This is in part owing to the fact that the language abounds in names like 'Pegasus', names having no st-referents. It is important to realize that one can produce such cases at will. For example, I imagine an owl standing before me. I shall call him 'Gordel'. What is 'Gordel' the name

of? It is the name of an imaginary owl, something I have just imagined. I can talk about Gordel as though he existed (elsewhere than in my imagination). Now there are true and false statements to be made about Gordel: that he is an omniscient owl is true; that he is a pig is false. I can draw pictures of Gordel. I can tell people about him. (I may even begin to believe that he exists: you may be persuaded of it too.) That nominative relations are actually found in connection with few proper names in E is also, and perhaps primarily, owing to the fact that few names in E are unique and related to one and only one particular st-referent. We tend to use the same name over again to name different things. Hence material regularities are of greater importance in connection with the utterances of E. They too, however, present difficulties.

Even though material regularities are sometimes found in connection with demonstratives in E, there are all sorts of cases in which no such regularities can be found, e.g. such utterances as 'That idea is puzzling.', 'This problem is too difficult.', 'These matters needn't concern us.'. This is not to say that these occurrences of 'this', 'that', and 'these' have no referents but it is to say that these occurrences of 'this', 'that', and 'these' have no st-referents. Evidently hunting for st-referents is not a profitable undertaking. But there are still more serious limitations on generalizations about material regularities to be found in connection with elements of the form 'the . . .'. First, however, there are complications to be dealt with.

122. The words 'this', 'that', 'then', 'there', when subjected to morphological analysis yield a morphemic segment 'th-' with demonstrative meaning plus various residual elements with unique meanings. 'The' belongs to this group.

For reasons which need not concern us, some philosophers concerned with problems of logic have been inclined to construe certain utterances in which 'the' occurs as equivalent to certain utterances in which 'the one and only' occurs. Thus it has been said that we should not say 'A is the son of B.' if B had other sons beside A. But it is written:

Now David was the son of that Ephrathite of Bethelehem-judah, whose name was Jesse; and he [Jesse] had eight sons: and the man went among men for an old man in the days of Saul. [I Samuel 17:12]

(Of course a single counterexample proves nothing but such examples are everywhere at hand.) It is perhaps worth noting that the opposite of what is said about 'the' may be true of 'a', viz. that we do not say '*A* is a son of *B*.' if *B* has no other son than *A*.

123. It is said that 'the' is the "definite article" while 'a' is the "indefinite article": this is something of a muddle. 'The' more clearly contrasts with 'some' than with 'a'.

The contrast between 'the' and 'a' is not, despite the unfortunate customary labels, a simple binary contrast with respect to definite/indefinite. That is in fact roughly the contrast between 'the' and 'some'. 'The' and 'a' have markedly different distributions in *E:* 'The water was pleasant.' but not 'A water was pleasant.'. 'The' ranges over both mass nouns ('water', 'rice',) and count nouns ('bean', 'nail'). 'A' does not. 'A' contrasts with the affix '-s': 'a bone' as opposed to 'bones'.

This is not to say that one might just as well refer to the suffix '-s' as an "indefinite article." The contrast between 'the' and '-s' is not the same as that between 'the' and 'a'. One can combine 'the' and '-s' as in 'the books' but one cannot so combine 'the' and 'a': 'the a book' would be odd just as 'a books' would be odd. So one can characterize 'the' as definite, 'a' as indefinite singular, and '-s' as plural.

Like 'a', 'some' contrasts with 'the' with respect to being indefinite, but unlike 'a', 'some' like 'the' ranges over both mass nouns ('some water') and count nouns ('some bean'). Again, like 'the', 'some' ranges over both singular and plural. If 'the' is to be classed as the "definite article" then 'some' should be classed as the "indefinite article" for that is the only striking contrast between 'the' and 'some'.

(It must be noted, however, that it is far from clear that 'some' is a single word and hence the fairly simple contrast with 'the' may be only apparent. For 'some' in 'I want some beans.' is phonemically distinct from 'some' in 'Some strange fellow is looking for you.', the difference being that between /sŏm/ and /sǝm/. Just so one says and rightly that 'conv*ict*' and '*con*vict' are two different words. Furthermore, 'some' in the former utterance appears to differ in meaning from 'some' in the latter utterance, for only the former 'some' can have paired with it 'a quantity of'.)

124.   Slightly variant forms of material regularities are occasionally to be found in connection with elements of the forms 'the . . .', 'some . . .', 'a . . .', and '___ + -s . . .'. Since they all offer more or less the same problems I shall concentrate on elements of the form 'the . . .'.

That material regularities are to be found in connection with demonstratives in E is a weak generalization. But that material regularities are to be found in connection with expressions of the form 'the . . .' in E is such a weak generalization that it is not clear that it is warranted at all.

The difficulty is this. Since material regularities are correlations between linguistic elements and their st-referents, if a material regularity is found in connection with a particular linguistic element and if in a particular case that element occurs without an st-referent, then the utterance in that case must be deviant to a certain degree owing to a deviation from a material regularity. So if I say 'This book looks wet.' and there is no book to look at, the utterance is deviant. Thus if a material regularity could be found in connection with elements of the form 'the . . .', in those cases in which no st-referents could be found, utterances in which these linguistic elements occur must be deviant.

But there are indefinitely many sorts of cases which seem to be and indeed are perfectly in order and yet in which no st-referent can be found, e.g. the phrase 'the difficulty' in 'The difficulty is not easily avoided.'. Nothing spatiotemporal can in general be paired with 'the difficulty' in utterances of the form 'The difficulty is not easily avoided.'. Again, 'the plot' in 'The plot is too complicated.' can hardly have anything spatiotemporal paired with it.

These cases are worth noting and considering for they indicate that what is significant here are conditions and not merely spatiotemporal referents. The phrases 'the difficulty' and 'the plot' in the examples cited above can be said to be referring expressions. They each have a referent even though they do not have spatiotemporal referents. If the utterance 'The difficulty is not easily avoided.' is uttered , then generally there is some difficulty to be dealt with. The condition that there be a difficulty to be dealt with is one that may or may not be satisfied. If it is not satisfied in a particular case then in that case the utterance is deviant to a certain degree. But if the condition is satisfied, that does not mean that there is something spatiotemporal to be found that can be paired off with the expression 'the difficulty'. To speak of "the referent of the phrase 'the difficulty' " is to speak of the hypostatization of a condition.

125.   A further difficulty is found in the fact that quite often an element of the form 'the . . .' will occur as syntactic subject in an utterance and yet the speaker is not referring. Thus it is far from clear that one is warranted in classing expressions of the form 'the . . .' as referring expressions. Whether or not a particular expression of the form 'the . . .' is a referring expression depends on rather subtle factors.

An utterance like 'The president cannot vote.' is thoroughly ambiguous in this respect. The speaker might be wanting to say something about a particular person, e.g. that this person cannot vote owing, perhaps, to illness. Or he might be wanting to say that no one who holds the office of president can vote owing, perhaps, to a prohibition to that effect in the constitution and he might say this at a time when the office of president is vacant. This indicates that whether or not a referent (spatiotemporal or otherwise) can be found cannot be determined by the syntactic form of the utterance, e.g. the fact that the phrase 'the president' occurred as syntactic subject is not sufficient.

In the latter case when the speaker said 'The president cannot vote.' he might just as well have said 'No one who holds the office of president can vote.' or 'Whoever may be president, he cannot vote.' or 'If anyone is president then he cannot vote.'. In such cases it would be clear that the speaker was not referring. (The point of so-called "nominalistic reductions" is simply that they serve to make clear what speech act is being performed.) If in saying 'The president cannot vote.' one is not referring to anyone it can be seen in this way: by asking 'If you are referring, whom are you referring to?' for one cannot refer without referring to something (or some things) or someone (or certain ones). That there is no answer to the question indicates that one is not referring. Compare this with 'The horse captured by Bellerophon has wings.': 'What horse are you referring to?'—'Pegasus.'.

It might seem that matters of tense provide the determining factor, e.g. even though 'The president cannot vote.' is ambiguous, 'The president will not vote.' seems unambiguous. That is an illusion. The utterance could have been uttered without deviation by one of the framers of the constitution while discussing the role of the chief executive. Again, it might seem that an utterance like 'The president was bald.' or 'The president is a fool.' is unambiguous even out of context: here, surely, one can find a referent and one can claim oddity, or at least a deviation, if none is to be found. This illusion can be dispelled by the comparison with 'The cat is a domestic animal.' and 'The pterodactyl was winged.': in such cases no referents need be found and yet the lack of referents does not yield oddity or even deviation. It so happens that being bald or a fool is and was irrelevant to being president. But this is a fact about the constitution, not about the language.

Again, the actual existence of a likely referent cannot be the determining factor. Someone at the time of Louis XIV who said 'I want to see the king of France.' would most likely have been wanting to see Louis XIV. But someone who said 'I want to be the king of France.' need not have been wanting to be Louis XIV: to want to be Louis XIV is one thing but to want to be the king of France might be another. 'I want to be the king of France.' could be uttered without deviation today even though there is at present no king of France.

126.   What I have called "nominative relations" and "material regularities" are essentially relations between spatiotemporal entities and linguistic elements associated with the speech acts of referring and of making a reference. Such relations and regularities are to be found in connection with only some elements of E and these only on occasion. It should by now be clear that a semantic analysis of E simply in terms of spatiotemporal referents cannot even begin to get off the ground. But even apart from the arbitrary restriction to spatiotemporal referents a semantic analysis of E simply in terms of the conditions requisite for the performance of the speech acts of referring and of making a reference is equally hopeless. Few morphological elements of E refer to anything.

The phrase 'the author of the *Faerie Queene*' on occasion refers to a particular referent, viz. Spenser. But apart from the name, the constituents of this phrase, viz. 'the', 'author', and 'of', do not refer to anything. By and large, single words do not refer to anything; e.g. the word 'good' does not refer to anything, and neither does the word 'cow'.

There is, unfortunately, a confusion over this point that permeates all of the philosophy of language. It is said that the word 'cow' refers to an animal of such-and-such a sort. That is at best an unfortunate metonym. The word 'cow' refers to nothing at all. If one says 'Cow is in the field.' then if 'cow' is not a proper name, one is uttering an odd utterance. The word 'cow' can be used in combination with other morphological elements to refer to something, e.g. 'the cow', 'a cow', 'cows' (i.e. 'cow' $+$ '-s'). Sometimes when the word 'cow' occurs in a morphological construction, it, the construction, is employed to refer to a cow. But sometimes not. I say 'He wants some cow dung.': I am not referring to a cow, I am referring to a person.

(Of course I can manage not to see this by telling myself over and over again "The word 'cow' is a name, so it must be the name of something.")

127. To deny that the word 'cow' refers to anything at all is not to deny that there are procedures by which we can associate the word 'cow' with a certain set of spatiotemporal entities.

The expression 'this cow' in 'This cow is hungry.' can be said to be a referring expression. It refers to a demonstratively determined member of a special set of spatiotemporal referents. This indicates that occurrences of 'cow' in certain referring expressions in E are related to a distinct set of st-referents. Consider the different sets of st-referents associated with the utterances 'That cow is brown.', 'Those cows are feeding.', 'This cow is hungry.', 'That cow is not hungry.'. Occurrences of 'cow' in referring expressions in E are (in general) then related to members of a certain set of referents extrapolated from the sets of st-referents associated with the utterances noted. (It should be noted that no simple method of extrapolation will do here; e.g. consider the three utterances 'That black cow is hungry.', 'That white cow is not hungry.', and 'That brown cow is licking the tree.'. If we consider the sum of the sets of referents associated with these utterances we see that it includes a tree as well as cows. If we consider the logical product we have the null set. To pick out all and only cows we shall have to associate certain conditions with the word 'cow' and then pick out those and only those spatiotemporal entities that satisfy the relevant conditions. And this is simply to say that we can relate the word 'cow' to an appropriate set of spatiotemporal entities only if we know either what meaning 'cow' has in English or what a cow is.)

But there is a limit to how far one can go in this direction. 'Cow' in 'A cow is a domestic animal.' or elements like 'unicorn', 'griffin', can hardly be related to some appropriate set of spatiotemporal entities. Consider the hippocat, where a hippocat is an animal exactly like an hippopotamus except that it has whiskers exactly like a big cat. Like unicorns, hippocats are nonexistent. But unlike unicorns there are not even pictures of hippocats to be found. 'Hippocat' cannot sensibly be related to a set of spatiotemporal entities. 'Hippocat' occurs in 'I should like to see a hippocat.' and this utterance can be related to a set of st-referents, viz. that constituted by speakers of the language associated with E who refer to themselves, but the connection is not attributable to the element 'hippocat'.

128. That a semantic analysis of E simply in terms of the conditions requisite for the performance of the speech acts of referring and of making a reference is hopeless should not be surprising. Such a simple form of analysis could be fruitful only if meaning and reference were the same and they are not.

That meaning and reference cannot be identified has been known since the time of Panini, has been a matter of public knowledge since the time of Frege. (One should mention here the oldest example on record, the expression 'śaśaviṣāṇaḥ', the horns of a hare, discussed by the Hindu grammarians and held to have meaning despite the lack of a referent.) But it is still useful to have another clear proof of the difference. 'This' and 'that' ('I' and 'you', 'we' and 'us') provide such a proof. Both 'this' and 'that' can be connected with a set of st-referents. Roughly speaking, 'this' is connected with a set of demonstratively determined "proximate" st-referents, whereas 'that' is connected with a set of demonstratively determined "remote" st-referents. But these two sets may in fact have exactly the same members. This can be seen as follows. Suppose there are two cats in the room, one seated at one end near me and the other seated at the opposite end. I say 'This cat and that cat look somewhat alike.'. I then walk to the opposite end of the room and say 'This cat likes fish but that cat prefers meat.'. The point is simply that whatever can be referred to by 'this' may at another time be referred to by 'that'. Hence 'this' and 'that' may be connected with one and the same set of st-referents. Nonetheless, it is obvious that 'this' and 'that' (or 'I' and 'you') do not have the same meaning in E. Hence meaning and reference cannot be identified.

IV

TRUTH CONDITIONS

129.   A speaker of the language associated with E looks at the cat on the mat and says 'Witchgren is on the mat.'. A state regularity is to be found in connection with the utterance type. The utterance is connected with a declarative-speech act. If such an utterance is uttered then generally a certain state of affairs obtains in our limited world, viz. one characterizable in terms of the satisfaction of the conditions requisite for the performance of the declarative-act in question. Thus if the utterance is to be uttered without deviation from a state regularity there must be something named 'Witchgren' that is being referred to by the speaker and there must be some situationally determined particular mat that the speaker is making a reference to.

But in so far as we are concerned simply with the performance of a declarative-act, it is not necessary that that which is named 'Witchgren' be in the specified relation to the mat in question; more simply, it is not necessary that Witchgren be on the mat. If in uttering 'Witchgren is on the mat.' the speaker is making an assertion then he is doing so whether Witchgren is on the mat or not. If Witchgren is not on the mat then the speaker is making a false assertion: presumably a false assertion is an assertion (and thus unlike a decoy duck or a cigar-store Indian).

130.   The speech act of making an assertion is of little interest here in contrast with the speech act of making a true assertion. Yet these are not two distinct acts. One cannot make a true

assertion without making an assertion. Even so, the act of making a true assertion is obviously of greater importance here in that it necessitates the satisfaction of relatively strong conditions.

'True' is a notoriously difficult word. It is connected with all sorts of puzzles; e.g. it has been said that the customary usage of 'true' and 'false' in English leads to contradictions. It would simplify matters enormously if we could leave the word alone. But we cannot. There is a connection between an utterance like 'Witchgren is on the mat.' and certain specific declarative-acts, such acts as those of making a true assertion, making a true statement, giving a correct description, giving a true account. If in general there were no such connections between the declarative utterances of *E* and the performance of such specific speech acts, it would be vastly more difficult (though not necessarily impossible) to provide a semantic analysis of the utterances of *E*.

131. If someone says 'The book on the table belongs to George.' and there is a book on the table and it does belong to George, we may say that what was said was true. If there is a book on the table but it does not belong to George, we may say that what was said was not true or was untrue or was false. But if there is no book on the table, we do not say that what was said was either true or untrue or false.

(Though these differences are largely ignored by philosophers there are differences between 'not true', 'untrue', and 'false'. 'True' and 'false' are not simple opposites. Unlike either 'not true' or 'untrue', 'false' invokes a factor of deceit. Thus one speaks of 'a false front', 'a false face', but not of 'an untrue front'; one says 'He is not true to his word.' but not 'He is false to his word.', 'He played me false.' but not 'He played me untrue.'; to say 'He is not a true friend.' is not to say 'He is a false friend.'; one says 'The (billiard) cloth is untrue.' but not 'The cloth is false.'; and so on. The difference between 'not true' and 'untrue' is of course that between a denial and an affirmation.)

Roughly speaking, 'true' and 'false' are employed primarily in connection with what is expressed by predicates of some utterances in declarative form. Less roughly speaking, 'true' and 'false' are primarily employed in connection with the non-referential aspect of utterances uttered in the performance of some declarative-speech acts. If in saying 'What George stated is true.' one is making a statement then one is making a statement about a statement.[1] If one says 'What George stated is false.' and if a criticism is therewith expressed, the criticism expressed is a criticism of the speech act, not of the utterance uttered in the performance of that speech act. But such a criticism of a speech act performed in the uttering of that utterance is appropriate only if the utterance in question meets certain minimum conditions, e.g. that it does not constitute a deviation from regularities pertaining to certain matters of reference. (N.B.: 'e.g.' and not 'viz.'.)

132.   Neither sentences nor utterances are either true or not true. But if we were generally to employ the word 'truc' in

---

[1] For a contrary view see P. F. Strawson, "Truth," *Analysis*, IX (1949), 83–97. Strawson there claims that "to say an assertion is true is not to make any further assertion at all; it is to make the same assertion" (p. 83). He holds this to be a true but "inadequate thesis" (p. 84). I take it to be false. If George asserts that he hates a loose use of words and I then say 'What George asserted is true.', I need not have made any assertion at all. I might have made a comment, or a remark, or I might even have made a statement. Perhaps what Strawson wanted to say was 'To assert that an assertion is true is not to make any further assertion at all; it is to make the same assertion.' and perhaps also 'To state that a statement is true is not to make any further statement at all; it is to make the same statement.': neither claim is true. For example, suppose I have absolutely perfect faith in George, I know him to be the soul of honor, and I believe him to be as infallible as the pope. If someone says to me 'I cannot believe George's statement.', I may reply 'I say that what George stated is true.' even though I do not know what George stated. It would be curious to suppose that in making this statement about what George stated, about George's statement, I am not really making a statement about George's statement but somehow making the very same statement even though I do not know what it is.

connection with utterances, we could do so consistently only in connection with utterance tokens.

Suppose at time *a* I say 'The cat is on the mat.' and, at *a*, the cat is on the mat. Then say the utterance is true. Suppose at time *b* I say 'The cat is on the mat.' and, at *b*, the cat is not on the mat. Then say the utterance is not true. Since one and only one utterance is in question, the utterance 'The cat is on the mat.' will be said to be both true and not true. Therefore it is neither.

This does not show that we do not ordinarily speak of utterance types as either true or false. At best, it shows only that we cannot do so without inconsistency. That we are consistent is another matter.

But it is not true in every sense of the word 'utterance' that the utterance uttered at *a* is the same as the utterance uttered at *b*. There is one utterance type but two utterance tokens. It is still open to us to say that utterance tokens are true or false. This would lead to oddities.

(The case is somewhat different with sentences. Suppose we write the sentence 'The cat is on the mat.' on a blackboard at *a* and, at *a*, the cat is on the mat. A moment later, at *b*, while the sentence is still on the board, the cat is not on the mat. Apparently one and only one sentence token is in question: hence sentence tokens cannot be said to be either true or false without inconsistency. The difference here is owing to the fact that sentence tokens, unlike utterance tokens, are enduring entities. This difficulty, however, is easily avoided by attending only to what is sometimes spoken of as "an initial temporal slice of the sentence token" and predicating 'true' or 'false' of it.)

We generally do not employ the words 'true' and 'false' in connection with utterance tokens. To do so would lead to oddities. If one is told that the statement 'Caesar crossed the Rubicon.' is true then one knows that if anyone at anytime makes that statement, he makes a true statement. But if one were told that the utterance token 'Caesar crossed the Rubicon.'

is true, it would still be open to one to ask 'Is the utterance token 'Caesar crossed the Rubicon.' true?' for in asking that question one utters a different utterance token of the type 'Caesar crossed the Rubicon.'.

But both inconsistencies and resultant oddities are irrelevant here. It is simply and immediately a deviation from regularities to be found in connection with the corpus E to say ' 'The cat is on the mat.' is a true utterance.': this is a deviant utterance. Statements, assertions, and so forth are true or not true but not utterances and not sentences.

Statements and utterances need not be confused. A statement is made by uttering an utterance in an appropriate way and in an appropriate situation. Statements but not utterances can be retracted, denied, etc. Identifying statements and utterances can engender nothing but confusion (primarily by way of a reaction, an appeal to "propositions," "abstract entities").

But neither are statements to be identified with assertions, nor assertions with contentions, nor contentions with descriptions, nor descriptions with remarks, nor remarks with comments, and so on. If in glancing at a painting in a gallery one says 'That has lovely pigmentation.', one is making a comment, not a statement. If while walking through the gallery one glances out of a window and says 'It's a lovely day.', one is remarking on the weather, not commenting, not stating, not asserting, not describing. In uttering 'I suppose things have gotten a bit out of hand.' the speaker may be making a statement but hardly an assertion. One says 'He should retract his statement.' but not 'He should retract his assertion.'. To say 'The president made a statement to the press.' is not to say 'The president made an assertion to the press.'. Statements or descriptions may be inaccurate but not assertions. And so on. There are differences here and on occasion these differences are significant (and on occasion not, but this is not such an occasion).

133. If the utterance 'The door was open.' is uttered then generally (or in a standard case) some situationally determined particular door was open. If the door in question was not open

then the assertion, or statement, etc., made (if one is made) in uttering the utterance is false while the utterance constitutes a deviation of a certain degree from a state regularity (or projection). Thus making a false statement involves a certain degree of deviation from a state regularity (or projection). Any utterance, the uttering of which in an appropriate way and in an appropriate situation constitutes the making of a false statement, or a false assertion, or the giving of an incorrect account, or an incorrect description, etc., is *ipso facto* deviant to a certain degree (which need not be confused with being deviant *tout court*).

There is an important asymmetry between utterances that can be employed in saying something true and those that can be employed in saying something not true or untrue or false. Any utterance whatever can be uttered in an inappropriate way or in an inappropriate situation. But it is not the case that any utterance whatever can be uttered without a certain degree of deviation, e.g. not 'He will and will not do it.'. There is a difference between utterances here: some lend themselves to deviation more so than others.

Given the present nature of horses, the utterance 'Horses moo.' can be employed in saying something untrue but it cannot without oddity be employed in saying something true (e.g. the utterance is correlated with or forms some part of a code). 'Horses have horns.' is another utterance of the same sort. But consider the utterance 'The horse mooed and shook its horns while giving milk.'. If someone simply said 'The horse mooed.' or 'The horse has horns.' or 'The horse has horns and is shaking them.' or 'The horse gave milk.', we might in some situation reply 'No, that is not true.'. But when these utterances are compounded, when the persons says 'The horse mooed and shook its horns while giving milk.', what would be said would not be untrue: it would be odd.

The compounding of utterances that can be employed in saying something untrue, unlike the compounding of utterances that can be employed in saying something true, leads directly to oddity attributable to the use of particular words.

134. The fact that an utterance employed in saying something untrue does exemplify a certain degree of deviation from a semantic regularity (or projection) is the principal reason why if someone says something too obviously untrue we may be inclined to wonder whether we have properly understood him or whether he understands what he is saying.

If someone says 'I have just been decapitated.', one would take him to be joking, or telling a story, or speaking nonliterally, etc., or if he were apparently in earnest and wanting to speak literally, one would assume he simply did not know what the word 'decapitated' means. I find it difficult (but not impossible) to envisage a case in which one could say in reply 'That is untrue.'.

The line between something untrue and something that is neither true nor untrue is much like the line between a poor screwdriver and something that is not a screwdriver at all. Imagine an object shaped exactly like a screwdriver but made of extremely brittle glass. Such a thing would make a very poor screwdriver. I should say that it was a glass replica of a screwdriver, thus not a screwdriver at all. If, however, it were made of unbreakable glass, I should refer to it as 'a glass screwdriver', thus a screwdriver of a certain kind, viz. one made of glass.

135. Uttering an utterance in the making of a false statement is one way (among innumerable ways) of deviating to a certain degree from a state regularity (or projection). But to say that the utterance is deviant to a certain degree is not to say that the uttering of the utterance constitutes a misuse of words. To say that it did would most likely be to misuse 'misuse'. Some deviations occur owing to a misuse of words but not all and not even many.

One speaks of a "misuse" of a word or phrase by way of criticizing the person's use of the word or phrase in question, thus by way of criticizing the performance of a certain speech act. But one can sensibly make such a criticism only if one supposes or presupposes that the person in question has the relevant intention.

If one sees a person grasp a screwdriver by the tapered end, press the handle against the head of the screw, and turn the screwdriver without altering the position of the screw, one can say that the person is misusing the screwdriver on the supposition that the person is thereby trying to drive in the screw. But if the person knows full well that one cannot so drive in a screw but is doing this simply to amuse himself, one cannot sensibly charge him with a misuse of the screwdriver. At the best one might charge him with an abuse of the tool for he might thereby damage the handle. In order for the person's action to constitute a misuse of the screwdriver it is necessary that he have the relevant intention and that his intention is likely to be frustrated owing to his use of the tool. If even when gripping the handle properly he is unable to drive in the screw owing, say, to the toughness of the wood, that would not constitute a misuse.

'Misuse' is a term of criticism employed in connection with various acts including speech acts. Before one can sensibly charge another with a misuse of a word it is necessary to determine what speech act the person takes himself to be performing. If I were to utter 'Hello!' on leaving a person, my utterance would be odd but I could hardly be charged with misusing the word. If I were to say it, it could only be by way of a bad joke. But someone unfamiliar with the use of 'hello' in English might so misuse it. If I say 'It was raining.' with a view to making a true statement about the weather and it was not raining then, since my failure to achieve my purpose is not attributable to my use of words, I cannot be said to be misusing words. For it is not as though what led me into error was lack of information about the words. Nonetheless, the uttering of the utterance constituted a deviation to a certain degree from a state regularity (or state projection).

136.   That an utterance employed in making a false statement is deviant to a certain degree may seem objectionable to some. So I shall say something more about it.

One is apt to feel that if I say 'The door is open.' when the door is not open, because say the wind blew it shut when my back was turned, then even though what I say is not so that it is not so is, as it were, the world's fault, not mine. My utterance was perfectly in order. Whereas if I say, pointing to the hat on the mat, 'The hat has hurt its paw.', one feels that something queer is going on here and that it is is my fault. It is not that the world has failed to co-operate with me but that I am asking too much of it. Hats have not got paws to be hurt and I ought to know that. So if I say 'Caesar did not cross the Rubicon.' that utterance is deviant because I know and you know that I know that he did. But if I say 'It will rain.' and mean it but it does not rain then that does not show that the utterance was deviant for this time it was the world's fault.

I have no great objection to such talk. For no matter whether utterances employed in making false statements, in saying what is not so, and the like are deviant to a certain degree or not, one can associate certain conditions, or truth conditions, with such utterances only by means of projections (see below) based on regularities to be found in connection with sets of utterance tokens employed in making true statements, or in saying what is so, etc. To put the matter very simply, if someone says 'The door is open.' and the door is open then I may have at least a chance of noticing the open door and in some way relating the condition that there be something open to the utterance in question. But if someone says 'The door is open.' when the door is not open, I am not going to find it easy to relate the condition that there be something open to the utterance. Later of course it will be possible to do so on the basis of projections based on regularities.

Even though I have no great objection to such talk, I do not choose to indulge in it myself. I am not concerned with apportioning blame. I do not use the phrase 'deviant to a certain degree' as a term of criticism. An utterance is uttered under certain conditions. Certain conditions I take to be relevant in connection with a given utterance. If the utterance is uttered and the conditions that I take to be relevant are not satisfied then in that case I say the utterance is deviant to a certain degree. Precisely why the conditions were not satisfied is for the time being irrelevant. At a later stage in the analysis one may find that certain types of deviation have characteristic signals, e.g. a contour indicating irony when I say 'That is an intelligent book.' meaning quite the opposite. False statements unlike ironic comments have no characteristic signals or markers. And of course there can be no syntactic basis for a distinction between utterances employed in making true statements and utterances employed in making false statements since such a division clearly can separate utterance tokens of the same type. But all of this is irrelevant. I am not here concerned simply with syntactic deviations but with nonsyntactic semantic deviations as well.

137.   If the utterance 'The door is open.' is uttered then (perhaps) generally some situationally determined particular door is open. Thus a state regularity may be found in connection with the utterance. That state regularities can be found in connection with many syntactically nondeviant whole utterances of E should by now be obvious. But it should also be obvious that state regularities cannot be found in connection with all utterances of E.

No regularity can be found in connection with u_i if u_i has not been uttered before or has been uttered infrequently. Thus no regularity can be found in connection with any utterance that is included in the corpus simply owing to the fact that it was elicited from an informant or that it was uttered once or twice in the presence of the analyst. *A fortiori* no state regularities can be found pertaining directly to such utterances.

138.   This sort of difficulty can be dealt with by considering not simply state regularities but "state projections" (see 62 ff. above). State projections take the following form: given that a syntactically nondeviant whole utterance of E is uttered then, in a standard case, certain conditions are satisfied. The difference between a state regularity and a state projection is simply that the latter does not involve a reference to what is generally the case.

The utterance 'I wish I had a hippocat.' has in fact rarely been uttered. Consequently it is not true that if the utterance is uttered then generally the condition that someone wants an animal exactly like a hippopotamus except that it has whiskers exactly like a big cat is satisfied. What is generally the case evidently has nothing to do with the case.

What one can say is that if the utterance is uttered in accordance with the regularities to be found in connection with the corpus E then, primarily on the basis of composition, it is clear that certain conditions must be satisfied. Thus if the utterance 'I wish I had a hippocat.' is uttered then, in a standard case, the condition that someone wants an animal exactly like a hippopotamus except that it has whiskers exactly like a big cat is satisfied. It should be noted that to know precisely what conditions can be associated with an utterance like 'I wish I had a hippocat.' it is necessary to know what meaning "hippocat' has in (my) English (idiolect). Consequently in discussing questions of meaning, I shall begin by ignoring state projections. (See 160 ff. below.)

139.   Strong state regularities cannot be found in connection with what I shall call "determinate" utterances. By 'a determinate utterance' I mean an utterance that can be employed in making an assertion, or statement, etc., and such that if it is employed in making a statement precisely what statement is made is not dependent on the context in which the utterance is uttered. Thus 'He is here.' is not a determinate utterance for such an utterance can be employed in one context to make a statement about one person and employed in another context to make a statement about a different person, thus a different statement in each case. In contrast, 'George K. crossed the Hudson at 2 A.M. on October 20, 1943.' is a determinate utterance (assuming that there is one and only one George K. and one and only one Hudson).

Logicians who speak of sentences rather than statements, assertions, and the like as being true or false presumably are concerned with and have in mind determinate utterances or sentences. It is an important fact that no significant state regularities can be found in connection with determinate utterances.

140.   Consider the determinate utterances 'George K. crossed the Hudson at 2 A.M. on October 20, 1943.' and 'George K. crossed the Missouri at 3 A.M. on October 30, 1945.'. I shall assume that George K. did in fact cross the Hudson at the designated time and that he did not in fact ever cross the Missouri. A state regularity could conceivably be found in connection with each utterance for if either utterance is uttered then generally certain conditions might be satisfied, viz. those under which the performance of the declarative-speech acts in question can be performed. But there is of course a difference between these two utterances: if in uttering the former one is making a statement then one is making a true statement, but if in uttering the latter one is making a statement then one is making a false statement. The stated state regularities to be found in connection with each of these utterances would hardly be significant for they would fail to reflect the striking difference between the two utterances, viz. that one can and the other cannot be employed in making a true statement. Such regularities may be characterized as "weak."

We might attempt to remedy the defect as follows: if the utterance 'George K. crossed the Hudson at 2 A.M. on October 20, 1943.' is uttered then generally the conditions requisite for the performance of a declarative-speech act are satisfied and the condition that George K. have crossed the Hudson at 2 A.M. on October 20, 1943 is satisfied. Since we cannot in the other case say that the condition that he have crossed the Missouri is satisfied, for he did not, we have acounted for the striking difference between the two utterances. But this will not do at all.

To say 'If the utterance 'George K. crossed the Hudson at 2 A.M. on October 20, 1943.' is uttered then (generally?) the condition that George K. have crossed the Hudson at 2 A.M. on October 20, 1943 is satisfied.' is not to state a relevant semantic regularity. It is not generally the case that the condition is satisfied: the condition is satisfied once and for all. The irrelevance of the "regularity" can be seen in the fact that it is impossible for a speaker to deviate from the "regularity," thus the "regularity" must be deemed irrelevant on the grounds of conventionality (see 58 above).

141. The difficulty here is again easily dealt with in terms of state projections rather than state regularities. If the utterance 'George K. crossed the Hudson at 2 A.M. on October 20, 1943.' is uttered then, in a standard case, the condition that George K. have crossed the Hudson at 2 A.M. on October 20, 1943 is satisfied.

A determinate utterance can be associated with the satisfaction of a particular so-called "truth condition" by means of a projection on the basis of composition. For considerations of composition provide one with reasons for pairing 'the condition that George K. have crossed the Hudson at 2 A.M. on October 20, 1943' rather than say 'the condition that Japan be across the Pacific from California' with the utterance 'George K. crossed the Hudson at 2 A.M. on October 20, 1943.'. Since both conditions are in fact satisfied one can say trivially that if the utterance 'George K. crossed the Hudson at 2 A.M. on October 20, 1943.' is uttered then the condition that George K. have crossed the Hudson at 2 A.M. on October 20, 1943 is satisfied and the condition that Japan be across the Pacific from California is satisfied. The irrelevance of the latter condition cannot be determined simply by noting the conditions under which the utterance 'George K. crossed the Hudson at 2 A.M. on October 20, 1943.' is uttered. It can be determined by an appeal to composition.

But furthermore, since a determinate utterance has a particular truth-condition associated with it by means of a projection on the basis of composition, since projections are based on regularities and since the relevant regularities cannot be found in connection with determinate utterances, it follows that a determinate utterance has a particular truth-condition associated with it by means of a projection from regularities to be found in connection with a corpus of nondeterminate utterances.

142. Strong state regularities cannot be found in connection with utterances pertaining to spatiotemporally distant matters

outside of our relatively limited four-dimensional world. Thus no strong state regularity can be found in connection with 'Caesar crossed the Rubicon.'. But again, the difficulty is easily dealt with in terms of a state projection.

If the utterance 'Caesar crossed the Rubicon.' is uttered then, in a standard case, the condition that Caesar have crossed the Rubicon is satisfied. The condition in question can be said to be satisfied and is in fact satisfied even though it cannot be said to be satisfied in our relatively limited four-dimensional world. That such a condition is satisfied is established in whatever way we do in fact establish historical matters, thus by complex procedures involving both theoretic and observational considerations. But that the condition in question is to be associated with the utterance in question is determined on the basis of composition. There can, of course, be no question of relating 'Caesar' directly to a spatiotemporal referent. Caesar no longer exists. Consequently we must proceed by associating certain conditions with the name 'Caesar', thus by considering the information-content of the name (see 110 ff. above).

If the utterance 'Caesar crossed the Missouri.' is uttered then, in a standard case, the condition that Caesar have crossed the Missouri is satisfied. It follows that there is no standard case for the uttering of the utterance 'Caesar crossed the Missouri.'. But since the condition that Caesar have crossed the Rubicon is satisfied, there can be a standard case for the uttering of the utterance 'Caesar crossed the Rubicon.'.

143. State projections will seem puzzling, or so I am inclined to suppose, only if one becomes ensnarled in nonsensical problems about "the reality of the past"; e.g. if one supposes that since the consequent conditions of certain projections can be shown to be satisfied only on the basis of what is to be found in our relatively limited four-dimensional world, thus on the basis of present conditions, then, somehow, the conditions that are really relevant to the utterances in question are the present conditions and not the projected conditions. And proceeding in this way one may begin to wonder whether in saying 'Caesar

crossed the Rubicon.' one is talking about the past or about the present, and one may even begin to wonder how it is possible to talk about the past, and even finally conclude that one cannot talk and it does not make any sense to talk about the past. And since philosophic problems are monotonous in their similarity, one can in a similar vein begin to suppose that in talking of a person's dream one is somehow really talking about what the person says when he wakes up and not about something that happened while the person was sound asleep. And so one can suppose that in talking of a person's feelings one is somehow really talking about the person's movements. And so on.

The confusion here results from the wholly unwarranted assumption that the relevant conditions are not those indicated by a projection on the basis of composition but other conditions.

144.   All of this means that here there will be no great problem about the "analytic" and the "synthetic." Consider statements (2), (3), and (4):

   (2)   The statement that Caesar crossed the Rubicon is true only if Caesar crossed the Rubicon.

   (3)   The statement that Antony made love to Cleopatra is true only if Antony made love to Cleopatra.

   (4)   The statement that Caesar crossed the Rubicon is true only if Antony made love to Cleopatra.

All three statements are true, but (2) and (3) are "analytic," (4) is "synthetic." The truth of (2) and (3) can be determined by considering the regularities to be found in connection with E and by considering matters of composition that enable one to associate the particular truth-conditions with the utterances in question. (But see 170 below.) To establish the truth of (4) it is then necessary to undertake a historical investigation to determine the truth of the statement that Caesar crossed the Rubicon and of the statement that Antony made love to Cleopatra.

There is, furthermore, no problem here in answering questions like "Is the statement that nothing is both red and green all over analytic or synthetic?" The answer is: it is synthetic and in fact false. There is nothing odd or even deviant about the utterance 'That is red and green all over.', e.g. in a case in which the referent of 'that' is a red and green striped ball. Of course the person who says that the statement that nothing is both red and green all over is analytic would also say that the case of the striped ball is not a case in point: that is not what he meant by 'all over.' Even so, there is nothing odd or deviant about the utterance 'That is red and green all over.'.

The temptation to suppose that the statement that nothing is both red and green all over is analytic instead of in fact false and synthetic arises, I believe, out of the following consideration. If the utterance 'That is red.' is uttered then in a standard case the condition that the referent of 'that' be not green is satisfied. But from the fact that the condition that the referent of 'that' be not green is satisfied it does not follow that the condition that the referent of 'that' be green is not also satisfied. So one tries to give 'all over' a special sense such that it will preclude the possibility that the condition that the referent of 'that' be green be satisfied.

The temptation to suppose that the statement that nothing is both red and green all over is analytic may also be owing to a confusion of the attribution of a characteristic negatively characterized with the denial of the attribution of a characteristic. The point here is, in a way, simply this: it is not self-contradictory to say 'That is both red and not red.': a red and green striped ball is again a case in point. To say that something is not red is, on occasion, to attribute to it a relatively specific characteristic even though the characteristic in question is negatively characterized. This need not be confused with the denial of an attribution, e.g. saying that it is not the case that what is in question is red. Thus to say 'That is not red.' is, on occasion, to affirm that the referent of 'that' has a characteristic negatively characterized, whereas to say 'It is not the case that that is red.' is to deny that the referent of 'that' has a certain characteristic.

If I say 'It is and it is not the case that that is red.' I contradict myself for I both affirm and deny that that is red, and that is absurd. But if I say 'That is both red and not red.' I need not be contradicting myself: I may be attributing to it two distinct characteristics.

145.   That state regularities cannot be found in connection with many utterances of E is obvious. It may seem equally obvious that, in particular, state regularities are not to be found in connection with either so-called "tautologies" or "contradictions." That is in fact the case but I doubt that it is particularly obvious.

If tautologies and contradictions are specified syntactically, i.e. such that certain utterances are so classed in virtue of their syntactic structure, then two distinct regularities can be found in connection with such utterances. But in so far as the relevance of regularities is decided on the basis of considerations of composition, neither of these regularities can be deemed relevant.

If either a tautology or a contradiction is uttered then, in certain contexts, the utterance is subject to interpretation or construal by the hearer. This is owing to the fact that there is, as it were, a certain principle of exegesis employed by the speakers of the language associated with E. The principle in question is remarkably like one employed by Aquinas in the interpretation of scriptures: "If a theory can be shown to be false by solid reasons, that theory cannot be held to be the sense of Holy Scripture." [2] Roughly speaking, the principle is this: construe what is said in such a way that, with a minimum of interpretation, it is significant. Hence utterances that do not appear to be significant from the vantage point of a logical system, e.g. 'It is raining and it is not raining.', 'Business is business.', 'a rose is a rose is a rose', are significant in English owing to the operation of this exegetical principle. Thus if the utterance 'He will and he will not do it.' were to be uttered in a certain context, it would most

[2] *Summa Theologica* I, Q. 68., Art. 3.

likely be construed as an utterance of the form 'He, George, will and he, Josef, will not do it.'.

That a tautological or contradictory utterance is subject to interpretation or construal by the hearer is, however, not a relevant regularity. It is rather a sign of a deviant utterance. That an utterance is likely to be construed indicates that it is deviant as it stands, for if it were not deviant there would be no need to construe it. (It is sometimes said that every utterance must be construed or interpreted by the hearer if the hearer is to understand it. That is simply false if 'interpreted' and 'construed' mean what they usually mean, viz. interpreted and construed.)

If either a tautological or a contradictory utterance is uttered then, generally, one or more persons are reasoning deductively. Thus one says 'Suppose utterance type u_i is true or false. Then u_i is both true and false. Therefore it is neither.'. There is nothing odd about the utterance type 'Then u_i is both true and false.'. The utterance was uttered in the course of an argument proceeding by *reductio ad absurdum*. Philosophy being what it is (which is a tautology of the first type calling for construal or interpretation) *reductio ad absurdum* arguments are easy to provide and frequently to be encountered in philosophical discourse.

That tautological and contradictory utterances are frequently uttered in a context in which persons are reasoning deductively is not a relevant regularity. That such utterances are uttered in such cases is itself owing to the fact that by means of projections tautological and contradictory conditions can be associated with tautological and contradictory utterances respectively. Thus it is owing to the fact that a contradictory utterance has contradictory conditions associated with it that it is possible to give a *reductio ad absurdum* argument. State projections can be found for both tautological and contradictory utterances though with this difference: there can be no standard case for the uttering of a contradiction since it calls for the satisfaction of contradictory conditions. (In this respect contradictions resemble determinate false statements.)

146. A state regularity cannot be found in connection with utterances employed in propounding paradoxes. 'What I am now at this very moment saying is false.' is an odd utterance type.

It is necessary to distinguish between an utterance token and an utterance type primarily in connection with (nonsyntactic) semantic deviation. The utterance token 'The is in here.' is syntactically deviant. It follows that every token of the type is syntactically deviant and hence the utterance type is syntactically deviant. The distinction between syntactically deviant utterance tokens and syntactically deviant utterance types is therefore superfluous, for an utterance token is syntactically deviant if and only if the correlative utterance type is syntactically deviant.

If the utterance token 'Pass the salt!' is uttered on meeting someone in the street, the token is likely to be semantically deviant. But not every token of this type is semantically deviant, e.g. a token of the type 'Pass the salt!' that is uttered at the dinner table, etc. On the other hand, 'What I am now at this very moment saying is false.' is a semantically deviant utterance type in that every token of the type is deviant, indeed odd.

147. An utterance type may be semantically deviant and yet not evidently so. This fact has been a source of uneasiness to some: such uneasiness calls for therapy, not semantic analysis. That an utterance leads to contradiction constitutes a proof that the utterance is semantically deviant, and the so-called "semantic paradoxes" can be formulated in English.

The fact that the semantic paradoxes can be formulated in English has led some philosophers, primarily logicians, to the conclusion that English is in a muddled state. Some have, I believe, gone so far as to say that English is "inconsistent." What that is supposed to mean is difficult to say. To suggest that English may be inconsistent is, as it were, to liken a natural language to a logistic system. There is of course something of an analogy between the two.

Generally speaking, a logistic system is constituted by a set of primitive symbols, axioms, formation rules, and transformation rules. Still generally speaking, a logistic system may be said to be inconsistent if a contradiction is derivable in the system. There is something analogous to some of this to be found in connection with a natural language. The grammatical utterances of English are, as it were, its well-formed formulas, for the syntactic regularities of English correspond (more or less) to the formation rules of a logistic system. Furthermore, there is something of an analogue of the transformation rules of a logistic system to be found in any natural language. The semantic regularities (or projections) pertaining to such elements as 'and', 'or', are analogous to transformation rules; e.g. generally if a statement made by uttering u_i at time a would be true and if a statement made by uttering u_j at time a would be true then a statement made by uttering $u_i +$ 'and' $+ u_j$ at time a would be true. Again, in so far as 'brother' and 'male sibling' are synonymous, there is in English an analogue of a transformation rule of a logistic system in virtue of which one can derive 'He has a male sibling.' from 'He has a brother.'. (There is of course a disanalogy here in that both the formation and transformation rules of a logistic system generally are syntactic whereas the analogues of formation rules in a natural language are syntactic while the analogues of transformation rules are semantic. But the disanalogy does not suffice to refute the analogy.)

Since the analogues in English of transformation rules in a logistic system are essentially semantic regularities (or projections) pertaining to the elements of English, the claim that English is inconsistent must essentially be a claim to the effect that the syntactic and semantic regularities (or projections) of English lead to a contradiction. Thus to claim that the antinomy of the liar proves that English is inconsistent is to claim that the semantic regularities pertaining to 'true' and 'false' are analogous to transformation rules that, in conjunction with other analogues of formation and transformation rules to be found in English, lead to a contradiction.

148.   Consider the following utterance:

(5)   What I am now saying is false.

Utterance (5) is paradoxical in that if in uttering (5) one is making a statement then if that statement is true it must be false and if it is false it must be true. Granted that (5) is paradoxical, what is responsible for the fact? That the word 'false' is not solely responsible is shown by (6):

(6)   What he is now saying is false.

No paradox follows from (6). This suggests that "self reference" is the source of the difficulty. But no paradox follows from (7):

(7)   What I am now saying is not to be repeated.

Hence "self-reference" is not in itself an explanation.

Utterance (6) seems to point to 'I am' as the source of the difficulty, whereas (7) seems to point to 'false'. But (6) shows that 'false' cannot be said to be solely responsible for the difficulty, while (7) shows that 'I am' cannot be solely responsible. Just so, (8),

(8)   What I say is false.

is not necessarily paradoxical, and thus (8) points to 'am now . . . ing'. But the right conclusion is that here, as everywhere in language, difficulties arise owing to a combination of factors, not to any single factor. The problem is to locate the factors primarily responsible.

Consider (9):

(9)   It is good that he will and will not do it.

Utterance (9) is evidently odd. Has the word 'good' anything to do with the oddity of (9)? The answer must be yes. Notice that the substitution of 'not possible' for 'good' in (9), viz. 'It is not possible that he will and will not do it.', deprives the utterance of oddity. The substitution of 'nonsensical to say', 'absurd to suppose', 'unreasonable to believe', for 'good' in (9) has the same effect. But since this is so, the occurrence of the word 'good' in (9) must contribute to its oddity. However, it is clear that the word 'good' contributes merely a minor factor. The major factor is evidently the utterance part 'he will and will not do it' since this utterance part can occur as a whole utterance and would, in many cases, be odd by itself.

All this indicates that in order to detect the major factor responsible for the oddity of a particular utterance, it is necessary to reduce, as it were, the odd utterance to its simplest form. It is obvious that 'He will and will not do it.' is deviant in precisely the same way as 'He is and is not here.'. In short, the oddity of (9) is simply a case of the general oddity of utterances of the form 'p and not p.' when such utterances are uttered apart from an argument proceeding by a *reductio ad absurdum*. That an utterance of this form is odd is owing to the meaning of 'and', 'not', and that assigned to 'p', and the order of the terms. The paradox we are considering is in its simplest form:

(10) (10) is false.

Hence the paradox is owing to the meaning of 'is', 'false', the reference of '(10)', and the order of the terms. Since altering the order of the terms does not eliminate the difficulty, e.g. 'Is (10) false?' is equally perplexing if '(10)' is here self-referential, the paradox must be owing primarily to the meaning of 'false', 'is', and the reference of '(10)'.

The paradox is not a proof that the self-reference of '(10)' is in any way objectionable. I am not saying there are no grounds for an objection to self-reference. Perhaps there are such. But they are not provided by this paradox. But neither is the paradox a proof that the word 'false' is in any way objectionable. The paradox does constitute a proof that the combination (effected by 'is') of the self-referential '(10)' together with the word 'false' is objectionable. The precise nature of the difficulty can be found only in an investigation of both self-reference and the meaning of the word 'false'.

The question of the consistency of English can be now posed in a simple way: do the syntactic and semantic regularities (or projections) of English preclude the combination of the self-referential '(10)' with 'false'? Or alternatively, is (10) a deviant utterance? If (10) is deviant, it cannot serve to establish the inconsistency of English and there is no problem here. All that follows is this: if we were to attempt a definition of 'false', we should have to account for the fact that the occurrence of the word in the environments '(10) is . . . .' (where '(10)' refers to the resultant whole utterance and is thus self-referential), 'What I am now at this very moment saying is . . . .', etc., would constitute a deviant utterance type. It will follow from the definition of 'false' that such environments as these are closed to the word. It cannot fail to follow. For suppose we define 'false' as f, and it does not follow from the fact that 'false' means f that 'false' cannot occur in these environments: then 'false' cannot be defined as f, given that the environments in question are closed to 'false'. But if (10) were not a deviant utterance, it would follow that the environments in question were not closed to 'false' and that would mean that English must be inconsistent. So the question is: is (10) deviant?

The following is a regularity to be found in connection with English: if u_i is uttered by way of making a statement then generally that statement does not lead to a contradiction. Utterance (10) deviates from this regularity. So I say this: the paradox constitutes a proof that (10) is deviant. The difference between a logistic system and my language can be put thus: if in a logistic system I come across a contradiction, I cross out the system. But if in my language I find a contradiction, I cross out the contradiction.

149.   That state regularities are to be found in connection with many declarative utterances of E is simply a fact: it could have been otherwise.

A state regularity can be found in connection with a particular declarative utterance of E only if that utterance is not infrequently uttered. In the ideal case, a state regularity is readily found in connection with a declarative utterance if the utterance is frequently uttered and if in uttering the utterance the speaker is saying something true about something in the immediate context of utterance. Actually, however, an ideal case is hard to come by. Many utterances are infrequently uttered, speakers talk about matters outside of the immediate context of utterance, they lie, make mistakes, and so forth.

It is sometimes said that one reason not to lie is that if all the speakers of the language were to lie at every possible opportunity they would soon have no language to speak. Why that is supposed to be a reason not to lie I cannot say. But anyway it is not true. Even if the speakers of a language were to lie at every possible opportunity, state regularities might still be found in connection with the declarative utterances they uttered; e.g. the speaker, pointing to a blue harpsichord, says to a color-blind person 'That harpsichord is green.': even if the speaker is lying in so saying, he has managed to convey a certain truth, viz. that what he is pointing at is a harpsichord.

But the more serious confusion here is the supposition that truth conditions and not simply conditions are of fundamental importance in the speaking and understanding of a language. I can see no reason why every declarative utterance uttered by the speakers of a certain language might not be deviant. That they were deviant could be established on the basis of projections from regularities to be found in connection with nondeclarative utterances of the language. There is no reason why the declarative utterance must be, as it were, the standard meter rod of a language (see 74 ff. above).

150.   State regularities are to be found in connection with nondeclarative as well as declarative utterances.

An utterance like 'Shut the door!' is connected with an imperative-speech act. If such an utterance is uttered then generally a certain state of affairs obtains in our limited world, viz. one characterizable in terms of the satisfaction of the conditions requisite for the performance of the imperative-act in question. Thus there will be an open door; the hearer will be in a position to and will be capable of shutting the door in question, and so forth.

An utterance of the utterance 'Shut the door!' may be deviant in indefinitely many ways; e.g. the utterance is uttered in a

situation in which there is no hearer. Or it is uttered in response
to 'The door *is* shut.'. Or the speaker vehemently shook his head
while uttering the utterance. Or there is no door to be shut. Or
the door is known by all concerned to be fixed fast. And so on.
The phrase 'and so on' is essential here. The list cannot be completed. The paths of deviation are unlimited and innumerable.
Case studies of aphasics, science fiction, can here supplement
one's limited imagination.

   There are nice problems in connection with imperative-acts
that we can note but need not worry over. Suppose one is in a
position of authority; one utters the utterance 'Shut the door!',
and this utterance is addressed to a subordinate. If the door is
in fact open, the hearer is in a position to and is capable of
shutting it, etc., then it seems clear that one has issued an order.
But suppose the door is already shut, or suppose the utterance
is addressed to a person who is manifestly incapable of shutting
the door: has one issued an order?

   Let me say that if the door is in fact open, the hearer is in a
position to and is capable of shutting the door, and so forth then
"optimum conditions" for the issuing of the order are satisfied.
I am inclined to suppose that in everyday discourse one would
not be said to have issued an order if the optimum conditions
were clearly not satisfied. This is to say that a pronounced deviation from optimum conditions is probably enough to lead
us to refuse to characterize the speech act performed as the issuing of an order. (If one could order the door to be shut even
when the door is already shut, it would follow that in such a
case it would be impossible to obey the order: it would be curious to speak of an order that could not conceivably be obeyed.
But I do not suppose that this proves anything.)

   What is interesting here is that there is no specific term in *E*
with which to criticise the performance of an imperative-speech
act. If one utters the utterance 'Shut the door!' when the door
is shut but with a view to getting the hearer to shut the door,
something has gone wrong. But there is no familiar word for
what has gone wrong. If someone says to me 'Shut the door!'
and the door is already shut, I cannot (without oddity) reply

'You are mistaken.'. I may say 'You are confused.' but that is not a specific criticism of the performance of the speech act.

It is not surprising that there is no specific term with which to criticise the performance of an imperative-speech act. We would have little use for such a term: in general things do not tend to go wrong in the performance of such an act.

151.   I want to say that either state regularities or state projections can be found in connection with or for virtually all syntactically nondeviant whole utterances of E.

I cannot here prove that this is so for such questions do not here admit of proof. If it were granted that sets of conditions can be and in fact are correlated with the individual elements of E that have meaning in English, it would then follow that either state regularities or state projections could be found in connection with or for virtually all syntactically nondeviant whole utterances of E. For every such utterance could then be correlated with a set of conditions such that the set in question was some function of the sets of conditions correlated with the constituents of the utterance. But that sets of conditions can be and in fact are correlated with the individual elements of E that have meaning in English is precisely what I am primarily concerned to show.

Even though I cannot hope at this point to show that either state regularities or state projections can be found in connection with or for virtually all syntactically nondeviant whole utterances of E, it may help to consider an objection to what I am saying. In this way both what I am saying and what I am not saying may become clearer.

152.   What is apt to trouble some philosophers here is the fact that virtually no restrictions have been made on the nature of the conditions that may enter into (a statement of) a state projection.

I said (in 81 above) that state regularities take the following form: given that a syntactically nondeviant whole utterance of E is uttered then generally certain conditions are satisfied. The restrictions that have been made on the nature of the conditions that enter into state regularities are first that they be recurrent, secondly that they be not infrequently satisfied, and thirdly that whether or not they are in fact satisfied be confirmable or disconfirmable on the basis of what is to be found in our relatively limited four-dimensional world. Thus there are fairly strong restrictions on the nature of the conditions that may enter into state regularities and in consequence all sorts of conditions are ruled out, e.g. that Antony made love to Cleopatra.

In so far as a state regularity can be found in connection with a declarative utterance, if that utterance is employed in making a statement then the statement made is and must be confirmable or disconfirmable. For if w_i is paired with u_i directly on the basis of state regularities to be found in connection with the corpus E then it must be possible to determine whether or not the conditions associated with w_i are in fact satisfied. But this means that it must be possible to determine whether or not the conditions associated with u_i are in fact satisfied. Hence if u_i is employed in making a statement that statement must be open to confirmation or disconfirmation. Thus the requirement that the pairing of w_i with u_i be confirmable or disconfirmable directly on the basis of regularities to be found in connection with the corpus E entails the requirement that, if u_i can be employed in making a statement, that statement must be confirmable or disconfirmable. Consequently if one were rashly to suppose that only regularities are relevant in understanding a language one would be led to the view that if a statement is not in fact confirmable or disconfirmable then the statement must be devoid of significance. Alternatively, to insist that the conditions associated with u_i are relevant in a semantic analysis if and only if whether or not the conditions are satisfied is confirmable or disconfirmable would be tantamount to adopting the so-called "verification theory of meaning": it should be clear that that theory is rejected here.

The conditions that enter into state projections are not subject to the same restrictions as those that enter into state regularities even though every projection is ultimately based on regularities. If w_i is paired with u_i on the basis of a state regularity and if w_j is paired with u_j on the basis of a state projection from the regularity then the only restriction here is that the pairing of w_j with u_j be confirmable or disconfirmable on the basis of what is to be found in our relatively limited four-dimensional world. This, however, is only to say that in so far as the pairing of w_j with u_j is an instance of projection then it must ultimately be based on regularities. This is not to say that whether or not the conditions associated with w_j are in fact satisfied must be open to confirmation or disconfirmation. It is not even to say that whether or not the conditions associated with w_j are satisfied must at least in theory be open to confirmation or disconfirmation.

It is true that in so far as the pairing of w_j with u_j is based on the pairing of w_i with u_i the structural similarity between w_j and w_i must be a reflection of the structural similarity between u_j and u_i. But this does not mean that the conditions that enter into state projections must be markedly similar to the conditions that enter into state regularities. This is owing (at least in part) to the fact that similarity is an intransitive relation. For suppose w_k is paired with u_k on the basis of a state projection from the pairing of w_j with u_j, while w_j is paired with u_j on the basis of a state projection from the state regularity pairing w_i with u_i. Then in so far as w_j and w_i must be structurally similar one may expect the associated conditions to be similar in some respects. Consequently one may expect the conditions associated with w_k and w_j to be similar in some respects. But it does not follow that the conditions associated with w_k and w_i must also be similar in the same respects.

If w_j is paired with u_j on the basis of a state projection from the state regularity pairing w_i with u_i, it is possible that it may not be possible either in fact or in theory either to confirm or to disconfirm whether or not the conditions associated with w_j are in fact satisfied. If that is the case, then if u_j is employed in making a statement that statement will be neither confirmable nor disconfirmable. Thus the statements 'The dream he cannot ever recall is about you.', 'Everything has increased in size proportionally.', etc. may be neither confirmable or disconfirmable.

Even so such utterances are significant. (But I would not suggest that apart from considerations of theory their significance is of any significance.)

153.   But the objection is that the analysis of u_j is unintelligible if it consists in pairing w_j with u_j when the conditions associated with w_j are such that it is not possible either in fact or in theory to determine whether or not they are satisfied.

An unsupported objection such as this is difficult to deal with in any satisfactory way. I am inclined simply to deny it. But I do not suppose that that would persuade anyone. Yet it does seem clear that understanding a condition is not the same as knowing how to determine whether or not it is satisfied. If one says 'I'll do it on the condition that George approves of it.' there is no difficulty in understanding the condition even though there may be difficulty in determining whether or not the condition is satisfied. If one says 'I'll do it on the condition that Caesar would have approved of it.' there is still no difficulty in understanding the condition though there would be considerable difficulty in determining whether or not it was satisfied. And if I say 'I'll do it on the condition that the last living man, were he born yet, would approve of it.' there is still, I believe, no difficulty in understanding the condition though I do not see how it is possible even in theory to determine whether or not the condition is satisfied. Of course it is a silly condition but what does that matter?

154.   A further objection that might be made here is that projections are essentially irrelevant in a semantic analysis of a language for it may mistakenly seem that statements of projections do not provide one with further nonsyntactic semantic information.

Consider what is involved in formulating a metalinguistic statement of a regularity about a language in the language in question. One first notes that if u_i is uttered then generally certain conditions are satisfied. Then one notes that if u_w is uttered then generally certain conditions are satisfied. And then it is necessary to find that if the conditions associated with u_i are satisfied then generally the conditions associated with u_w are satisfied. Finally, taking u_w as w_i, one can say that w_i is paired with u_i.

But how is one to formulate a metalinguistic statement of a projection? Suppose w_i is paired with u_i as indicated, and no regularity can be found in connection with u_j. The problem is to find w_j such that the structural similarity between w_j and w_i will be a reflection of the structural similarity between u_j and u_i. Consequently w_j must be the value of some function over u_i, w_i, and u_j. But this seems to indicate that the metalinguistic statement of a pairing of w_j with u_j can provide no nonsyntactic semantic information not already provided by the metalinguistic statement of the pairing of w_i with u_i. This, however, is not the case.

The metalinguistic statement that w_i is paired with u_i can be said to provide semantic information about u_i only in so far as the hearer understands what is said in uttering w_i. If not knowing what the word 'dicteur' means in French one finds that in *Larousse* it has paired with it 'celui qui dicte' one will still not know what the word means if one does not understand what is said in uttering 'celui qui dicte'. But given that a pairing of w_i with u_i is semantically informative about u_i then the metalinguistic statement of a projection pairing w_j with u_j on the basis of the pairing of w_i with u_i is semantically informative about u_j. For a statement to that effect is essentially a statement of a complex pairing of w_i with u_j, where w_j serves to indicate the precise relation between u_j and w_i. Thus one is told that if u_j is uttered then, in a standard case, conditions related to those associated with w_i are satisfied. This does provide semantic information about u_j.

V

MEANING

155. Meaning is essentially a matter of nonsyntactic semantic regularities, so I am inclined to suppose (and so I said in 40 above). If you like, this is a theory of mine that serves to account for certain facts, or what I take to be facts, about the matter, e.g. that 'to' in the utterance 'I want to go through Istanbul.' cannot be said to have meaning in that utterance. This theory can be developed, expanded, to account for still further facts, or what I take to be facts, about the matter.

156. If m_i, a morphological element of E that presumably has meaning in English, occurs in and has meaning in u_i then it is reasonable to suppose that for $j \neq i$ there is a u_j such that m_i occurs in and has meaning in u_j and such that m_i cannot sensibly be said to differ in meaning in each case. More generally, if we consider the various utterances of the distributive set for m_i in E, viz. the syntactically nondeviant whole utterances of E in which m_i occurs, it is reasonable to suppose that m_i will not differ in meaning in each and every case.

157. That 'to' cannot be said to have meaning in the utterance 'I want to go through Istanbul.', and that if an element has meaning in English it may be presumed not to differ in meaning in each and every utterance, indicates that there are two sets of elements of E that are relevant in determining whether or not a given morphological element has meaning in English.

The first set is a subset of the set of syntactically nondeviant whole utterances of E in which it occurs, thus a subset of the distributive set for the element in E. The second set is a subset of the set of contrastive elements in virtue of which the morphological identity of the element in question can be established. Thus if the element in question is the word 'good', the first set includes such utterances as 'That is good.', 'What good is that?', 'She is good to me.', whereas the second set includes such utterances as 'That is fine.', 'That is pleasant.', 'That is mine.', 'What use is that?', 'What man is that?', 'She is mean to me.'. Note that the second set in question could be characterized as a subset of the distributive set for the environments of a subset of the distributive set for 'good' in E. But I shall refer to it as a subset of the contrastive set for the element in question.

The intuitive basis for this move is twofold. First, as I have said, it seems reasonable to suppose that a morphological element of E that has meaning in English will not differ in meaning in each and every utterance of E. Consequently it is necessary to consider at least a subset of the set of syntactically nondeviant whole utterances in which it occurs, thus a subset of its distributive set in E. Secondly, the significance of what is said depends on what is not said. The utterance actually uttered stands in contrast with and takes its shape from what is not but could without deviation be uttered. The fact that 'excellent', 'splendid', and the like are available and yet not employed serves to determine the significance of 'That is a good painting.'. I would not say 'Guernica is a good painting.': it is a magnificent painting. Neither would I say 'Fouquet's picture of Agnes Sorel as the Madonna is a good painting.': it is an exquisite painting. (Aestheticians manage to enrich the appearance of their analyses by impoverishing the language.) Again, consider: 'Answer: is she beautiful or ugly?'. Neither alternative need do yet if one has a forced option one can (on occasion) choose. Yet you must understand that if I say 'beautiful' under such conditions she need not rival Helen. So one might say that every natural language forces the option for any natural language has a limited lexicon and it imposes these limits on its speakers. And that one has no option with respect to the uttering of 'to' in the environ-

ment 'I want . . . go through Istanbul.' again indicates that
'to' in the resultant whole utterance does not have meaning.[1]

158. I said (in 37 ff. above) that the set M, the set of elements
of E that presumably have meaning in English, certainly includes a very large proper subset of the set of elements yielded
by the procedures of some sort of morphological analysis. That
the set of morphological elements is not wholly included is
established on the basis of such elements as 'to' in 'I want to go
through Istanbul.'. But so far no reason has been given, no evidence has been offered, in support of the claim that M does in
fact include a very large subset of the set of morphological elements of E.

That M does include such a subset is no doubt obvious. But
obvious or not, it is something to be explained. For why is it
that the distributional procedures of morphological analysis
serve to characterize a set of elements having such a striking
intersection with the set of elements of E that presumably have
meaning in English? This is not an accident; neither is it a miracle. Any theory of meaning that fails to account for and explain
the fact is *ipso facto* an inadequate and unilluminating theory.
(That the question is generally overlooked in discussions of
meaning is, I believe, largely owing to the fact that it has been
mistakenly supposed that a morphological analysis of a corpus
necessarily involves consideration of what meaning the elements
in question may have.)

If whether or not an element of E has meaning in English depends on certain semantic features of what I have called its
distributive and contrastive sets, it follows at once that for an
element of E to have meaning in English it must be associated
with a distributive and contrastive set. But since morphological

[1] See de Saussure, *op. cit.* Also see Jakobson, *op. cit.*, pp. 55–82, in
particular, pp. 58–62. Attention to de Saussure's operations of combination and selection would lead one in an obvious way to focus on what
I have called the distributive and contrastive sets for m_i in E. In this
sense, the analysis being presented here is, I believe, essentially Saussurian
in approach.

elements may be identified on the basis of distributive and contrastive features, it also follows that every morphological element of E satisfies at least one condition for having meaning in English. Consequently there is good reason to suppose that whether or not a morphological element of E has meaning in English depends on whether or not the relevant semantic features are to be found in connection with its distributive and contrastive sets.

159. Still further confirmation is to be found at once for the view that whether or not a morphological element of E has meaning in English depends on whether or not the relevant semantic features are to be found in connection with its distributive and contrastive sets.

Words are generally said to have meaning or to have a meaning; not utterances and not sentences. We speak of understanding what is said and of knowing the meaning of words. We do not generally speak of "understanding a word" or of "knowing the meaning of what is said."

The utterance 'What does the sentence 'George is inclined to go to the cinema.' mean?' sounds odd to me. 'What does that sentence mean?' is a somewhat special question. It seems appropriate primarily in connection with short phraselike sentences in a foreign language. Thus 'What does 'Es regnet.' mean?' is not at all odd. This should not be surprising: if it is primarily words and phrases that have meaning or have a meaning in a language then in so far as a sentence approximates a word or phrase it will not seem or sound odd to ask about its meaning. But neither utterances nor sentences can in general be said to have or not to have meaning or to have or not to have a meaning. One cannot show or even try to show that two sentences differ in significance in the way one can show or try to show that two words differ in meaning; e.g. that 'assert' and 'state' differ in meaning is indicated by the fact that 'assert' but not 'state' occurs without oddity in the environment 'He is going to . . . himself.'. One cannot in this way show that two sentences, e.g. 'He stated his views.' and 'He asserted himself.', differ in significance. One can show that the two sentences differ in significance by showing that they have different syntactic structures or that their constituents differ in meaning (or in significance).

The utterance 'One can show that two utterances (sentences) differ in significance.' need not be confused with the somewhat odd utterance 'One can show that two utterances (sentences) differ in meaning.': 'meaning' and 'significance' differ in meaning, which is not to say ' 'Meaning' and 'significance' differ in significance.'. So one says 'The remark is of no significance.' but not 'The remark is of no meaning.'. Though we do sometimes ask 'What is the meaning of that remark?', we do not (generally) say that a remark has a meaning. If we do say of a certain remark that it has a meaning (but not 'has meaning.'), we are likely to mean that there is some significance to be attached to it: in this way we single it out from other remarks which, though of a familiar and unobjectionable sort, would not be said to have a meaning, which is not to say they would be said not to have a meaning.

The everyday use of the word 'meaningless' is to the point. The proposal to ban atomic weapons may be said to be meaningless. But this is not to say that if a senator says 'Let us ban atomic weapons!' his words have no meaning, and it is certainly not to say that his words do not have meaning. The proposal may be said to be meaningless because there is no possible way of enforcing such a ban save the self-defeating one of threatening atomic attack. But one knows perfectly well what the senator is saying, why he is saying it. Indeed, he probably knows that what he is proposing is meaningless. There may still be good reasons to propose it: diplomacy thrives on meaningless and lengthy statements. It is better to keep talking than to start fighting.

(Again, it is perhaps necessary to insist that there are differences between 'meaningless', 'senseless', 'nonsensical', 'pointless', 'absurd', 'ridiculous'. One says 'It is senseless to build a garage when you don't expect ever to have use for it.' but not 'It is meaningless to build a garage when you don't expect ever to have use for it.'. And to be told that one has engaged in a non-sensical discussion is not as bad as being told that one has engaged in a senseless discussion. And so on.)

In contrast, single words are not generally said to be meaningless. What would be an example of a meaningless word? Someone might say ' 'Faith' is a meaningless word.': it is not irrelevant that that would be a cynical remark. A word has meaning: that which does not have meaning is (generally) not a word but a nonsense syllable, or set of syllables, or a proper name. Although a decoy duck is not a duck, a meaningless proposal is a proposal (likely to be acted on).

That words primarily, but not utterances or sentences, are generally said to have meaning is a fact, yet not, as it were, an inevitable fact, about language. Phonemes, morphemes, words, phrases, sentences, utterances, are all relatively arbitrary units singled out and employed in the analysis of language. If we were not the sort of creatures we are, if we could remember it or hold it in mind, we might tend to focus on some unit larger than an utterance, say a speech, or conversation, and then talk of the or a meaning of an utterance with respect to this larger unit. We might have been the sort of creatures that would be apt to talk in this way. But we are not and do not.

That words primarily, but not utterances, are generally said to have meaning in English should not be surprising: that a word has a distributive set in E is obvious; that utterances have a distributive set in E is not obvious. It is a matter of what we can remember, of what we can hold in mind.[2]

[2] Whether the significance of a sentence is a function of the meaning of its constituents is one of the oldest questions in semantic theory. The ancient Hindu grammarians were divided on this point: the so-called "Padavādins" maintained that the Padas, or parts of speech, were essentially the elements having meaning, whereas the so-called "Vākyavādins" maintained that the Vākya, essentially a sentence, was the only real element and, according to the grammarian Bhartrhari, there is no division of the signification of a Vākya. Wittgenstein's echo, "Nur der Satz hat Sinn; nur im Zusammenhange des Satzes hat ein Name Bedeutung" (*Tractatus*, 3.3), of Frege's dictum "Nur im Zusammenhange eines Satzes bedeuten die Wörter etwas" (*Die Grundlagen der Arithmetik*, sec. 62),

160.   I want to say that an element of E's having meaning in English is in some sense a function of some nonsyntactic semantic features of its distributive and contrastive sets. But the matter is somewhat complicated. It is necessary to introduce a relatively precise notation here.

Let $d_1(m_i)$, $d_2(m_i)$, . . . , $d_n(m_i)$ be utterances of the distributive set for m_i in E. Let $d_1(m_i) \mid m_1$, $d_1(m_i) \mid m_2$, . . . , $d_1(m_i) \mid m_n$, $d_2(m_i) \mid m_1$, $d_2(m_i) \mid m_2$, . . . , $d_2(m_i) \mid m_n$, . . . , $d_n(m_i) \mid m_1$, $d_n(m_i) \mid m_2$, . . . , $d_n(m_i) \mid m_n$ be utterances of the contrastive set for m_i in E. For example, if m_1 is 'tiger', if m_2 is 'lion', and if $d_1(m_1)$ is 'That is a tiger.', then $d_1(m_1) \mid m_2$ is 'That is a lion.'. Thus the vertical line '$\mid$' indicates that the utterance $d_1(m_1) \mid m_2$ is obtained by putting m_2 for m_1 in the environment of $d_1(m_1)$. If m_1 is 'tiger' and if $d_1(m_1)$ is 'That is a tiger.' I shall on occasion write 'That is a (tiger).' where the parentheses serve to indicate the appropriate substitution point.

It should be noted that the above enumeration of the utterances of the contrastive set for m_i in E is, as it stands, defective in that it suggests both that each morphological element of E contrasts with every other morphological element of E, which is clearly false, and that m_i in $d_i(m_i)$ contrasts with precisely the same elements as m_i in $d_j(m_i)$, which is likely to be false. For example, let d_1('good') be 'What good is that?', let m_3 be 'use', and let d_2('good') be 'That is a good tool to have.'. Then d_1('good') contrasts with d_1('good') $\mid m_3$ but d_2('good') does not contrast with d_2('good') $\mid m_3$ for that is the syntactically deviant utterance 'That is a use tool to have.'. Consequently m_3 must be excluded from the enumeration of the contrastive set for 'good' in E relative to d_2('good').

This defect of the enumeration can be avoided by stipulating that in the enumeration of the contrastive set for m_i relative to $d_i(m_i)$ contrasting elements are to be numbered in terms of alphabetic precedence relative to $d_i(m_i)$. Consequently one can-

is simply a latter-day expression of the Guru school of the Mīmāmsakas (philosophers, not grammarians), in particular the doctrine of Anvitābhi-dhānavāda, according to which Padas have what meaning they have only in the context of a sentence.

not assume that m_n in $d_i(m_i) \mid m_n$ is identical with m_n in $d_j(m_i) \mid m_n$, for there is no reason to assume that the n-th contrast relative to $d_i(m_i)$ is identical with the n-th contrast relative to $d_j(m_i)$. Ambiguities can be avoided by writing 'm_{jn}^i' for the n-th contrasting element relative to m_i in $d_j(m_i)$. Thus the superscript 'i' indicates that the element in question contrasts with m_i, the first subscript 'j' indicates that it contrasts with m_i in $d_j(m_i)$, and the second subscript indicates that it is the n-th contrast for m_i in $d_j(m_i)$, where order is determined by alphabetic precedence. However, I shall not bother to put in the appropriate superscripts and subscripts since it is obvious in each case what they must be; e.g. '$d_2(m_i) \mid m_n$' should be written '$d_2(m_i) \mid m_{2n}^i$'. I shall simply assume that 'm_n' in that expression is an abbreviation for 'm_{2n}^i'.

We may assume (on the basis of Parts III and IV) that some of the utterances of the distributive and contrastive sets for m_i in E may have sets of conditions associated with them by means of state regularities. But it should also be clear that state regularities cannot be found pertaining to all the utterances of the distributive and contrastive sets for m_i in E. Since projections are irrelevant at this point (see 138 ff. above), we must restrict our attention to proper subsets of the distributive and contrastive sets for m_i in E, viz. to those proper subsets in connection with the members of which state regularities can be found. Thus we shall be concerned with syntactically nondeviant whole utterances that have sets of conditions associated with them on the basis of state regularities. I shall employ braces, '{' and '}', to indicate that I am referring to a set of conditions. Thus I shall write: $d_i(m_i)$ has associated with it the set of conditions $\{d_i(m_i)\}$, $d_i(m_i) \mid m_j$ has associated with it the set of conditions $\{d_i(m_i) \mid m_j\}$, and so on.

161. It has sometimes been supposed that whether or not two words differ in meaning depends on whether or not the substitution of one for the other preserves the truth value of a statement, the making of which involved using one of these words with others. The futility of such a criterion in connection

with E should be obvious: it is inapplicable to the question whether or not two occurrences of the same word differ in meaning.

There can be no question whether the "substitution" of 'division' in 'The division is happy.' for 'division' in 'The division is incorrect.' preserves the truth value of the statement that the division is correct. Furthermore, the fact that we have here two occurrences of the same word rather than two different words is irrelevant. Consider the "substitution" of 'bear' in 'I see a bear.' for 'bear' in 'I cannot bear it any longer.': here we have two different words, not merely two occurrences of the same word.

162.   Even so, it might seem that there is a simple criterion for whether or not elements m_i and m_j differ in meaning in English, viz. m_i and m_j differ in meaning in English if and only if $\{d_i(m_i)\}$ is not identical with $\{d_i(m_i) \mid m_j\}$. But this won't do at all.

There are cases in which $\{d_i(m_i)\}$ is identical with $\{d_i(m_i) \mid m_j\}$ and yet m_i and m_j differ in meaning in English. Thus $\{$'The glass is exactly half (full).'$\}$ is identical (or virtually identical) with $\{$'The glass is exactly half (full).' $\mid$ 'empty'$\}$ (i.e. the conditions associated with 'The glass is exactly half full.' are identical (or virtually identical) with the conditions associated with 'The glass is exactly half empty.') and yet 'full' and 'empty' differ in meaning in English. Thus one says 'Fill it half full.' but not 'Fill it half empty.', and consider the difference between the two imperatives 'Keep on pouring until it is half empty!' and 'Keep on pouring until it is half full!'.

And still further, there are cases in which $\{d_i(m_i)\}$ is not identical with $\{d_i(m_i) \mid m_j\}$ and yet m_i and m_j do not or need not differ in meaning in English. Thus let 'regit' be an exact synonym for 'tiger' and consider the utterance 'The word 'tiger' begins with the letter 't'.'. Clearly $\{$'The word '(tiger)' begins with the letter 't'.'$\}$ is not identical with $\{$'The word '(tiger)' begins with the letter 't'.' $\mid$ 'regit'$\}$.

163.   If we consider the sets of conditions associated with utterances of the distributive set for m_i in E, viz. $\{d_1(m_i)\}$, $\{d_2(m_i)\}$,

. . . , $\{d_n(m_i)\}$, we may hope to find a common factor. But it seems fairly clear that for suitably chosen elements there will be no obvious factor. Consider the following pair of 'tiger'-s:

(1)   That is a tiger.

(2)   I want a tiger.

I want to say that 'tiger' in (1) does not or anyway need not differ in meaning from 'tiger' in (2). The question is: what entitles one to say it?

It is clear that {'That is a tiger.'} is not only not identical with {'I want a tiger.'} but the two sets do not seem even to resemble one another. And although the intersection (i.e. the logical product) of the two sets may not be null it is not at all obvious that it is not null. In the one case one can expect to find a tiger or something resembling a tiger but in the other case one can only expect to find a person wanting a tiger. So there is a problem here.

164.   There is a difference between {'That is a tiger.'} and {'I want a tiger.'}. But there is also a difference between {'That is a tiger.'} and {'That is a lion.'}, and there is a difference between {'I want a tiger.'} and {'I want a lion.'}. And more to the point, there does not seem to be any difference between the difference between {'That is a tiger.'} and {'That is a lion.'} and the difference between {'I want a tiger.'} and {'I want a lion.'}.

More generally, the difference between $\{d_i(m_i)\}$ and $\{d_i(m_i) \mid m_x\}$ sometimes seems to be identical with the difference between $\{d_j(m_i)\}$ and $\{d_j(m_i) \mid m_x\}$. And this is so in a great many cases though not in all cases. But now consider the matter in an even more general way.

165.   The particular relation between $\{d_i(m_i)\}$ and $\{d_i(m_i) \mid m_x\}$ that is pertinent here is simply the particular difference between the two sets of conditions contributed by $\{d_i(m_i)\}$. The total difference between the two sets can be construed as a set of conditions, viz. the set constituted by the logical sum less the logical product of the two sets in question. Thus if the two sets are a and b then $a\bar{b} + \bar{a}b$ constitutes the total difference be-

tween a and b (where $\bar{a}$ is the complement of a, and $\bar{a}b$ is the logical product of b and the complement of a). But the relevant difference here relative to m_i is that constituted by the logical product of $\{d_i(m_i)\}$ and the complement of $\{d_i(m_i) \mid m_x\}$. I shall speak of this difference between $\{d_i(m_i)\}$ and $\{d_i(m_i) \mid m_x\}$ as the relevant difference in so far as I am concerned with questions of meaning pertaining to m_i in E.

Some of the utterances of the distributive set and some of the utterances of the contrastive set for m_i in E can have sets of conditions associated with them by means of state regularities. These sets will differ from one another in various ways. More precisely, letting D_{ij} be the relevant difference between the set of conditions associated with $d_i(m_i)$ and that associated with $d_i(m_i) \mid m_j$ (thus D_{ij} is the set of conditions constituted by the logical product of $\{d_i(m_i)\}$ and the complement of $\{d_i(m_i) \mid m_j\}$), we have the following differences to consider: D_{11}, D_{12}, . . . , D_{1n}, D_{21}, D_{22}, . . . , D_{2n}, . . . , D_{n1}, D_{n2}, . . . , D_{nn}. (For example, D_{2n} is the set constituted by the logical product of $\{d_2(m_i)\}$ and the complement of $\{d_2(m_i) \mid m_n\}$. Finally, let Dm_i be the set of the sets D_{11} . . . D_{nn} relative to m_i in E.

166.   We must take care not to confuse sound and sense. Not every member of Dm_i has something to do with whether or not m_i has meaning in English.

If m_1 is 'tiger', m_2 is 'lion', and $d_2(m_1)$ is 'The word 'tiger' begins with the letter 't'.', then the difference between $\{d_2(m_1)\}$ and $\{d_2(m_1) \mid m_2\}$ has nothing to do with whether or not m_1 has meaning in English. It has nothing to do with whether or not m_1 and m_2 differ in meaning in English. That the difference here is irrelevant to questions of meaning can be seen in the fact that the contrastive set for 'tiger' in E relative to the utterance 'The word 'tiger' begins with the letter 't'.' is constituted by utterances including every word in E. More simply, the difference here is obviously a matter of spelling, not of meaning.

167.   And now one can see that talk about "referential opacity," of "intensional" and "extensional contexts," is something of a muddle.

Consider the following inferences:

(3) $a = b$
     $\Phi(a)$
     Therefore: $\Phi(b)$

(4) The morning star and the evening star are one and the same planet, viz. Venus.

The morning star has a noxious atmosphere.

Therefore: the evening star has a noxious atmosphere.

(5) George's lucky star and Josef's lucky star are one and same planet, viz. Venus.

George's lucky star has a noxious atmosphere.

Therefore: Josef's lucky star has a noxious atmosphere.

The schema of (3) is clearly a valid inference schema. Even so, I am inclined to suppose that (4) is not a valid inference even though (5) is a valid inference. What holds true of and in symbols need not hold true of or in words. Words are thicker than symbols.

Suppose there were a physical theory to the effect that if a planet can be seen in the morning then it has a noxious atmosphere, but if it can be seen in the evening then it has a nonnoxious atmosphere. The first premise of (4) would then indicate that Venus must have a variable atmosphere. Hence the premises of (4) might be true and yet the conclusion false. I am inclined to suppose, however, that (5) is a valid inference for I think no such dodge is possible in connection with (5).

The reason why (4) is not valid while (5) is valid is simply this: the significant difference between 'the morning star' and 'the evening star' is the difference between 'morning' and 'evening' (or possibly between 'morn-' and 'even-'). Let m_4 be 'morning' and let m_5 be 'evening'. Then consider the difference between Dm_4 and Dm_5. An inference like (4) is valid if and only if the premises serve to establish that the difference between Dm_4 and Dm_5 is irrelevant. I am saying that the difference between Dm_4 and Dm_5 is relevant in (4) and that the premises of (4) do not serve to establish that the difference is irrelevant. Hence (4) is an invalid inference. On the other hand, (5) is a valid inference in that the analogous difference in (5) is irrelevant.

More generally, one can validly infer $d_i(m_i)|m_x$ from $d_i(m_i)$ if and only if the difference between Dm_i and Dm_x is irrelevant. Thus from 'That is a tiger.' one can, as it were, "infer" 'That is a tiger.' without the aid of a further premise for no further premise is required to establish that the difference between Dm_1 and Dm_1 (i.e. between D'tiger' and D'tiger') is irrelevant for there is no difference. From 'Leo is a lion.' one can infer 'Leo is a tiger.' if and only if the difference between D'lion' and D'tiger' is irrelevant. That the difference is irrelevant can be made explicit by an additional premise. So one argues validly from 'Leo is a lion.' and 'A lion is a tiger.' to 'Leo is a tiger.'.

168.   The differences between sets of conditions associated with utterances of the distributive set and sets of conditions associated with utterances of the contrastive set for m_i in E depend on matters of sound, spelling, and syntax, as well as on matters of meaning.

> I am unable, yonder begger cries,
> To stand, or move; if he say true, hee *lies*.

To understand what is done in and by using a word it is necessary to attend to phonetic, phonemic, morphological, and syntactic factors, as well as nonsyntactic semantic factors. And still more may be required: 'Don't forget your etiquette if you wish to get into high society!' can be a play on the etymological doublet of 'etiquette', viz. 'ticket'. For a word has a history and its history may be relevant.

This is why it is wrong to say "The meaning of a word is its use in the language" for the use of a word depends on many factors many of which have nothing to do with questions of meaning. (That "the meaning of a word is its use in the language" is not even a good slogan.)

A word has a certain sound (or sounds), it is pronounced in a

certain way (or ways), it is spelt in a certain way (or ways), it
has a certain grammatical classification (or classifications), it has
a certain history, it has certain phonetic or phonemic or morphological resemblances to other words, and so forth. Consequently it seems clear that only a proper subset of Dm_i can be
relevant in connection with questions of meaning pertaining to
m_i in E.

Let Sm_i be the proper subset of Dm_i that is relevant in connection with questions of meaning pertaining to m_i in E. The
problem then is to specify as precisely as possible the set Sm_i.

169.   If a difference between $\{d_i(m_i)\}$ and $\{d_i(m_i)|m_x\}$ is irrele-
vant in connection with questions of meaning pertaining to m_i
in E, the explanation is to be found in the irrelevance either of
$d_i(m_i)$ or of $d_i(m_i)|m_x$ or of some of the conditions associated
with these utterances.

The trouble is this: we have cast our net far too wide. For
not only is not every utterance of the distributive set for m_i in E
relevant, but not even every semantically relevant condition associated with relevant utterances of the distributive set for m_i
in E is relevant in connection with questions of meaning pertaining to m_i in E. The reason for this is simply that understanding what is said always calls for something over and above
merely knowing what meaning each of the elements of an utterance may have, and often knowing just that is not required.
Thus one may understand what is said in saying 'The word
'anisotropy' is spelt with two 'o'-s.' and yet not know what meaning the word 'anisotropy' has in English. And merely knowing
what meaning the words may have won't enable you to understand even as simple a remark as 'He is tiger hunting.'. For example, suppose one is told that the following pairings may be
made by way of explicating what meaning the elements of the
utterance may have:

'he':   'some male referred to, which referent is in question
          being contextually determined'

'is':   'something implural characterizable at present in
          terms of something'

'tiger':   'large carnivorous striped quadrupedal feline'

'hunt-':   'go in pursuit of (a) wild animal(s) or game'

'-ing':   'continuous activity'

'.':   'assertive intonation contour'

Such a list at best enables one to get a hazy idea of what the utterance in question is all about. For what has been left out of the account are such facts as 'tiger hunting' is an endocentric construction with 'hunting' as the head, 'he is' is an exocentric construction, and so forth, and even more to the point, what has been left out is an explication of such constructions.

To take another example of a different kind, even if one understands all the constructions involved, merely knowing what meaning the words may have won't enable you to understand the remark 'England had at least one laudable bishop.': it is necessary to catch the pun. It might seem as though the principle of composition would necessarily serve to preclude a pairing of 'there was a bishop by the name of 'Laud' ' with 'England had at least one laudable bishop.'. But that is far from clear. 'Laudable' in 'England had at least one laudable bishop.' contrasts with 'intelligent', 'sensible', 'foolish', 'disgraceful'. Suppose it so happened that one could pun on each and every contrast. Of course the Anglican orders would then be filled by oddly named clergymen but that is of no importance. And it would then be less obvious that the pairing of 'there was a bishop by the name of 'Laud' ' with 'England had at least one laudable bishop.' would be precluded by considerations of composition. Or again, since every utterance of the word 'etiquette' can pun on its doublet 'ticket', it is not clear that the principle of composition would preclude pairing 'some female is interested in matters pertaining to admission to high society' with 'She's interested in matters of etiquette.'.

170.   I said (in 44 above) that the problem of finding regularities pertaining to m_i has two distinct but inseparable parts. We must find regularities pertaining to u_i and then we must attrib-

ute something about these regularities to the occurrence of m_i in u_i. But what should be clear by now is that these two problems really are inseparable. An analysis of a whole utterance cannot be completed without an analysis of the morphological elements of the utterance. For only in so far as an analysis of the morphological elements of an utterance is made can one determine the literal significance of the utterance.

To understand what is said it is often not enough to know what meaning the elements of the utterance may have and to understand the constructions employed. But that is enough if one is concerned only to grasp the literal significance of a syntactically nondeviant utterance. The word 'literal' is from Latin via French and it has the etymological meaning of according to the letter. The etymological meaning of the word is to the point here. With respect to a syntactically nondeviant utterance u_i, an utterance (or utterance part) w_i can serve to express the literal significance of u_i if and only if the pairing of w_i with u_i can be construed as a direct function of the syntactic structure of u_i and of the meaning of the morphological elements of u_i. But this means that what meaning a word has cannot be a simple function of the significance of the utterances in which it occurs. If we are to determine the literal significance of an utterance, we must first determine what meaning the morphological elements of the utterance may have.

For example, although the principle of composition has an important critical function, one cannot tell by appealing to the principle what the literal significance of an utterance like 'I want a hippocat.' is: at best one can be lead to suppose that whatever is paired with 'I want a hippocat.' will be structurally similar to whatever is paired with 'I want a tiger.'. Since no regularities can in fact be found in connection with 'I want a hippocat.', whatever is paired with that utterance can be so paired only on the basis of composition, as a projection. But a knowledge of syntactic structure is not enough to enable one to explicate the literal significance of the utterance 'I want a hippocat.': obviously one must know what meaning 'hippocat' has in (my) English (idiolect).

And this means that our problem still is: how are we to specify Sm_i?

171. I propose to speak of a phonetic or orthographic "transform" of a segmental morphological element of E (thus here excluding the suprasegmental element of contour). I shall say that a is a phonetic or orthographic transform of b if and only if the following conditions are satisfied. First, a is phonetically or orthographically distinct from b. Secondly, a is not an element of E. Thirdly, a is introduced into E as a variant of b and such that a is to have exactly the same distribution in E as b had prior to the introduction of a (in so far as this is possible in accordance with the syntactic regularities to be found in E). And fourthly, a is to be constituted of exactly the same number of morphological elements as b and in exactly the same order.

Thus if b is 'male sibling' then 'elam gnilbis' may be a transform of b but not 'gnilbiselam'. Furthermore, if 'elam gnilbis' is a transform of 'male sibling' then 'elam' is a transform of 'male' and 'gnilbis' is a transform of 'sibling'. It should be noted that once both a and b become elements of E they will at once have different distributions in E. Thus let 'nood' be a transform of 'good': then 'good' but not 'nood' can occur in 'Is a nood thing a . . . thing?'.

In so far as the difference between $\{d_i(m_i)\}$ and $\{d_i(m_i) \mid m_x\}$ is a function of a difference, say, in spelling, that difference will not remain invariant under transformations of spelling. More generally, a difference between $\{d_i(m_i)\}$ and $\{d_i(m_i) \mid m_x\}$ is irrelevant in connection with questions of meaning pertaining either to m_i or to m_x if that difference is not invariant under all phonetic and orthographic transformations. It is as though we were concerned with the word's soul, its meaning, and its soul is that which remains invariant under all transformations of its body.

Thus let p, q, and r, be variables for transforms of d_i, m_i, and m_x, respectively. Then the difference between $\{d_i(m_i)\}$ and $\{d_i(m_i) \mid m_x\}$ is irrelevant in connection with questions of meaning pertaining either to m_i or to m_x in E if the difference is not identical with the difference between $\{p(q)\}$ and $\{p(q) \mid r\}$ for every p, q, and r. It is perhaps worth stating that, in case this talk of a phonetic or orthographic transform seems puzzling, all such talk is essentially an elaborate *façon de parler*. Thus instead of saying that the difference between $\{d_i(m_i)\}$ and $\{d_i(m_i) \mid m_x\}$ is irrelevant in connection with questions of meaning pertaining either to m_i or to m_x in E if it is not invariant under all phonetic or orthographic transformations, one can say that the difference is irrelevant if the difference can be made out to be a function of phonetic or orthographic factors.

To say that the difference between $\{d_i(m_i)\}$ and $\{d_i(m_i) \mid m_x\}$ is irrelevant if it is a function of phonetic or orthographic factors is simply to extend a principle already employed in morphological analysis. For example, if we were concerned simply with words rather than with morphological elements, one could say that the contrastive set for 'tiger' in E relative to the utterance 'That is a tiger.' does not include such an utterance as 'That is a (tiger).' | 'elephant', for the utterance 'That is a elephant.' is syntactically deviant. Since 'elephant' begins with a vowel, the sandhi form 'an' of the morpheme 'a' is compulsory. But since we are concerned primarily with morphological elements, and not simply with words, we can say that 'tiger' in 'That is a (tiger).' contrasts with 'That is a (tiger).' | 'elephant' with the understanding that 'That is a (tiger).' | 'elephant' is equivalent to 'That is an elephant.': thus 'a' in 'That is a tiger.' and 'an' in 'That is an elephant.' are allomorphs of the single morpheme 'a'. Just so, we can say that 'Where are the (cat)-s?' contrasts with 'Where are the (cat)-s?' | 'dog' even though the phoneme /s/ occurs in 'Where are the cats?' while the phoneme /z/ occurs in 'Where are the dogs?', for again, /s/ and /z/ are allomorphs of the plural morpheme '-s'. And again, we can say that 'possible' in 'That is im-(possible).' contrasts with 'decent' in 'That is im-(possible).' | 'decent' owing to the fact that 'im-' and 'in-' are allomorphs of a single negative morpheme. Thus 'That is im-(possible).' | 'decent' is equivalent to 'That is indecent.'. And still again, we can say that 'boy' in 'The (boy)-s took the book.' contrasts with 'The (boy)-s took the book.' | 'man', where this latter utterance is to be equivalent to 'The men took the book.', this being so on the basis of a morphophonemic rule that enables us to rewrite 'man' + the plural morpheme '-s' as 'men'. Just so, 'walk' in 'The boys (walk)-ed it home.' contrasts with 'The boys (walk)-ed it home.' | 'take', where the latter utterance is to be equivalent to 'The boys took it home.', this on the basis of a morphophonemic rule that enables us to rewrite 'take' + the past tense morpheme '-ed' as 'took'.

172.   But the mere fact that a difference between $\{d_i(m_i)\}$ and $\{d_i(m_i) \mid m_x\}$ cannot be made out to be a function of phonetic or orthographic factors does not suffice to show that the difference is relevant in connection with questions of meaning pertaining to m_i in E. For such a difference can throw light on such questions only if the structure of the utterance in which m_i occurs is the same as the structure of the utterance in which m_x occurs. That is not always the case.

The difference between {'Where is the orange (flower)?'} and {'Where is the orange (flower)?' | 'grower'} (i.e. between the set of conditions associated with 'Where is the orange flower?' and the set of conditions associated with 'Where is the orange grower?') is not relevant in connection with questions of meaning pertaining to 'flower' in E. And neither is the difference between {'Where is the red (flower)?'} and {'Where is the red (flower)?' | 'sympathizer'}. For in each case the structure of the relevant constructions has been altered. The expressions 'the orange flower' and 'the orange grower' differ in structure, a difference which is usually (but not invariably) signalized by a difference in contour. The expressions 'the red flower' and 'the red sympathizer' also differ in structure. In each case the difference is owing (in part) to the fact that an extra morphemic element has been introduced, viz. '-er', for '-er' is a morphemic segment of 'grower' and 'sympathizer' but not of 'flower'. In consequence, 'orange' in one case and 'red' in the other shift in meaning.

173.   We can finally say that Sm_i is that proper subset of Dm_i such that the members of Sm_i cannot readily be made out to be

a function of phonetic or orthographic or structural factors. This means that the relevant subsets of both the distributive and contrastive sets for m_i in E have now been drastically restricted in membership. The extent of the restriction can be sketched as follows.

From the entire distributive and contrastive sets for m_i in E we first selected (in 160 above) only those utterances in connection with which state regularities could be found. Thus all novel or relatively rare utterance types were ignored. Furthermore, even though many determinate utterance types may have been selected, viz. those frequently uttered, only weak regularities can be found in connection with such utterances (see 140 above). Then from these proper subsets of the distributive and contrastive sets for m_i in E we have selected only those utterances such that the nonsyntactic semantic differences between them cannot readily be made out to be a function of phonetic or orthographic or structural factors. This means that we are left with only a fragment of the distributive and contrastive sets for m_i in E. I propose to speak of this fragment as "the core set" for m_i in E. And I propose to speak of the logical sum of the core sets for all morphological elements of E as "the semantic core" of E.

It should be noted that not every word of E will occur in the semantic core of E. Alternatively one can say that the core set for some elements of E is the null set. To take one obvious example, it is clear that the relevant subset of Dm_i relative to the nonce word 'hippocat', viz. S'hippocat', is nothing but the null set. This is only to say that it is impossible to determine what meaning 'hippocat' has in (my) English (idiolect) simply by considering regularities to be found in connection with utterances of the distributive set for 'hippocat' in E. Very simply, there are no regularities (either relevant or irrelevant) to be found. Nonce forms like 'hippocat' and 'regit' represent an extreme type of case. But less extreme cases are everywhere at hand. No relevant regularities are in general likely to be found in connection with utterances of the distributive sets for such forms as 'anisotropy', 'poultice', 'sartorial', 'turbit'. Consequently these words, and thousands of others, will not occur in the semantic core of E. The words that will occur are of course primarily those having a relatively high frequency of occurrence in the corpus, 'the', 'to', 'is'.

174. I cannot say whether the logical distinction made here between the semantic core of a corpus and the corpus itself has any bearing on questions of linguistic ontogeny, on the development of a child's ability to speak and understand a language. I am inclined to think there is a connection but these are difficult matters beyond the scope of this essay.

I shall speak of two different levels in the analysis of meaning, where the levels in question are differentiated in terms of the operations of analysis (and synthesis) performed at each level. Possibly these levels correspond to psychological stages in the development of a child's ability to understand a language. Possibly not. In the absence of evidence and in default of sensible means or methods of confirmation or disconfirmation, speculation over such matters seems pointless.

175. Before I can state the conditions under which a morphological element of E has meaning in English I find it necessary to introduce a stronger preliminary notion, that of having "rudimentary meaning" in English. This is a stronger notion in that if m_i has rudimentary meaning in English it follows that m_i has meaning in English, but if m_i has meaning in English it does not follow that m_i has rudimentary meaning in English.

Rudimentary meaning is a matter of a morphological element's having meaning in the semantic core of the corpus. First, m_i has rudimentary meaning in the core utterance $d_i(m_i)$ if and only if the logical sum of $S_{i1} \ldots S_{in}$ is not null. This is to say if and only if the logical sum of the relevant differences, relative to m_i, between $\{d_i(m_i)\}$ and $\{d_i(m_i) \mid m_1\}$, between $\{d_i(m_i)\}$ and $\{d_i(m_i) \mid m_2\}$, between $\{d_i(m_i)\}$ and $\ldots$, and between $\{d_i(m_i)\}$ and $\{d_i(m_i) \mid m_n\}$ is not null.

Secondly, since difference in meaning is I believe clearly a matter of degree (so one says things like 'That is closer to but not exactly what it means.'), m_i in $d_i(m_i)$ differs in rudimentary meaning to a certain degree from m_i in $d_j(m_i)$ if and only if the logical sum of S_{i1} . . . S_{in} differs from the logical sum of S_{j1} . . . S_{jn} to that degree.

Thirdly, m_i has rudimentary meaning in English if and only if m_i has rudimentary meaning in $d_i(m_i)$, $d_j(m_i)$, . . . , and in $d_n(m_i)$, and m_i in $d_i(m_i)$ does not appreciably differ in rudimentary meaning from m_i in $d_j(m_i)$, . . . , $d_n(m_i)$. Thus to have rudimentary meaning in English, m_i must have rudimentary meaning in various utterances of its core distributive set and it must not appreciably differ in rudimentary meaning in these utterances.

176. The first level in the analysis of meaning is complete when one has determined the rudimentary meaning of the morphological elements of the semantic core of E. It is then possible to advance to and to operate at a more sophisticated level.

Given the rudimentary meaning of the morphological elements of the semantic core, we can gradually associate sets of conditions with all syntactically nondeviant whole utterances of E. For it is then possible to formulate state projections pertaining to the novel or infrequently uttered utterances excluded from the semantic core. Furthermore, and more significantly, at this level it is possible to deal with metalinguistic utterances like 'A bachelor is an unmarried man.'. Such an utterance can be connected with the speech act of defining the meaning of the word 'bachelor', thus with the speech act of making a metalinguistic statement about the word 'bachelor'. Consequently at this level of analysis and on the basis of such an utterance we can tentatively (but only tentatively) pair 'unmarried man' with 'bachelor' and we can associate the condition of being an unmarried man with utterances of the distributive set for 'bachelor' in E.

This, however, is not to say that we are forthwith entitled to say ' 'Bachelor' means unmarried man in English.'. We are entitled to say that only if we can show, first, that the utterance 'A bachelor is an unmarried man.' is not deviant in that it can without deviation be employed in making a true statement, and, secondly, that the statement 'A bachelor is an unmarried man.' is in fact a metalinguistic statement about the word 'bachelor' and not, as 'A bachelor is a lonesome person.' or 'A man is a featherless biped.' would be, simply a statement about bachelors or about men. Consequently the mere fact that we find such an utterance in the corpus does not entitle and certainly does not commit us to accepting a particular definition of 'bachelor'. Thus despite the metalinguistic (incomplete) sentence in the *Shorter Oxford English Dictionary* pertaining to the word 'inspect', which sentence may be presumed to be the counterpart of an utterance included in our corpus, we need not (and I do not) accept the dictionary's definition.

177.   The method of tentatively sorting out metalinguistic from nonmetalinguistic utterances can be illustrated here in connection with the utterance 'A man is a featherless biped.'. A statement made in uttering such an utterance in some appropriate way and in some appropriate situation would surely be true. Consequently our problem here is to determine whether or not the utterance can sensibly be construed as metalinguistic and in particular whether such a statement can sensibly be construed as a metalinguistic statement about the word 'man'. It cannot. This can be seen as follows.

If we construe the statement as a metalinguistic statement about 'man', as in fact providing an analysis of 'man' by pairing 'featherless biped' with 'man', it is necessary to determine whether or not the (supposed) analysis is a partial or a complete analysis; e.g. one could pair 'man' with 'bachelor' by way of a partial analysis of 'bachelor', whereas the pairing of 'unmarried man' with 'bachelor' could constitute a complete analysis of 'bachelor'. A complete analysis yields an equivalence, 'A person is a bachelor if and only if the person is an unmarried man.', whereas a partial analysis yields only a one way implication, 'If a person is a bachelor then the person is a man.'.

First, assume that 'featherless biped' is paired with 'man' by way of a complete analysis of 'man'. Then consider such non-deviant utterances as 'A creature exactly like a chicken save for being featherless would be a featherless biped.', 'A plucked chicken is a featherless biped.', which could be employed in making true statements. Here 'man' cannot without deviation occur in the environments that 'featherless biped' occurs in. Furthermore, that 'man' cannot occur in these environments is not explicable in terms of nor is it attributable to phonetic or orthographic or structural factors. We obviously cannot associate the condition of being a man with these utterances.

Secondly, assume that 'featherless biped' is paired with 'man' by way of a partial analysis of 'man'. Then consider such non-deviant utterances as 'Try to act like a man!', 'A one-legged man crossed the street.', 'A man born with only one leg would be something of a freak.', some of which could be employed in making true statements. Here 'featherless biped' cannot without deviation occur in these environments that 'man' occurs in. Again, the fact that it cannot is not explicable in terms of nor is it attributable to phonetic or orthographic or structural factors.

Thirdly, it is necessary to remember that the analysis here is in connection with morphological elements and not simply words. Although there may be or are semantic differences between various occurrences of 'man', it is still necessary to consider the entire distributive set for 'man' in the corpus. Consequently it is necessary to consider such utterances as 'He's a manly fellow.', 'She wore mannish clothes.', 'It was a manful deed.', 'He finally attained manhood.'. 'Man-' in these utterances is a simple stem combined with the derivational affixes '-ly', '-ish', '-ful', '-hood'. It is also necessary to consider such phrasal compounds as 'man-eater', 'manhole', 'manslaughter'. It is obviously unprofitable and unilluminating to attempt to associate the condition of being a featherless biped with an utterance like 'She wore mannish clothes.'. Notice that the pair 'man' and 'mannish' is matched by such pairs as 'baby' and 'babyish', 'freak' and 'freakish', 'boy' and 'boyish', 'tiger' and 'tigerish', 'fool' and 'foolish'. Consequently, if we associate the condition of being a featherless biped only with utterances of the distributive set for the word 'man' but not the stem 'man-' in *E*, we must consider whether or not the resultant pairings would be in accordance with considerations of composition.

Fourthly, it is necessary to notice that a statement like 'A man is a featherless biped.' can be related to such statements as 'Men are featherless bipeds.', 'Men generally are featherless and bipedal.', 'Men are characteristically featherless and bipedal.', but not to such statements as 'All men are featherless bipeds.', 'Every man is a featherless biped.', 'Any man whatsoever is a featherless biped.'. For again, a freakish man born with only one leg would not be a featherless biped. Such a creature would be a freakish man and not merely a manlike freak. If we were to class 'A man is a featherless biped.' as a metalinguistic statement about the word 'man', we should then be virtually committed to classing virtually all general statements as metalinguistic.

Evidently the hypothesis that 'featherless biped' may be paired with 'man' by way of either a partial or a complete analysis of 'man' is not a fruitful one. So for the time being we tentatively (but only tentatively) conclude that the statement 'A man is a featherless biped.' is not to be construed as a metalinguistic statement about the word 'man' and that if it is so construed it appears to be in error. No final conclusion is possible here until an explication of having meaning in English has been provided and until it has been determined precisely what meaning 'man' has in English and how what meaning it has is related to the condition of being a featherless biped.

178.   It is now possible to state more or less precisely the conditions under which a morphological element of E has meaning in English. We now assume that all utterances of the distributive and contrastive sets for m_i in E may have sets of conditions associated with them. Let C_{ij} be the relevant difference between the set of conditions associated with $d_i(m_i)$ and that associated with $d_i(m_i) \mid m_j$; thus C_{ij} is the set of conditions constituted by the logical product of $\{d_i(m_i)\}$ and the complement of $\{d_i(m_i) \mid m_j\}$, and such that C_{ij} cannot readily be made out to be a function of phonetic or orthographic or structural factors. (It should be noted that C_{ij} may not be identical with S_{ij} even in

cases in which $d_i(m_i)$ and $d_i(m_i) \mid m_j$ are core utterances. For possibly only weak regularities were found in connection with $d_i(m_i)$ and $d_i(m_i) \mid m_j$, whereas at the second level of analysis it was possible to associate a stronger set of conditions with the utterances. Thus at the first level of analysis even though certain conditions could have been associated with the utterance 'George crossed the Hudson at 2 A.M. on October 20, 1943.', once projections became available a stronger association could be made (see 140 above). We now have the following differences to consider: C_{11}, C_{12}, . . . , C_{1n}, C_{21}, C_{22}, . . . , C_{2n}, . . . , C_{n1}, C_{n2}, . . . , C_{nn}. (For example, C_{2n} is the set constituted by the logical product of $\{d_2(m_i)\}$ and the complement of $\{d_2(m_i) \mid m_n\}$.) Finally, let Cm_i be the set of the sets C_{11} . . . C_{nn} relative to m_i in E. (Thus I shall, on occasion write 'C'tiger' ', 'C'lion' '.)

We can now say first, m_i has meaning in $d_i(m_i)$ if and only if the logical sum of C_{i1} . . . C_{in} is not null. Thus 'to' in 'I want to go through Istanbul.' does not have meaning in that utterance.

Secondly, m_i in $d_i(m_i)$ differs in meaning to a certain degree from m_i in $d_j(m_i)$ if and only if the logical sum of C_{i1} . . . C_{in} differs from the logical sum of C_{j1} . . . C_{jn} to that degree.

Finally, m_i has meaning in English if and only if m_i has meaning in $d_i(m_i)$, $d_j(m_i)$, . . . , $d_n(m_i)$, and m_i in $d_i(m_i)$ does not appreciably differ in meaning from m_i in $d_j(m_i)$, . . . , $d_n(m_i)$. Thus to have meaning in English, m_i must have meaning in various utterances of its distributive set and it must not appreciably differ in meaning in these utterances. Alternatively one can say that m_i has meaning in English if and only if it has a nonnull set of conditions C_{ij} . . . C_{mn} associated with it in various utterances of its distributive set. Or still again, m_i has meaning if and only if Cm_i has nonnull members, or if and only if m_i has associated with it some nonnull set of conditions.

The vagueness of this account may seem objectionable but I am not concerned with so-called "rational reconstruction." I am concerned with an accurate representation: a clear picture of a blurred line must be blurred in one sense and not in another.

179.   Since the word 'synonym' has loomed large in contemporary discussions of meaning, it may help to say something about the matter here.

The elements m_i and m_j are synonyms if and only if m_i and m_j arc distinct words not in complementary distribution and Cm_i and Cm_j are the same set or are markedly similar sets; m_i and m_j are exact synonyms if and only if m_i and m_j are distinct words not in complementary distribution and Cm_i and Cm_j are one and the same set, thus identical.

The restriction that m_i and m_j be distinct words not in complementary distribution calls for explanation. If we were to consider plural affixes such as '-s' and '-en', in so far as they have meaning they evidently do not differ in meaning, indeed, they are allomorphs of the plural morpheme. But I do not believe that the word 'synonym' is used in connection with affixes. If we consider the word 'a' as in 'That is a book.' and the word 'an' as in 'That is an etching.' we find that one virtually never occurs in an environment in which the other occurs, thus the forms are in complementary distribution. I am inclined to suppose that the word 'synonym' is not used in connection with forms in complementary distribution.

Given such a restriction, it is fairly clear that there are virtually no exact synonyms in English. Why should there be? Let 'thater' be an exact synonym of 'that': when would we have occasion to use 'thater' instead of 'that'? 'Thater' will find no place in the language for it is superfluous. But this is not to deny that on occasion at least 'brother' and 'male sibling' may be exactly synonymous. To say that 'brother' and 'male sibling' are exactly synonymous is not to say that they are exact synonyms: they are not synonyms, either exact or otherwise. 'Synonym' and 'synonymous' are not synonyms, neither are they synonymous.[3]

---

[3] E. A. Nida states as "a principle of semantic analysis" that "No morphemes or combinations of morphemes are identical in meaning." He adds: "This principle means that there are no real synonyms, i.e. forms which have identical meanings" (*op. cit.*, p. 151). His reasons for adopting such a dubious "principle" of analysis are based on what I take to be a

180. Does a proper name like 'Witchgren' have meaning in English? I said not but what does that matter. The question is whether or not a name like 'Witchgren' satisfies the conditions for having meaning in English. If it does then something is wrong with my theory or with my intuitions.

Consider the utterance 'Witchgren is on the mat.': let this be d_1('Witchgren'). Does 'Witchgren' have meaning in d_1('Witchgren')?

'Witchgren' has meaning in d_1('Witchgren') if and only if C_{11} . . . C_{1n} is not null. Thus there must be a contrasting element, m_x, such that the logical product of $\{d_1$('Witchgren')$\}$ and the complement of $\{d_1$('Witchgren') $\mid m_x\}$ is not null, and such that the relevant difference between $\{d_1$('Witchgren')$\}$ and $\{d_1$-('Witchgren') $\mid m_x\}$ is invariant under phonetic and orthographic transformations of d_1('Witchgren') and d_1('Witchgren') $\mid m_x$, and such that the difference cannot readily be made out to be a function of structural factors.

Taking d_1('Witchgren') $\mid m_x$ as d_1('Witchgren') $\mid$ 'he' it is clear enough that the logical product of $\{d_1$('Witchgren')$\}$ and the complement of $\{d_1$('Witchgren') $\mid$ 'he'$\}$ is not null. The fact that 'Witchgren' in 'Witchgren is on the mat.' does contrast with 'he', 'dust', 'water', is I believe the principal reason why so many philosophers are inclined to suppose that proper names do have meaning in English. And if one adopts the slogan that "the meaning of a word is its use in the language," one can then hardly avoid supposing that proper names generally do have meaning in English. (Thus Wittgenstein writes: ". . . the *mean-*

confusion of 'meaning' and 'connotation'. He writes: ". . . the alternant pronunciations of duty (1) /duwtiy/ and (2) /dyuwtiy/ carry certain distinct connotations. In some circumstances the form /dyuwtiy/ induces an unfavorable response from the listener, who interprets it as pedantic or associated with people whose culture he does not appreciate. On the other hand, among a certain small set of speakers of American English the form /duwtiy/ is a mark of educational and cultural inferiority" (p. 151). Notice that the contrast Nida points to between /duwtiy/ and /dyuwtiy/ is not proportional to the contrast found between /huw/ and /hyuw/, between /muw/ and /myuw/, etc.; thus it conflicts with the principle of composition.

ing of a name is sometimes explained by pointing to its bearer." [4] This is true only in rare and special cases, e.g. a certain person is named 'Blue-nose' and he has a blue nose. It is, however, not infrequently the case that whom the speaker means in using a name is explained by pointing to the person of whom it is a name. Thus if I say 'George is coming.' and am asked 'Whom do you mean?', I may point to George by way of an answer.)

The fact that the logical product of $\{d_1(\text{'Witchgren'})\}$ and the complement of $\{d_1(\text{'Witchgren'}) \mid \text{'he'}\}$ is not null proves nothing. The important question then is whether the relevant difference between the two sets of conditions is invariant under phonetic and orthographic transformation. To answer this question we must determine what conditions are associated with $d_1(\text{'Witchgren'})$, i.e. with 'Witchgren is on the mat.'.

What conditions are associated with 'Witchgren is on the mat.'? If 'Witchgren is on the mat.' is true then something named 'Witchgren' is on the mat. (But it does not follow that if 'Something named 'Witchgren' is on the mat.' is true then Witchgren is on the mat. There is no reason why one could not name an owl 'Witchgren', in which case if Witchgren the owl were the creature in question, it would not follow that Witchgren the cat would be on the mat.) But it also seems to be the case that if 'Witchgren is on the mat.' is true then, in so far as 'Witchgren' in *E* has the information-content of being a tomcat, a particular tomcat is on the mat. Consequently there seem to be (at least) two different and distinct regularities or projections that may be relevant. We may say that if 'Witchgren is on the mat.' is uttered then (generally or in a standard case) a particular tomcat is on the mat, or we may say that if the utterance is uttered then (generally or in a standard case) something named 'Witchgren' is on the mat. It should be obvious that the latter regularity or projection is irrelevant here in connection with questions of meaning since such a regularity or projection will not be invariant under phonetic or orthographic transformations. Consequently, 'Witchgren' has meaning in English if and

---

[4] *Philosophical Investigations*, p. 21. "Und die *Bedeutung* eines Namens erklärt man manchmal dadurch, dass man auf seiner Träger zeigt."

only if the former regularity or projection is relevant. So the question is this: is the former regularity or projection relevant?

To decide this it is necessary to determine whether or not it accords with the principal of composition, thus we must determine whether or not a pairing of 'a particular tomcat is on the mat' with 'Witchgren is on the mat.' is in accordance with the principle of composition.

Consider the utterance 'Dragel is on the mat.' where 'Dragel' is the name of an owl and has the information-content of being an old grey owl. (Dragel was created old and grey.) If 'Witchgren is on the mat.' has paired with it 'a particular tomcat is on the mat' then in virtue of the apparent structural similarity between 'Witchgren is on the mat.' and 'Dragel is on the mat.' we require an equal similarity between 'a particular tomcat is on the mat' and whatever is to be paired with 'Dragel is on the mat.'. But if 'Dragel is on the mat.' has paired with it 'a particular old grey owl is on the mat' while 'Witchgren is on the mat.' has paired with it 'a particular tomcat is on the mat', the pairings will fail to accord with the principle of composition. Furthermore, suppose 'Glywellyn' in E has the information-content of being a tomcat. Then consider the statement 'Glywellyn is on the mat.'. If the utterance employed in making that statement has paired with it 'a particular tomcat is on the mat' then in so far as 'Witchgren is on the mat.' and 'Glywellyn is on the mat.' are different statements and may differ in truth value, since both utterances are paired with one and the same utterance, the pairings fail to indicate how such a difference in truth value is possible. Finally, if 'Witchgren is on the mat.' has paired with it 'something named 'Witchgren' is on the mat', if 'Dragel is on the mat.' has paired with it 'something named 'Dragel' is on the mat', and if 'Glywellyn is on the mat.' has paired with it 'something named 'Glywellyn' is on the mat', then all three pairings accord with the principle of composition and there is no problem of explicating the possibility of differences in truth values.

What's in a name? There is nothing in a proper name. It has an information-content but even so, it is all sound and if the sound is changed the name is changed. Notice that one can say 'George is so called after his father.' or (what is different) 'George is so named after his father.': so one uses the name both to say something about a person and to say something about the name itself, thus one "uses" and explicitly "mentions" the name simultaneously. And one can do this with any proper name whatever. But one cannot in general do this with words. One can say 'Meowing is so called because of the way it sounds to us.'. But what is there to say about 'then' in this way?

181.   Consider a pair of 'bear'-s:

(6)   That is a bear.

(7)   I can't bear it.

'Bear' in (6) not only differs in meaning from 'bear' in (7) but it is a different word. The two occurrences of 'bear' are clearly allomorphs of different morphemes in that they have markedly different distributions in E in this sense: if we were to formulate the distribution of 'bear' in E, two markedly different formulas, or one complex formula having markedly different parts, would have to be given. Analogously, two different distributive sets can be associated with 'bear' in E in the following sense. Let 'raeb' be a transform of 'bear' in (6) and let 'areb' be a transform of 'bear' in (7). Then the distributive set for 'bear' in E can be sorted into two virtually exclusively subsets, viz. those utterances that we are inclined to pair off with members of the distributive set for 'raeb' in E and those that we are inclined to pair off with members of the distributive set for 'areb' in E. (The two sets will be virtually but not absolutely exclusive, e.g. the utterance 'I can't bear that bear.' will be a member of both sets.)

182.   Consider a pair of 'division'-s:

(8)   The division is incorrect.

(9)   The division is marching.

Unlike the pair of 'bear'-s, this pair of 'division'-s is only one word. But like the pair of 'bear'-s, this pair of 'division'-s differ in meaning to such an extent to warrant our saying *tout court* that they differ in meaning.

That the pair of 'division'-s, unlike the pair of 'bear'-s, is one word can be seen as follows. Let 'noisivid' be a transform of 'division' in (8) and let 'onisivid' be a transform of 'division' in (9). Then the distributive set for 'division' in E can be sorted into two subsets, viz. those utterances that we are inclined to pair off with members of the distributive set for 'noisivid' in E and those that we are inclined to pair off with members of the distributive set for 'onisivid' in E. But, unlike the case of 'bear', the two subsets are not virtually exclusive. Not only does 'The division is studying division.' belong to each set but 'I want to see the division.', 'Which division?', 'The division is incomplete.', belong to each set. Even the utterance 'Lieutenant George's division.' belongs to each set.

The difference between 'division' in (8) and 'division' in (9) must show up somewhere. If on the basis of the fact that the distributive set for 'division' in E is not neatly divisible into two exclusive subsets we say that we have one word then the difference shows up when we add that the one word differs in meaning in each case. This indicates that either we say that the two relevant occurrences of 'division' are allomorphs of homonymous, and therefore different, morphemes, or we say that they are homonymous allomorphs of the same morpheme. I shall follow what I take to be common usage at this point and say that in the case of 'division' we have to deal with one word that differs in meaning or, alternatively, that we are concerned with homonymous allomorphs of the same morpheme.

Let 'division' be m_4, and let $d_1(m_4)$ and $d_2(m_4)$ be (8) and (9) respectively. That m_4 in $d_1(m_4)$ differs in meaning from m_4 in $d_2(m_4)$ follows from the fact that the logical sum of $C_{11} \ldots C_{1n}$ differs from the logical sum of $C_{21} \ldots C_{2n}$. Since the difference is extreme, it warrants our saying *tout court:* m_4 in one case differs in meaning from m_4 in the other case. That there is an extreme difference to be found should be obvious: $C_{21} \ldots C_{2n}$ will include conditions pertaining to troops, army groups, and the like, none of which will be included in $C_{11} \ldots C_{1n}$. But there are complications here: it is necessary to proceed slowly and carefully.

183.   That 'division' in (8) differs in meaning from 'division' in (9) should be obvious. It may seem equally obvious that 'division' in (8) has a different meaning from 'division' in (9). That is indeed the case but I cannot believe that it is at all obvious.

(A word of warning may be necessary here about my use of the locutions 'differ in meaning', 'has a meaning', and the like. From the fact that I am prepared to say and do say ' 'Division' in (8) has a different meaning from 'division' in (9).' it does not follow that I am prepared to say or that I do say ' 'Division' in (8) has a meaning.' or ' 'Division' in (8) has a meaning in English.'. On the contrary, I do not say and I am not prepared to say that. Just so, though one says 'George and Josef have a different attitude about the matter.' it does not follow that one says 'George has an attitude about the matter.': one does not. No doubt the difference here is slight but I believe that it is of some significance.)

Consider a pair of 'brother'-s:

(10)   He is not literally my brother.

(11)   She has been a brother to me.

It is perhaps obvious that 'brother' in (10) differs in meaning to a considerable degree, and so differs in meaning, from 'brother' in (11). 'Brother' in (10) can have 'male sibling' associated with it, whereas 'brother' in (11) can have 'comrade', 'friend', associated with it. Furthermore, the difference between 'brother' in (10) and 'brother' in (11) appears to be as considerable as the difference between 'division' in (8) and 'division' in (9). Consequently, if we say not only that 'division' in (8) differs in meaning from 'division' in (9) but that 'division' in (8) has a different meaning from 'division' in (9), it might seem as though we must say that 'brother' in (10) has a different meaning from 'brother' in (11). But as against this, I want to say that even though 'brother' in (10) does differ in meaning from 'brother' in (11), it is not the case that 'brother' in (10) has a different meaning from 'brother' in (11): it is the case that 'brother' in (10) has a different sense from 'brother' in (11).

184. That 'division' in (8) can rightly be said to have a different meaning from 'division' in (9) is owing to the fact that 'division' in E has (at least) two different meanings. The difference between 'bear' and 'division' in this respect would show up in an adequate dictionary in this way: whereas 'bear' calls for (at least) two entries, 'division' (so far) calls for one entry with two headings. That 'division' in E calls for one entry with two headings is owing to the fact that it is a single word having (at least) two meanings. And that 'division' in E can rightly be said to have (at least) two meanings is owing to the fact that C'division', the relevant set of sets of conditions associated with 'division' in E, is neatly divisible into two relatively distinct and different proper subsets having what I shall call "a complementary association" with the utterances of the distributive set for 'division' in E.

Let C^1'division' and C^2'division' be two proper subsets of C'division' such that the members of C^1'division' include conditions pertaining to army groups, whereas the members of C^2'division' include conditions pertaining to matters of arithmetic. Then to say that C^1'division' and C^2'division' have a complementary association with utterances of the distributive set for 'division' in E is to say this: if C_{ij} is the relevant difference between $\{d_i(\text{'division'})\}$ and $\{d_i(\text{'division'}) \mid m_j\}$ then generally C_{ij} is a member of either C^1'division' or C^2'division' but not both.

Consider C'brother': it is true enough that C'brother' may be neatly divisible into (at least) two relatively distinct and different proper subsets for we can discern C^1'brother' whose members include conditions having to do with acting in a characteristic fashion, viz. brotherly, and we can discern C^2'brother' whose members include the condition of being male or of being a sibling. But unlike C^1'division' and C^2'division', C^1'brother' and C^2'brother' do not have a complementary association with utterances of the distributive set for 'brother' in E.

The difference can be seen thus: the utterance 'Lieutenant George's division.' may in a given case have associated with it either conditions pertaining to army groups or conditions pertaining to matters of arithmetic. Thus the utterance lends itself to ambiguity. But consider (12):

(12)   I wish I had a brother.

What is he wishing for? A male sibling? Or a person who will act in a characteristic fashion towards him? Or both? If one says truly 'I want to see Lieutenant George's division.', one probably wants to see either an army group or a bit of arithmetic. To answer the question 'Which do you mean: an army group or a bit of arithmetic?' by saying 'Both.' would be somewhat curious. But an answer to the analogous question about (12) might well be 'Both.'.

185.   'Brother' in (10) and 'brother' in (11) differ in meaning to such a degree as to warrant our saying *tout court:* they differ in meaning. The same may be said of 'division' in (8) and 'division' in (9). But the differences between 'brother' in E and 'division' in E warrant our saying certain things about the two occurrences of 'division' that cannot rightly be said about the two occurrences of 'brother'. Thus we can say that 'division' in (8) has a different meaning from 'division' in (9), whereas we can at best say that 'brother' in (10) has a different sense from 'brother' in (11).

To talk of the sense of a word is, as it were, to talk of the word branching off in a certain direction. The etymological forebear of 'sense', viz. the French word 'sens', is suggestive, and so is the current use of 'sens' in 'Sens obligatoire!', 'Sens unique!'. To say that here a word has one sense, there another, is, as it were, to say that here the word branches off in one direction, there another. To say that 'brother' has (at least) two different senses in English is, as it were, to say that (at least) two main branches can be found in connection with 'brother' in English. If the word 'brother' were a tree, it would have a single trunk with (at least) two main branches, but if 'division' were a tree, it would have two trunks joined at the roots, whereas the pair of 'bear'-s would be a pair of trees.

186.   The distinction between 'x has a different meaning from y.' and 'x has a different sense from y.' is not particularly subtle. Neither is the distinction between 'x and y differ in meaning.' and 'x and y differ in sense.'; e.g. 'brother' in (10) and 'brother' in (11) differ to such an extent as to warrant our saying *tout court:* they differ in meaning. But 'brother' in (10) and 'brother' in (12) do not differ to that extent. They differ but only to such an extent as to warrant our saying that they differ in sense. And the same may be said of 'brother' in (11) and 'brother' in (12).

All of this is easily explicable in terms of the strength of the intersection of the relevant sets of conditions. In so far as the relevant sets of conditions associated with 'brother' in (10) and 'brother' in (11) have a virtually null intersection, the two occurrences of 'brother' differ in meaning. In so far as the relevant sets of conditions associated with 'brother' in (10) and 'brother' in (12) differ and yet have a nonnull intersection, the two occurrences of 'brother' differ in sense. And of course from the fact that two occurrences of a word differ in sense it does not automatically follow that they have different senses.

187.   That frequently a word has here one sense, there another, is an important, a vital, fact about words. But it is horribly difficult to explain. I do not claim to explain it fully here. But I do claim to be able to begin to explain it on the basis of the theory of meaning being presented here.

An element m_i can have associated with it a set of sets of conditions Cm_i. Think of m_i as a jewel, of each member of Cm_i as one facet. Then which facet catches the light depends on contextual and linguistic environmental features, thus on its setting. So one says 'He's my brother.' or 'He's been a brother to me.' or 'He's a brother of the order.': in each case, if it is a standard case, a different facet of the word is turned to catch the light. And this, so far, is simple enough: that the utterance 'He's a brother of the order.' does not have associated with it the condition of being a sibling is owing to the fact that the environment in which 'brother' here occurs, viz. 'He's a . . . of the order.', serves to cancel any such association. Again, someone says 'Cow is coming.': then in a standard case 'Cow' is a proper name for that it is, is indicated by the combinative features.

But matters become vastly more complex when we consider deviant utterances, e.g. syntactically deviant utterances such as 'I wrote it a grief ago.' or 'The men grief the women.', or a semantically deviant utterance such as 'He's a *bright* fellow.' uttered in making an ironic comment. 'Grief' in 'I wrote it a grief ago.' serves to indicate a measure of time, but I do not suppose that this could be said to be a "sense" of the word 'grief'. Again, 'bright' in the ironic comment serves to indicate stupidity, yet this could not be said to be a "sense" of the word 'bright'. That 'grief' and 'bright' serve to indicate what they do in these cases is clearly owing to a complex interaction of various syntactic and semantic factors. More specifically, the significance of the deviant utterances in question is a function of the syntactic structures of the utterances and of the sets of conditions associated with those morphological constituents of the utterances that have meaning in English. Before it is possible to undertake a serious semantic analysis of such utterances it is necessary to develop a fairly clear concept of levels of grammaticalness, it is necessary to consider in some detail precisely how the syntactic structure of an utterance serves to determine the significance of the utterance. Such problems are beyond the scope of this essay.

188.   To say 'The word 'good' has meaning in English.' is not the same as saying 'The word 'good' has a meaning in English.'. Since the word 'good' can rightly be said both to have meaning in English and to have a meaning in English, it is not a good example here. So I shall switch to the word 'tiger'.

The word 'tiger' has meaning in English. But I am reluctant to say 'The word 'tiger' has a meaning in English.' for that may well draw the query 'What does 'tiger' mean?' and in response

to that I am inclined to say that it is not the case that 'tiger' has
a meaning in English. 'Tiger' has meaning in English but it is
not the case that 'tiger' means this or that.

The distinction between having meaning in English and
having a meaning in English is perhaps subtle or even over
subtle. Many speakers of my dialect make no such distinction.
I mean to make nothing much of it here. I mean only to explain
why it is that I am (and perhaps others are) inclined to make it.
The distinction, whether idiosyncratic or not, is suggestive. It
suggests that uttering an utterance of the form 'What does the
word '. . .' mean?' may, on occasion and depending primarily
on what fills the blank, constitute a deviation from regularities
to be found in or in connection with the language.

'What does the word 'tiger' mean?' is, I believe, a somewhat
deviant and perhaps even odd utterance, the uttering of which
constitutes a deviation from regularities to be found in or in
connection with the language. That the utterance sounds odd
is not owing to the fact that a great many adult speakers of my
dialect are familiar with the word 'tiger'. A great many adult
speakers of my dialect are not familiar with the word 'ousel' yet
'What does the word 'ousel' mean?' is a somewhat deviant utterance and sounds somewhat odd. And it is true that a great many
adult speakers of my dialect are familiar with the word 'perpendicular' yet 'What does the word 'perpendicular' mean?' is
not a deviant utterance and does not sound at all odd (to me
anyway). I am inclined to suppose that with some nouns like
'tiger' one asks, not 'What does the word 'tiger' mean?', but
rather 'What is a tiger?'. Whereas with some adjectives like
'good' one asks, not 'What is a good thing?', and not 'What is
good?', but rather 'What does the word 'good' mean?'. Why this
is so is something to be explained.

189.   An element m_i of E has meaning in English if and only if
it has associated with it a set of sets Cm_i such that the members
of Cm_i are nonnull sets of conditions, and these nonnull sets of
conditions do not appreciably differ from one another (see 178
above). In effect, this means that m_i has meaning in English if

and only if m_i has associated with it in various utterances of its distributive set a relevant nonnull set of conditions.

If m_i has meaning in English, to explicate what it means it is necessary in one way or another to characterize the relevant set of conditions, thus to characterize the members of Cm_i. But if it is not the case that m_i has a meaning in English, even though m_i has meaning in English, then there can be no question of explicating what m_i means for it is then not the case that it means this or that. Consequently, if there is, as I suppose, some sense to the distinction between 'has meaning in English' and 'has a meaning in English', one would expect there to be a difference between the character of the set of conditions associated with a word like 'tiger' and the character of the set of conditions associated with a word like 'good'. And, of course, a striking difference is to be found, a difference that neatly corresponds to the difference between 'having . . .' and 'having a . . .'.

190.   I say 'The word 'tiger' has meaning in English.'. If I am then asked 'What is a tiger?', I might reply 'A tiger is a large carnivorous quadrupedal feline, tawny yellow in color with blackish transverse stripes and white belly.' (derived from the entry under 'tiger' in the *Shorter Oxford English Dictionary*).[5] And now suppose someone says 'You have just said what the word 'tiger' means in English.': is that so? I think not.

Suppose in a jungle clearing one says 'Look, a three-legged tiger!': must one be confused? The phrase 'a three-legged tiger' is not a *contradictio in adjecto*. But if 'tiger' in English meant,

---

[5] The *Dictionary* gives: "1. A large carnivorous feline quadruped, *Felis tigris*, one of the two largest living felines. . . ." Thus a tiger is a feline, which is not to say that a tiger is feline, which would be somewhat curious. Consequently 'feline' should occur as a noun in the definition; hence I write 'a large carnivorous quadrupedal feline'. Notice that so construed the condition indicated by 'feline' in the definition is a necessary one: it is not possible for an animal to be a tiger and yet not be a feline. Whereas if 'feline' occurs in the definition as an adjective, the indicated condition is not a necessary one: it is possible for an animal to be a tiger and yet not be feline, just as a man need not be manly.

among other things, either quadruped or quadrupedal, the phrase 'a three-legged tiger' could only be a *contradictio in adjecto.*

Unlike the word 'tiger', the word 'brother' not only has meaning in English but it has a meaning in English and one can say what it means; thus: 'In one sense, the word 'brother' means male sibling.'. The word 'brother', unlike the word 'tiger', has associated with it a set of necessary and sufficient conditions. Technically speaking, 'brother', unlike 'tiger', can be defined *per genus et differentiam.*

The word 'tiger' has associated with it a set of conditions a, the word 'brother' has associated with it a set of conditions b. The difference between a and b is this: my tiger need not satisfy every condition of a; it may be my tiger nonetheless; but my brother could not be my brother if he did not satisfy every condition of b. Another way of saying this is: it is not hard to describe something that would be a freakish tiger and something else that would be a tigerlike freak; but what would be examples of a freakish brother and of a brotherlike freak? A brother who, say, ate bats might count as a freakish brother. But what would count as a brotherlike freak? (And notice that 'He has an old tiger.' is not deviant but 'He has an old brother.' is odd.)

191. If m_i has a meaning in English there can be a question of explicating what it means. But if m_i has meaning in English and it is not the case that m_i has a meaning in English, there is then no question of explicating what it means for it is then not the case that it means this or that. But this is not to say that there is then no question to be asked.

To ask the right question is no easy matter. A foreigner, learning to speak the language, might ask 'What does 'tiger' mean?'. One could not answer that question though one could tell him what he is wanting to know. So one could perhaps reply ' 'Tiger' in English has the same meaning as '. . .' in your language.', filling the blank with a close equivalent in his language. Or one could reply by saying 'A tiger is a large carnivorous. . . .'. Thus in either case one rejects, as it were, the question 'What does 'tiger' mean?' and instead offers an answer in the former case to 'What meaning does 'tiger' have in English?', in the latter case to 'What is a tiger?'. A foreigner may not know enough of the language to ask the right question.

One can ask different questions about or in connection with different elements of E. So one asks 'What does 'good' mean?' but not 'What does 'tiger' mean?'; 'What is a tiger?' but not 'What is a good?'. Since 'tiger' has meaning in English, if it were not the case that 'tiger' had different meanings in English, one could ask 'What is the meaning of 'tiger' in English?'. (Just so one passes from 'He has time to . . .' to 'The time he has to . . .'.) But one cannot ask 'What is the meaning of 'division' in English?': here the question is 'What are the meanings of 'division' in English?'.

Questions of the form 'What does '. . .' mean?', 'What is the meaning of '. . .'?', 'What does '. . .' mean in English?', are not general questions that can be asked of any element of E that has meaning in English. But neither are questions of the forms 'What is the definition of '. . .'?', 'What are the definitions of '. . .'?'. No doubt one can ask 'What is the definition of 'collision' in English?' but not 'What is the definition of 'then' in English?'.

Even so, there is a general sort of question that can be asked. If all one knows is that m_i has meaning in English then one can at least ask 'What meaning does m_i have in English?'

192.   That an element m_i of E has meaning in English is one thing: that it is possible to explain in detail precisely what meaning it has in English is another. But it is always possible to say something.

It would be naïve to suppose that there must be, or even can be, one and only one way of expounding the meaning of words: could there be only one possible map of a given terrain? The way we map an area depends on the area, on our interests. So at one time we use one type of projection, at another time another. As Bentham long ago pointed out in his superb account of exposition, the variety of ways of expounding the meaning of words corresponds to the variety of words to be found in the language.[6]

An element m_i of E that has meaning in English has associated with it a nonnull set or sets of conditions. To explain what meaning m_i has in English it is necessary to characterize the relevant associated set or sets of conditions. And because there are various ways of doing this, there are various ways of answering a question of the form 'What meaning does m_i have in English?'. Even so, there is something of a general procedure that is generally applicable.

193.   In determining precisely what meaning m_i has or may have in English, the first step is to determine as precisely as possible the membership of its distributive and contrastive sets.

At the most elementary level this means that a grammatical characterization of the element in question is called for. Thus what one says in answer to a question about 'bear' will depend on whether a noun or a verb is in question, for, of course, nouns and verbs have profoundly different distributions.

At a less elementary level it is necessary to specify the distributive and contrastive sets with some care and with attention to details. Thus even though 'intend' contrasts with 'mean' in 'What does he mean?', it does not contrast with 'mean' in 'What does the word mean?'. Or again, though 'false' contrasts with 'untrue' in 'What he said was untrue.', it does not contrast with 'untrue' in 'The cloth is untrue.', and thus 'The cloth is false.' is excluded from the distributive set for 'false' in E.

The first step of the procedure is completed when one has compiled a list of utterances in accordance with the schema of 160 above, where the value of n is as large as is practical.

194.   It is possible to determine with great precision and in great detail the membership of both the distributive and contrastive sets for m_i in E and yet have no notion of what meaning m_i may have in English. By appealing to an informant, one may

[6] See his *Works*, VIII, 242–253.

be able to fill in the schema of 160 above in great detail. But if one knows nothing more than that about m_i, one cannot even begin to say what meaning m_i has in English.

If one determines that m_i and m_j have different distributions in E, and thus are associated with different distributive and contrastive sets, it does not follow that m_i and m_j differ in meaning in English. Of course, if m_i and m_j have markedly different distributions in E one then has some reason to suppose that they differ in meaning in English. Thus to point out that one says 'It is senseless to build a garage if you have no need of one.' but not 'It is meaningless to build a garage if you have no need of one.' is to point out a good reason for supposing that 'senseless' and 'meaningless' differ in meaning in English. But a mere difference in distribution is not in itself an adequate criterion of a difference in meaning. Such a difference establishes a difference in meaning if and only if the difference is not a function of orthographic or phonetic or structural factors. For example, the prefix 'im-' of 'impossible' and the prefix 'in-' of 'intolerable' have different distributions in E. Yet both 'im-' and 'in-' can be said to be allomorphs of a single morpheme and they do not differ in meaning. The difference in distribution is clearly a function of phonetic factors: first, they have complementary distributions, one never occurs in an environment in which the other occurs; secondly, the bilabial nasal m occurs before a bilabial sound like p, whereas the alveolar nasal n occurs before an alveolar sound like t or d. Again, even though 'brother' in 'He is a blood brother of the king.' may have paired with it and may be synonymous with 'male sibling', the phrase 'male sibling' cannot occur in that environment: 'He is a blood male sibling of the king.' would be somewhat odd. This difference in distribution is clearly owing to the structural difference between 'male sibling' and 'brother', the former being an attributive endocentric construction with 'sibling' as head and the construction being partially closed. Again, despite the obvious difference in meaning, 'happy' and 'unhappy' have almost identical distributive sets in E (but not quite, for one says 'He's a happy-go-lucky fellow.' but not 'He's an unhappy-go-lucky fellow.'). This similarity in distribution is clearly owing to the structural relation between 'happy' and 'unhappy'.

Furthermore, one may know what meaning m_i has in English and yet not be able to specify the membership of either the distributive or the contrastive sets for m_i in E. This is to say that one may know what meaning a word has in English and yet not know how or when to use it. Frege said: "Only in the context of a sentence do words mean something." [7] But as against this one can say ' 'Famulary' means of or belonging to servants.': here no reference either is or need be made to any utterance or sentence in which the word occurs. I know what 'famulary' means but I do not know how or when to use the word. Again, if someone tells me that 'ultus', a word of Latin, means revenge, do I know how to use the word? Only if I can speak Latin. These are surprising facts only when seen from the vantage point of a misguided theory.

195 The second fundamental step in determining what meaning m_i has or may have in English consists in determining the relevant nonsyntactic semantic differences between the relevant utterances of the distributive set and the relevant associated utterances of the contrastive set for m_i in E. Following Bentham, this may be referred to as "disambiguation."

Thus if it is determined that 'That is a tiger.' and 'I want a tiger.' are utterances of the distributive set for 'tiger' in E, and that 'That is a tiger.' contrasts with 'That is a lion.', 'I want a tiger.' contrasts with 'I want a lion.', it is then necessary to disambiguate the contrasting elements. And so one can say that a relevant difference between 'That is a tiger.' and 'That is a lion.' is that the set of conditions associated with the former utterance, but not the set associated with the latter utterance, includes the condition of being striped. Furthermore, that is also a relevant difference between the set of conditions associated with 'I want a tiger.' and the set associated with 'I want a lion.'. A relevant difference between wanting a tiger and wanting a lion is that in the former case one is wanting something striped.

[7] *Op. cit.*, sec. 62.

Disambiguation is, as it were, something of an art. No art is needed to disambiguate 'That is a tiger.' and 'That is a lion.': the differences there are obvious enough. But disambiguating near synonyms or nearly synonymous expressions is another matter. To disambiguate such expressions it may be necessary to formulate an hypothesis about the difference and then see whether the hypothesis serves to account for a difference in the distribution of the expressions. It is not possible to give rules for the formulation of hypotheses, but there are three important maxims that can be kept in mind: first, Occam's eraser, don't multiply senses beyond necessity; secondly, attend to the etymology of the words in question; thirdly, attend to matters of composition and structure.

196.   The etymology of a word is generally (but not invariably) suggestive. For this reason and this reason alone, appeals to etymology are of great help in determining what meaning a word has. Words are transformed and change meaning in time but they rarely throw off every trace of their former meaning.

Suppose it is said that 'He is free to leave.' and 'He is at liberty to leave.' are exactly synonymous expressions. The etymology of the words in question makes this at once implausible. 'Liberty' is a word of Latin origin introduced into English via Old French and introduced alongside a perfectly good Anglo-Saxon equivalent, viz. 'frēo'. So one at once suspects that 'liberty' will be connected with more formal matters than its Anglo-Saxon equivalent. (The same may be said of such pairs as 'commence' and 'begin', 'initiate' and 'start'.) And so one says 'They freed the lines.' but not 'They liberated the lines.'. To say 'He is free to leave.' is to indicate that he is not under physical restraint, but to say 'He is at liberty to leave.' is to indicate that he is not under restraint of office or position, thus a social restraint of some sort. (Thus the difference between 'freedom' and 'liberty' is analogous to the difference between 'justice' and 'fairness'.)

197.   Attention to matters of composition and structure corresponds largely to what Bentham spoke of as "etymologization." It has two distinct aspects: it may be necessary to attend closely

to the syntactic structure of the utterances in question and it may be necessary to attend to cognate elements and expressions.

Suppose it is said that 'I ought to do it.', 'I am obliged to do it.', and 'I should do it.', are synonymous expressions. That the first two are synonymous is at once extremely implausible. It is clear that 'ought' does not contrast with 'obliged' in the utterance 'I ought to do it.': the utterance 'I obliged to do it.' would be odd. The contrasting expressions are 'ought' and 'am obliged'. Consequently it is plausible to assume that 'I ought to do it.' and 'I am obliged to do it.' are synonymous expressions if and only if 'ought' and 'am obliged' are synonymous expressions, and that is implausible owing to the fact that 'ought' is an active form whereas 'am obliged' is a passive form. Furthermore, the corresponding active form of 'oblige', as in 'He obliged me by going.', does not contrast with 'ought': 'He ought me by going.' would be odd. Here the etymology of 'oblige' is suggestive for it suggests that 'oblige' will connect with matters of compulsion in a way that 'ought' will not. So one may formulate the hypothesis that the set of conditions associated with 'I am obliged to do it.' includes the condition of being in some sense compelled. Such an hypothesis then serves to explain why it is one can say 'I know I ought to give money to the local charity but I am not obliged to do so.'. It further serves to explain why 'I am obliged to do it.', unlike 'I ought to do it.', is in the passive voice: being compelled is, as it were, something that happens to one.

That it is a subtler matter to disambiguate 'I should do it.' and 'I ought to do it.' is indicated by the fact that the etymology of 'should' shows that it is related to the Teutonic type 'skal', I owe, to Anglo-Saxon 'scyld', guilt, and to German 'Schuld', guilt. Furthermore, 'should' and 'ought' have markedly similar distributions in E, and no striking difference in syntactic structure can be seen at once. Even so, there are differences to be seen if one is looking for them. 'Should' in 'I should do it.' does not contrast with 'ought' but with 'ought to'. 'To' does not have meaning in the utterance 'I ought to do it.' but that 'to' is required establishes a syntactic difference between 'ought' and 'should'. There are other differences worth noting. 'Should' contrasts with 'ought to' in 'I should *do* it *for* you.', uttered say in replying to 'How would I ever carry it?', and it also contrasts with 'ought to' in 'I *should* do it for you.', uttered say in response to the comment 'You needn't worry about it, I can do it myself.'. But there are obvious differences between the two cases. Furthermore, notice that neither 'I *should* do it if I were you.' nor 'I should *do* it if I were you.' are odd, and thus are quite unlike 'I ought to do it if I were you.' which is somewhat odd. So there are at least three things to be explained: what is the difference between 'I should *do* it *for* you.' and 'I *should* do it for you.' in the preceding cases, why does 'ought' call for the infinitive with 'to', and why doesn't 'ought to' contrast with 'should' in 'I should do it if I were you.'?

If one replies to 'How would I ever carry it?' with 'I should *do* it *for* you.', it seems reasonable to suppose that in so saying one is indicating what can or could be expected. But if in response to 'You needn't worry about it, I can do it myself.' one says 'I *should* do it for you.', it seems reasonable to suppose that one is indicating not what can or could be expected but what is to be expected. Presumably the shift is effected by the stress on 'should' in the given context. So the stress on 'shall' in 'I *shall* go to Istanbul.' is indicative of resolution, suggesting what is to be the case rather than simply what will be the case. Now consider the questions 'Do you think I should do it?' and 'Do you think I ought to do it?'. Suppose we say that in deciding whether or not one should do it, what is under consideration is not whether or not one is to do it but rather something about one's doing it, viz. whether or not in doing it one would be doing what is to be expected. Whereas in deciding whether or not one ought to do it, what is under consideration is whether or not one is to do it. Such an hypothesis serves to explain why 'ought', unlike 'should', calls for the infinitive with 'to': it indicates a shift in viewpoint. Cf. the difference between 'Is it pleasant to walk along the shore?' and 'Is it pleasant walking along the shore?'. Notice that one says 'It is cold walking along the shore.' but not 'It is cold to walk along the shore.'. The hypothesis also serves to explain why 'ought to' does not contrast with 'should' in 'Do you think I should crack-up under torture?' where what is in question obviously is not likely to be whether or not one is to do it but rather whether one's doing it can or could be expected. Finally, the hypothesis serves to explain why 'ought to' does not contrast with 'should' in 'I should do it if I were you.': if I were you then doing it would be something to be expected of me. But there is here no question of whether or not I am to do it and hence no question of whether or not I ought to do it.

198. The third and final step in determining what meaning m_i has or may have in English consists in consolidating the results of the second step, viz. in formulating the relevant nonsyntactic semantic differences between utterances of the distributive set and the associated utterances of the contrastive set for m_i in E. And this means that the final step consists in formulating a dictionary entry or something approximating to such an entry.

If one knows which utterances do and which do not belong to the distributive and contrastive sets for m_i in E, and if one knows what the relevant nonsyntactic semantic differences are in each case, then one certainly knows what meaning m_i has in English. Consequently this third step of formulating the relevant differences may seem superfluous. But that would be a naïve view.

Suppose it is said that the relevant difference between $\{d_i(m_i)\}$ and $\{d_i(m_i) \mid m_x\}$ is a. One way of testing such an hypothesis is to see whether or not a can also be said to be the relevant difference between $\{d_j(m_i)\}$ and $\{d_j(m_i) \mid m_x\}$, or between $\{d_j(m_i)\}$ and $\{d_j(m_i) \mid m_j\}$, and so on. For example, I suggested (in 197 above) that a relevant difference between 'I should do it.' and 'I ought to do it.' is that the set of conditions associated with the former utterance, unlike the set associated with the latter utterance, includes some condition pertaining to what can or could be or is to be expected. The hypothesis is initially plausible in that it at once serves to explain certain differences between the distributions of the words in question. But there are other cases to be dealt with. 'Should' occurs in 'I should like to have stayed longer.', 'I thought I never should have got out.': can we say that the sets of conditions associated with these utterances also include a condition pertaining to what can or could be or is to be expected? If we can, that strengthens the hypothesis, if we cannot, that weakens the hypothesis.

More significantly, without some sort of formulation of the relevant differences it will be impossible to explain deviant or odd uses of the words in question. For example, I am inclined to suppose that it is somewhat odd to say 'Caesar should have crossed the Rubicon.' whereas it is not the least bit odd to say 'Caesar should not have crossed the Rubicon.'. But how can odd or deviant uses be shown to be either odd or deviant without in some way formulating the relevant conditions associated with the words in question and then showing that they are not satisfied in the case in question?

199.   Formulating the relevant differences between the distributive and contrastive sets for m_i in E is essentially a matter of providing some characterization of a set of conditions. This is, of course, often extremely difficult to do. But there are various procedures that can be of help here. I shall mention two of them.

One procedure, particularly appropriate in connection with common nouns like 'tiger' and 'lion' may be called "paradigmatization." This can be described as follows. Imagine that your life and fortune depended on showing a bloody and irascible dictator an animal that was unmistakably a tiger. We may assume that the word 'tiger' in the dictator's idiolect and the word 'tiger' in your idiolect have no difference in meaning whatever. If you show the dictator an animal such that it is not the case that it is unmistakably a tiger then you get whatever you don't like, whereas if you show him something that is unmistakably a tiger then whatever you like. In such a case, would you prefer to show him an x such that x is striped or not striped? four-legged or three-legged? whiskered or unwhiskered? purple or black or neither? one inch high or two feet high? tangible or intangible? and so on. In this way one can easily formulate a dictionary entry such as 'tiger': a large carnivorous quadrupedal feline, tawny yellow in color with blackish transverse stripes, etc. (And in this way it would be a simple matter to formulate an objective measure for determining degrees of difference in meaning between certain elements common to different idiolects.)

The second procedure, and one that I shall employ in connection with the word 'good', is essentially indirect in character. It is the most powerful method of analysis that I know of. One proceeds first by considering and examining deviant uses of the words in question. Secondly, one must formulate some sort of hypothesis to account for the fact that the utterances in question are or seem to be deviant. Thirdly, one determines whether or not it is possible to generate deviant utterances on the basis of the hypothesis. Thus if I were concerned to define the word 'ought', the first step would be to formulate some hypothesis that would serve to account for the fact that 'I ought to do it if I were you.' is somewhat odd.

200.   I believe that the preceding verbal dust is worth sifting, otherwise I would not have scattered it. The theory of meaning that has been presented here may be a step in the right direction. But there are too many fictions involved.

It is of course a fiction to suppose that one can formulate sensible principles of analysis based on some measure of syntactic structural similarity when no such measure is available. Thus what I have called "principles" are in fact and at best nothing more than imprecise and vague maxims. They were brought into the discussion because despite their vagueness and imprecision they seemed fairly obvious to me and of utility in the evaluation and thus in the formulation of a semantic analysis of a corpus. But of course there must be many other principles that could be enunciated, that one employs in the course of evaluating and formulating a semantic analysis, perhaps without even realizing that one does so. That is often the way. But owing to the general vagueness and imprecision of the whole problem, I have not been concerned to determine what such principles might be. This vagueness and imprecision unfortunately but unavoidably permeates the entire account that has been given here. More generally, an adequate theory of semantic structure cannot be formulated until an adequate theory of syntactic structure is available to build on. There is a sense in which the converse is also true, thus a sense in which the formulation of an adequate theory of syntactic structure and of an adequate theory of semantic structure must go hand in hand.

201.   But here one is brought up against a fundamental question in the philosophy of language. It is senseless to speak of an adequate theory without considering what the theory is supposed to be adequate to or adequate for. In formulating the theory presented here I have had but one objective in mind, viz. that of determining a method and a means of evaluating and choosing between competing analyses of words and utterances. Given such an objective it is conceivable that it could serve to assess not only the adequacy of a semantic theory but of a syntactic theory as well. But there is no *a priori* reason why one must adopt such an objective. For what is fundamental to any natural language is the action and reaction and interaction of speakers and hearers. And so one could be concerned to predict this behavior, to say what (if anything) determines it. Judged from such a viewpoint the semantic theory presented here is, as far as I can see, unilluminating. Again, one could be concerned with the acquisition and the imparting of linguistic skills, with the learning and the teaching of a language. That a semantic theory adequate for the purposes of analysis would be adequate for such purposes is far from clear.

202.   Apart from the narrowness of the objective and the lack of an adequate syntactic theory, the semantic theory presented here loses in relevance what it gains in simplicity and coherence by its reliance on a synchronic account of language. A synchronic account of a language is at best a fiction: a language will not stay put to have its picture taken. The speakers of a language change their habits, alter their ways: their language alters with them. And it is not of much help to retreat to one's

own idiolect; it will not stay put either; it would be deplorable if it did: one grows and learns things, or so one hopes.

To view a language synchronically is, at best, to adopt a convenient methodological stance; at its worst, such a view can lead to obscurantism and obfuscation as it has done in contemporary philosophy. It is an extraordinary fact that in rightly opposing obscurantism contemporary philosophers have often become obscurantists: that it is in a good cause is hardly an excuse. To put the point bluntly, the utterances that contemporary philosophers, e.g. logical positivists, so-called "ordinary language philosophers," and others say are devoid of significance are not devoid of significance. The utterances they say are incomprehensible are not incomprehensible. It is too bad that they are not right for then there would be nothing to be alarmed about. But the danger of philosophical rubbish is that it is comprehensible and incomprehensibly contagious. Metaphysicians and theologians are generally no harder to understand than poets or novelists. There is as much philosophical rubbish in Dostoevski and Kierkegaard as there is in Hegel and Heidegger. The difference between a work of metaphysics and *Finnegans Wake* is that what is said in the former is likely to be false when interesting and platitudinous when true, whereas such questions are not likely to arise in connection with the latter.

An exclusively synchronic view of language is conducive not to philosophical rigor but to *rigor mortis* owing to a hardening of the categories. 'At exactly what moment during the time that he was sound asleep did the dream occur?', 'Does time bend back on itself?', 'There are infinitely many stars.': perhaps for the time being these are deviant utterances. But just wait: what could not be said yesterday is the idiom of today. We cannot say what will be said tomorrow.

An exclusively synchronic account of language necessarily fails to take account of the productivity of the available patterns, for productivity is visible only from a diachronic point of view. It should be obvious that attention to diachronic factors may enable one to get a better view of the synchronic situation.

So in general a historical perspective is often of help in appreciating the present moment. To mention only one example: some explanation is wanted for the fact that the etymology of a word often does and yet sometimes does not throw a great deal of light on what meaning it has at present in the language; e.g. one does not expect the etymology of 'mother' to be of much help and it isn't, whereas one does expect the differences between the etymologies of 'poor', 'bad', and 'evil', to be of help and they are.

I am inclined to suppose that the semantic theory presented here is open to and almost certainly requires supplementation by diachronic studies. For just as semantic analysis necessarily presupposes syntactic analysis, so any diachronic analysis necessarily presupposes distinct synchronic analyses. Consequently the theory presented here is at best tentative, a point of departure for the time being for the diachronic analysis that it requires for supplementation, and it is at best provisional pending a further development of syntactic studies.

203.   Finally, I am inclined to suppose, for the reasons given, that this entire essay is best thought of as an informal introduction to and sketch of a rigorous semantic theory. If progress is to be made, I believe that what must next be done is this: the semantic theory in question must be stated in a relatively formal way. This will involve a detailed and formal specification of the elements of the theory, viz. its primitive terms, relations, and operations.

If one approaches semantic theory in such a formal way all sorts of interesting and difficult questions emerge. For example, from the viewpoint of a general and formal semantic theory, it is far from clear that, as in this essay, the whole utterance is the most profitable unit of analysis. On the contrary, problems encountered both in discourse analysis and in transformational analysis suggest that a general semantic theory is perhaps best formulated in terms of elements of varying length, in particular, in terms of long, medium, and short elements. Long elements of the theory would correspond to discourses or texts, medium length elements to whole utterances or sentences, short elements to words or morphemes. In terms of such a theory one could then attempt to specify various operations that would map the analyses of shorter elements onto the analyses of longer elements, and vice versa. For example, given the analyses of the sentences of a given set, one would attempt to specify some operation on the given analyses that would yield analyses of the morphological constituents of the sentences. And given the analyses of the morphological constituents of a set of sentences, one would attempt to specify some operation on the given analyses that would yield an analysis of each sentence of the given set. (This is indeed the fundamental problem of mechanical translation.) Although I believe the rough outlines of such a theory have been sketched here, there is still an enormous amount of detailed work to be done.

VI

THE WORD 'GOOD'

204. 'Good' is traditionally said to be an adjective but the traditional term 'adjective' is not a term to be taken too seriously. An adjective in traditional grammar is said to be a word that modifies a noun, whereas a noun is said to be a word with a certain reference: thus a cross classification is involved, a confusion of syntactic and semantic factors.[1]

Owing to the fact that the class of adjectives is (on such an account) not a well-defined class, it is not possible to speak generally of the semantic function of adjectives. The naïve supposition that an attributive adjective serves to characterize the referent of the noun construction (if it has a referent) is easily shown to be false; e.g. to refer to "an utter fool," "a perfect stranger," "a complete idiot," is not to refer to anything having the characteristic of being "utter," perfect, or complete.

The classification of adjectives in traditional English grammars as attributive, appositive, and predicate adjectives, throws little light on the nature or function of adjectives since it is based simply on the position of the adjective in a sentence regardless of whether or not the position can be altered by syntactic transformations; e.g. 'orange' is an attributive adjective in 'That is an orange flower.'. But from that utterance one can derive by means of a syntactic transformation 'That flower is orange.'. Here 'orange' is a predicate adjective. That 'orange' is an

[1] See any traditional grammar, e.g. G. L. Kittredge and F. E. Farley, *An Advanced English Grammar*.

attributive adjective in 'That is an orange flower.' and a predicate adjective in 'That flower is orange.' is of little significance.
(I do not say it is of no significance.) There is, furthermore, a
striking difference between 'orange' in 'That is an orange
flower.' and 'orange' in 'That is an orange grove.' and this difference is not indicated in saying that in each case 'orange' is
an attributive adjective. Notice that one cannot in general derive 'That grove is orange.' from 'That is an orange grove.'.

But the most important defect in traditional grammar with
respect to adjectives concerns the operation of modification: an
attributive adjective is said to modify the noun it is in construction with. But that obscures the fact that there is an important difference between 'blue' in 'He is a blue little man.'
and 'blue' in 'He is a little blue man.'. This difference is not
indicated in saying that in each case 'blue' is an attributive adjective modifying 'man'. Notice that the ambiguity of 'He is
blue.', indicating either color or sadness, is related to the fact
that 'He is blue.' may be a derivative of either 'He is a little
blue man.' or 'He is a blue little man.'.

205. I shall say that a predicate adjective modifies the complete syntactic subject it is in construction with. Thus 'good'
in (1)

(1)   That painting is good.

modifies not 'painting' but 'that painting'. I shall say that an
attributive adjective modifies the constituent it is in construction with. Thus 'good' in (2)

(2)   That is a good bright painting.

modifies not 'painting' but 'a bright painting'. On the other
hand, 'bright' in (2) modifies 'a painting'.

The difference between 'blue' in 'He is a blue little man.'
and 'blue' in 'He is a little blue man.' is then that in the former
case 'blue' modifies 'a little man', whereas in the latter case it
simply modifies 'a man'. To say that in each case 'blue' modifies
'man' would be to introduce an ambiguity.

'Good' not only modifies other elements but the constructions it enters into are often modified and 'good' itself is often modified directly. Thus a construction that 'good' enters into in (3),

(3)   That is a real good table.

viz. 'a good table', is modified by 'real'. 'Good' itself is directly modified in (4)

(4)   That is good enough.

by 'enough', by 'for you' in (5)

(5)   That is good for you.

and by the comparative affix '-er' in (6)

(6)   That is better.

for 'better' in (6) is analyzable as 'good' + '-er'.

206.   Consider the two remarks

(7)   This is a good strawberry.

(8)   This is a good lemon.

Suppose that we suppose that for (7) to be true what is in question must be sweet, or if not sweet then at least not sour. Whereas for (8) to be true we suppose that what is in question must be sour. Consequently (7) and (8) would suggest contradictory conditions. But consider (9):

(9)   This is a good carving knife.

If we suppose that a good carving knife must be sharp, but that a good strawberry need be neither sharp nor not sharp, (7) and (9) would suggest independent conditions.

Utterance (7) contrasts with 'This is a (good) strawberry.' |'sour', and (8) contrasts with 'This is a (good) lemon.'|'sour'. If 'good' does not differ in meaning in each case then we can expect the relevant difference between {'This is a good strawberry.'} and {'This is a sour strawberry.'} to be identical or virtually identical with the relevant difference between {'This is a good lemon.'} and {'This is a sour lemon.'}. But if we suppose that for (8) to be true what is in question must be sour, whereas for (7) to be true what is in question must not be sour, it then follows that there may be little difference between {'This is a good lemon.'} and {'This is a sour lemon.'} but there is bound to be a considerable difference between {'This is a good strawberry.'} and {'This is a sour strawberry.'}.

Consequently we must either say either that (8) cannot have associated with it the condition of being sour or that (7) cannot have associated with it the condition of not being sour or that 'good' in (7) differs in meaning from 'good' in (8).

207.   And now someone may want to say that the word 'good' is fundamentally ambiguous, that it means one thing in (7), another in (8), and still another in (9). Such a move would not only be contrary to Occam's eraser, it would be absurd, for reasons which should be obvious by now.

If one were to say that (7–9) indicate that 'good' is fundamentally ambiguous, one would be forced to say the same about a great many other adjectives. 'Heavy' exhibits some of the features of 'good' just noted in connection with (7–9).

For example, a heavy car may weigh over 3,000 lbs., but a heavy pencil does not weigh over 3,000 lbs. Thus there may not be much of a difference between {'That is a (heavy) car.'} and {'That is a (heavy) car.'|'ton and a half'} whereas there is bound to be a considerable difference between {'That is a (heavy) pencil.'} and {'That is a (heavy) pencil.'|'ton and a half'}. One would not on that account suppose that 'heavy' must differ in meaning in each case. Notice that one might very well say ' 'A heavy car' means one thing and 'a heavy pencil' means another.' but this is not to say ' 'Heavy' in 'a heavy pencil' means one thing and 'heavy' in 'a heavy car' means another.'. Similar examples may be given in connection with such adjectives as 'real', 'tall', 'lovely', 'simple'. Whether or not such examples can be given in connection with a particular adjective is predictable on the basis of what I shall call the "rank" of the adjective.

208.   There are striking syntactic differences between adjectives like 'good', 'heavy', and 'red'. Consider the following utterances:

*(10)   That is a red heavy good table.

*(11)   That is a heavy red good table.

*(12)   That is a red good heavy table.

*(13)   That is a heavy good red table.

*(14)   That is a good red heavy table.

Each utterance of *(10–14) is odd (hence the asterisks). But

(15)   That is a good heavy red table.

(15) is not the least bit odd. Notice that *(12) when uttered aloud can be mistaken for (16)

(16)   That is a real good heavy table.

The reason for it is not hard to find. Whereas *(17)

*(17)   That is a good real table.

is quite odd, (3), 'That is a real good table.', is not the least bit odd (though perhaps a bit vulgar). Since 'real' precedes 'good' whereas 'red' follows 'good' in the above combination, it is natural to take 'red' in *(12) as 'real' (or as 'right' in some dialects).

The preceding examples indicate that there is an order among adjectives in English. By considering pairs of attributive adjectives we can assign relative ranks (with respect to relatively large classes of environments). Thus since one says 'That is a red wooden table.' and not *'That is a wooden red table.', if we assign 'wooden' rank a, we can assign 'red' rank b where $b > a$.

Some adjectives are of the same rank. Thus one can say either 'That is a deep wide pit.' or 'That is a wide deep pit.'. 'Deep' is of lower rank than 'good' for one says (18)

(18)   That is a good deep pit.

but not *(19)

*(19)   That is a deep good pit.

Indeed, 'deep' here almost sounds like 'damn' for 'damn' is of a higher rank than 'good' since one says (20)

(20)   That is a damn good pit.

but not *(21)

*(21)   That is a good damn pit.

(and here 'good' sounds like 'god' for the same reason).

(There seem to be different principles behind the ordering of adjectives in the attributive construction in question. It appears that adjectives a_1 and a_2 are likely to be invariant in order in such a construction, i.e. one finds $a_1 + a_2 + noun$ but not $a_2 + a_1 + noun$, if it is generally the case that a_1 has a greater privilege of occurrence than a_2 in combination with nouns and noun constructions. For example, one says 'a little white house' but not *'a white little house'. This appears to be connected with the fact that 'little' has the greater privilege of occurrence, and thus one says 'a little sonnet' but not *'a white sonnet', 'a little trip' but not *'a white trip'. Again, one says 'a pretty lace dress' but not *'a lace pretty dress', and so one can say 'a pretty speech' but not *'a lace speech', 'a pretty view' but not *'a lace view'.[2]

(However the ordering of adjectives in the construction in question is not as simple a matter as it may at first appear. One says 'He's an intelligent old man.' but not *'He's an old intelligent man.' and yet 'old' has a much greater privilege of occurrence than 'intelligent'. Again, one says 'a pious young girl' but not *'a young pious girl', and so on. Furthermore, it should be noted that one says 'a fat old man' but 'an old fat pig', whereas 'a fat old pig' might be uttered in speaking abusively of a man. Consequently it seems that environments like 'a . . . man', 'a . . . girl', introduce some special factors. Thus some principle other than simple privilege of occurrence must be at

2 I am indebted to my students J. Rizik and W. Ruddick for help in sorting adjectives.

work here. Semantically speaking, it appears to be one having something to do with natural kinds but I can provide no satisfactory syntactic characterization.)

209. That 'good' is a high-ranking adjective serves to explain certain differences between (1), 'That painting is good.', and (22) and (23)

(22) George is good.

(23) It is good that it is raining.

Although (1) and (22) are often said by philosophers to exemplify different "uses" of 'good', and thus 'good' in (1) is often said to have an "aesthetic sense" whereas 'good' in (22) is said to have a "moral sense," we in fact find that the contrastive sets for 'good' relative to each utterance are markedly similar. Thus 'good' in each case contrasts with 'red', 'heavy', 'ugly', 'pleasant', 'bad', 'poor', 'evil'. The reason for this is in part that (1) and (22) have an obvious structural similarity.

On the other hand, 'good' in (23) does not contrast with 'red', 'heavy', or 'poor'; a contrast with 'ugly' and 'evil' is uncertain; the only clear contrasts are with 'pleasant' and 'bad' (of the contrasts cited). Consequently there might seem to be some reason for marking off (23) as a special case in comparison with (1) and (22). And so one might be tempted to speak of two different classes of occurrences of 'good'. That would be a mistake.

The contrastive sets for 'good' relative to (1), (22), and (23), are all different. Thus 'good' contrasts with 'hungry' in (22) but not in (1), and 'good' contrasts with 'casein' in (1) but not in (22). The reason for the similarity between the contrastive sets for 'good' in (1) and (22) is to be found simply in the similarity of the elements modified by 'good' in each case. Thus 'good' serves to modify a proper noun in (22), 'George', and a noun phrase in (1), 'that painting'. Whereas 'good' in (23) serves to modify a noun clause, 'that it is raining'. Being a high-ranking adjective 'good' has a greater privilege of occurrence than such adjectives as 'red' and 'heavy'.

Not only does 'good' not contrast with 'red' in (23), it does

not contrast with 'red' in (2), 'That is a good bright painting.',
even though 'good' does contrast with 'red' in (24)

(24)   That bright painting is good.

Consequently, if one were to say that (23) is a special case of
some sort, one would also have to say that (2) is a special case
of some sort and, in short, that virtually every case is a special
case of some sort, which is absurd. (However, that 'good' does
not contrast with 'red' in (2) in no way indicates that 'good'
does not contrast with 'red' in (6), 'That is better.'.)

210.   I want to say that 'good' in E is essentially a modifier. But
there are utterances of E in which 'good' occurs and in which it
does not modify anything. Thus it is necessary to consider the
following utterances:

(25)   Good!

(26)   Very good, my lord.

(27)   Good morning!

(28)   The Good is sought after by all men.

The occurrence of 'good' in (25) offers no puzzles here: (25)
is generally a response utterance; e.g. someone says 'It is raining.' and one replies 'Good!'. On occasion, however, (25) may
be uttered in response to some feature of the situation and not
to a prior utterance. One may notice that it is raining and say
'Good!'. In either case, however, it is clear that (25) is intimately
related to an utterance like (23), 'It is good that it is raining.',
in which case 'good' can be said to modify 'that it is raining'.

Utterance (26), 'Very good, my lord.', is an interesting example of what might be called a conventional use of 'good'. We
may suppose that (26) is a response utterance, uttered by a
servant by way of acknowledging an order from his master. I
am inclined to suppose that this conventional use of 'good' to
acknowledge an order, command, and so forth is derivative from
a use of 'good' in which 'good' modifies something. I am not inclined to suppose that one could very well construe (26) as an
ellipsis for (29) or (30)

(29)   That is very good, my lord.

(30)   That, my lord, is very good.

for either (29) or (30) would suggest that the servant was giving
an independent opinion about the matter rather than simply
acknowledging an order. Presumably the uttering of either (29)
or (30) would be deemed presumptuous on the part of a servant.
It would be deemed presumptuous of him to voice an independent opinion about his master's order for, in so far as he is his
master's servant, he can have only one opinion about that which
his master has ordered, viz. that it is, indeed, very good. It is,
as it were, this conventional opinion that is being voiced in
(26), and by voicing it the servant thereby acknowledges the
order. Consider how curious it would be to adopt the locution
'Very bad, my lord.' as the conventional way of acknowledging
an order. But if (26) can be construed as a conventional form
of (29) or (30), it is then quite clear that it is intimately related
to and derivative from a use of 'good' as a modifier. What is
being modified can be determined in the context of utterance
by querying the word 'that' in (29) or (30), viz. by asking (31)

(31)   What is very good?

the answer to which might be (32)

(32)   That the carriage be brought at once is very good.

in which case 'good' modifies 'that the carriage be brought at
once'.

Although 'good' is a modifier in (33)

(33)   The good Berkeley was mistaken.

(33) is another interesting instance of what I take to be essentially a derivative use of 'good'. The use of 'good' in (33) appears to be related to the use of the stem 'good-' in (34) and (35)

(34)   The good-man Timothy entered the house.

(35)   Good-wife Marjorie came in too.

'Good-man' and 'good-wife' are etymological derivatives of
'good' originally having the sense of master and mistress of the

house, respectively. The patronizing and somewhat archaic tone of (33) is perhaps owing to and perhaps stems from its connection with the use of 'good-' in (34) and (35). The use of 'good-man' in the sense of master of a house is perhaps related to the use of 'good' in (36)

(36)   The goods are on the shelf.

where 'goods' originally had the sense of good things, property. Possibly a good-man was so-called owing to his being the master of good things, viz. property. The patronizing and somewhat archaic tone of (33) could then be explained on the grounds that in referring to Berkeley as 'the good Berkeley' one is thereby likening Berkeley to a good-man, the master of a small property, the property being some small thing associated with Berkeley, viz. his philosophical views.

Utterance (27), 'Good morning!', is an interesting case. It is fairly clearly a conventional greeting, but I am inclined to suppose it is related to a use of 'good' as an attributive adjective, as in (37)

(37)   Have a good morning!

On the other hand, (38)

(38)   Goodbye!

is a conventional parting utterance, but it is not, save by association, related to or derivative from any use of 'good'. Notice that unlike [gʊd] in 'Goodbye!', 'good' in 'Good morning!' contrasts with 'fine', 'lovely', 'splendid', 'terrible'.

Finally, (28), 'The Good is sought after by all men.', is evidently derivative from a use of 'good' as a modifier. But the difficulty is to explain the method of derivation and the logical relations involved. Etymologically speaking, such morphological constructions as 'The Good', 'goodness', 'goodity', are derivative from predicative or attributive occurrences of 'good'; but even if they were not, it would still be profitable to construe them as such: it is easier to explain what 'goodity' means in terms of what 'good' means and of what is indicated by '-ity' than it is to explain what 'good' means and what is indicated by '-ity' in terms of what 'goodity' means. However, since I am not here concerned to discuss the general question of the relation between morphological constructions of the form 'The . . . ', '. . .-ness', '. . .-ity', '. . .-hood', and their constituents, I propose to ignore (28).

211.   Since the word 'good' can be thought of as occurring in an utterance primarily as a modifier, e.g. in combination with a noun in an endocentric construction, the problem of expounding the meaning of 'good' is now essentially that of saying how it modifies whatever it does modify. Or to put the matter in another way, 'good' (or for that matter, any high-ranking adjective) can be thought of as analogous to a numerical function, while the various elements that it modifies can be thought of as so many arguments to the function yielding different values in different cases. The problem then is, as it were, to state the rule whereby one passes from the argument to the value of the function for the given argument.

And a way to begin is this: just as a numerical function can take only certain things as arguments to the function, viz. numbers, so 'good' can modify only certain elements satisfying certain conditions.

212.   Consider the following utterances:

(39)   That is a good ache.

(40)   That is a good corpse.

(41)   That is a good dewdrop.

(42)   That is a good molecule.

(43)   That is a good pebble.

(44)   That is a good entity.

(45)   That is a good inspiration.

(46)   That is a good twinge.

(47)   That is a good chill.

(48)   That is a good swamp.

Utterances (39–48) all sound somewhat odd, some more so than others. (43) sounds the least odd of all. Possibly it does not sound odd at all. Now compare (49–58) with (39–48):

(49)   That is a good feeling.

(50)   That is a good cadaver.

(51)   That is a good crystal.

(52)   That is a good pattern.

(53)   That is a good brick.

(54)   That is a good item.

(55)   That is a good idea.

(56)   That is a good reaction.

(57)   That is a good breeze.

(58)   That is a good pasture.

Here (40) and (50) are illuminating cases: (50) does not sound odd at all while (40) certainly does sound odd even though 'That is a lovely corpse.' does not sound odd. There is no difference between a corpse and a cadaver, but there is a difference between 'corpse' and 'cadaver' and the difference is apparently sufficient to have some bearing on the occurrence of 'good' in (40) and serves to differentiate it from (50). The words 'corpse' and 'cadaver' are very close synonyms, indeed almost exact synonyms. The only difference between them seems to be this: 'cadaver' is a word employed by persons who engage in the practice of medicine and it serves to characterize something answering to certain interests of those persons, viz. an interest in dissection. Again, consider the difference between (48) and (58): unlike the word 'swamp', the word 'pasture' serves to characterize something answering to certain interests. And again, there appears to be the same difference between (43) and (53). It is true that (43) may not sound very odd, but it certainly sounds odder then (53). The reason appears to be simply that 'brick' serves to characterize something generally answering to certain interests in a way that 'pebble' does not.

213.   Utterances (39–58) suggest the following hypothesis: if an element of an utterance is modified by 'good' then if the utterance is to be nondeviant the element modified by 'good' must there serve to characterize something that may or may not answer to certain interests.

This hypothesis serves to explain why (39–48) sound odd apart from special contexts. Notice that but for (45) the utterances fail to satisfy the indicated condition in an obvious way; (45) is a more interesting case in that the difficulty there is largely owing to the fact that the possibility that what is in question does not answer to certain interests is precluded. For it is not true that the word 'inspiration' is employed to characterize something that may or may not answer to certain interests. On the contrary, it serves to characterize something that very definitely does answer to certain interests.

The adequacy of the hypothesized condition receives confirmation from the fact that it is now possible to generate odd-sounding utterances by deliberately violating the condition. Thus (59)

(59)   That is a good gila monster.

sounds odd even though (60)

(60)   That is a good cat.

does not sound odd. The difference between the two utterances is simply owing to the fact that 'cat' unlike 'gila monster' serves to characterize something that may or may not answer to certain interests. Again, (61) unlike (62)

(61)   That is a good cardinal number.

(62)   That is a good number.

sounds quite odd. 'Cardinal number' is a phrase employed primarily by mathematicians but it does not serve to characterize something that may or may not answer to certain interests. On the other hand, (63)

(63)   That is a good proof.

does not sound at all odd owing to the fact that 'proof' does ordinarily serve to characterize something that may or may not answer to certain interests. Notice that even though (62) does not seem to be deviant, if one had to say which of the three utterances, (62) or (64) or (65)

(64)   That is a good telephone number.

(65)   That is a good number to play.

is most likely to be deviant, the choice would surely be (62). (Utterances (64) and (65) are interesting cases of a type that must later be examined more carefully.)

214.   The hypothesis under consideration is this: if an element of an utterance is modified by 'good' then if the utterance is to be nondeviant the element modified by 'good' must there serve to characterize something that may or may not answer to certain interests. But there is an obvious difficulty here that calls or seems to call for an obvious qualification.

Only an apparent counterexample is found in (66)

(66)   That was a good miss.

said, say, of a shot in basketball having all the virtues, as it were, of a good shot save that of going through the hoop. 'Miss' does not ordinarily serve to characterize something that may or may not answer to certain interests: on the contrary, (except for the pun) it ordinarily serves to characterize something that serves to frustrate certain interests. However, even though (66) is not deviant *simpliciter,* it is deviant to a slight degree. One can, I believe, feel the strain on 'miss', a strain owing to the fact that the word is here, somewhat unnaturally, serving to characterize something that may or may not answer to certain interests. A more natural way of saying much the same (though not exactly the same) thing is (67)

(67)   That was a good try.

But a genuine difficulty is to be found in the following case:

if instead of uttering (1), 'That painting is good.', one were to utter (68)

(68)   That is good.

while pointing at the painting, the utterance need not be or even seem to be deviant. Yet the word 'that' does not there serve to characterize something that may or may not answer to certain interests. Again, 'George' in (22), 'George is good.', does not there serve to characterize something that may or may not answer to certain interests. Yet neither (22) nor (68) are or even seem to be deviant.

There are (at least) two courses open to us at this point. On the one hand, we can alter our hypothesis to allow for these two cases, e.g. we could say that if an element of an utterance is to be modified by 'good' then if the utterance is to be nondeviant the element modified by 'good' must there either refer to or serve to characterize something that may or may not answer to certain interests. On the other hand, we could, for the time being anyway, adhere to our present hypothesis and treat (22) and (68) as special cases. The justification for treating or attempting to treat them as special cases will in part be that so far as our present hypothesis is concerned they cannot be anything else but special cases since they conflict with the hypothesis. So the questions are these: which alternative shall we choose? and what warrants the choice?

215.   Suppose we were to adopt the revised hypothesis: then suppose someone utters (69)

(69)   That one is good.

while pointing at a corpse. We cannot very well say that (69) would be deviant if uttered while pointing at a corpse and non-deviant while pointing at a cadaver for one points at a corpse if and only if one points at a cadaver: the class of corpses is identical with the class of cadavers. Nonetheless I am strongly inclined to say that (70)

(70)   That corpse is good.

sounds odd while (71)

(71)   That cadaver is good.

does not sound odd. Furthermore, even though (71) does not sound odd, I think that almost anyone who considers the matter carefully will agree that in comparison with (50), 'That is a good cadaver.', (71) does seem somewhat deviant. Just so, although neither (1), 'That painting is good.', nor (72)

(72)   That is a good painting.

are deviant, somehow (72) seems the more natural utterance. And the explanation for this is not hard to find. Even though 'painting' in (1) serves to characterize the referent of the phrase 'that painting', in so far as it is a constituent of a referring expression it serves primarily to delineate the referent in question by means of the characterization rather than, as in (72), to characterize a referent already and otherwise delineated.

   If we were to adopt the revised hypothesis we should not be able to discriminate between (69) uttered in reference to a corpse and (69) uttered in reference to a cadaver. And this means that we should not be able to discriminate between (70) and (71), for it is clear that 'one' in (69) can be a substitute for either 'corpse' or 'cadaver'. Clearly the occasional oddity of an utterance like (68), 'That is good.', depends not on what is referred to but on the indicated characterization of what is referred to. If (68) is uttered in reference to something characterized as a bit of dust then (68) would be odd, but if (68) is uttered in reference to the very same thing characterized as a sample, (68) would not be odd. Consequently, I am inclined to reject the revised hypothesis and instead adhere, for the time being, to the original hypothesis.

216.   Our hypothesis is this: if an element of an utterance is modified by 'good' then if the utterance is to be nondeviant the element modified by 'good' must there serve to characterize something that may or may not answer to certain interests. The

difficulty with the hypothesis is that (22), 'George is good.', (68), 'That is good.', and (69), 'That one is good.', do not meet the specified condition and yet neither (22) nor (68) nor (69) sound odd or even deviant.

Suppose we say that (22), (68), and (69) are special cases. If so, we must then determine whether or not anything warrants us in treating them as special cases apart from the fact that we can thereby save our present hypothesis. That there is some such warrant for treating them as special cases can be seen as follows.

Utterances like (22), (68), and (69) seem to be dependent on the context of utterance in a fairly obvious way. For in cases in which (22), (68), or (69) are uttered without deviation of any sort one can generally, in context, readily supply either an appropriate characterization of the referent in question or an appropriate modification of 'good'. Thus if (22) is uttered without deviation one can, in context, generally construe it as equivalent to some utterance similar to (73) or (74):

(73)   George is a good golfer.

(74)   George is good at tennis.

Just so, (68) and (69) can generally be similarly construed in context. Consequently I believe there is sufficient warrant for adhering to our original hypothesis and treating (22), (68), and (69), as special cases: one is certainly not straining unduly in doing so.

217.   Consider utterances (75-79):

(75)   Rubbish is good.

(76)   Misery is good.

(77)   Water is good.

(78)   Pleasure is good.

(79)   Paintings are good.

These all sound remarkably odd. Their odd sound is explicable in terms of our hypothesis for the elements modified by 'good' do not there seem to serve to characterize anything, let alone characterize something that may or may not answer to certain interests. Nonetheless, (80–84) are not and do not even sound odd:

(80)   Rubbish is good as fertilizer.

(81)   Misery is good for one's soul.

(82)   Water is good to drink.

(83)   Pleasure is good for one's soul.

(84)   Paintings are good to have.

Furthermore, it should be noted that given an appropriate context of utterance, (75–79) would not seem at all deviant, much less odd. For if one were talking about what is or is not good as fertilizer, or for one's soul, or to drink, remarks like (75–79) would not seem and indeed would not be the least bit deviant.

Utterances (75–84) indicate that we must extend our hypothesis as follows: if an element of an utterance is modified by 'good' then if the utterance is to be nondeviant then either the element modified by 'good' must there serve to characterize something or someone or some aggregate that may or may not answer to certain interests or 'good' must itself be modified.

The revised hypothesis serves to account for certain striking facts about some of the seventy-six nondeviant utterances of the distributive set for 'good' in E so far noted: it serves to account for the odd sound of (39–48), (59), (61), (62), (70), and (75–79).

These utterances are not odd or even deviant but they certainly sound odd at first. This is explicable in terms of the revised hypothesis. For example, (41), 'That is a good dewdrop.', sounds odd. But if one thinks of an appropriate context, i.e. one in which the word 'dewdrop' can serve to characterize something that may or may not answer to certain interests, the odd sound is no longer to be heard. Thus a context in which we are interested in photographing dewdrops would do. And thus (62), 'That is a good number.', no longer sounds odd as soon as one thinks of a number at roulette or a telephone number.

Furthermore, the revised hypothesis allows us to draw fine lines that are intuitively satisfactory. Thus if one had to choose, almost anyone who considers the matter carefully would say that (62) sounds odder than (64) or (65), that (22) sounds odder than (73) or (74), that (1) sounds odder than (72), that (70) sounds odder than (40), that (71) sounds odder than (50). And the reason is simply that in each case in the preferred utterance either the element modified by 'good' more clearly serves to characterize something that may or may not answer to certain interests or 'good' is itself modified by an element that serves to indicate the relevant interests. Thus in each case in the preferred utterance the relevant interests are more clearly indicated.

218.   The present hypothesis is about the distribution of 'good' in utterances of the distributive set for 'good' in *E*. But such a hypothesis clearly suggests a relatively simple hypothesis about the meaning of the word 'good', viz. that 'good' has associated with it the condition of answering to certain interests, which interests are in question being indicated either by the element modifying or the element modified by 'good' or by certain features of the context of utterance.

Since almost anything one can think of may or may not answer to certain interests, it is to be expected that 'good' has a very great privilege of occurrence. Thus the fact that 'good' is clearly a high-ranking adjective provides some confirmation for the hypothesis in question.

219.   Since the word 'interests' evidently is of some importance in the hypothesis under consideration, it is necessary to consider certain problems posed by the word.

In view of the philosophical tradition from the time of the first English translation of Aristotle onward, it would perhaps be plausible to formulate the hypothesis stated above in terms of "ends" rather than "interests"; i.e. to say that 'good' has associated with it the condition of being conducive to or constituting the attainment of certain ends. I have deliberately avoided such a formulation. When I say "interests," I mean interests; I do not mean ends.

I take an end to be something (an event, state of affairs, etc., but that need not concern us here) envisaged as consequent upon a course of action, something that would constitute a successful termination of that course of action. Thus ends and means are inextricably interwoven: to view something as an end is to view it as consequent upon some course of action, though not necessarily as consequent upon any particular course of action, and some course of action is conceivably a means to that end. (Although there is perhaps no need to discuss these matters, it need not be supposed that 'end', 'goal', 'aim', are exact synonyms: they are not.) Consider (85):

(85)   It is good that she is dead.

Here 'good' modifies 'that she is dead'. I take it that this clause may serve to characterize a state of affairs that may or may not answer to certain interests. One may be thankful that she is dead owing to the fact that one either had or took an interest in her welfare and one was distressed by the fact that she was in great pain; hence one may be thankful that she is released from suffering. The appositeness of the word 'interest' here may be questioned (but see below), but there can be no question about the word 'end': 'that she is dead' does not in any way (apart from the pun) serve to characterize anything that one need recognize as an end. Her death is not something that one need in any way seek after. One need take no steps whatever either to bring about or in any way to facilitate the occurrence of her death. Indeed, one could do all that was possible to prevent it and yet still say (85) after she was dead.

220.   Something must be said about my use of the word 'interest'. I mean to be using that word in an ordinary way. I shall assume that you know what that is, that you are familiar with the word. Since the word has been used in extraordinary ways by philosophers it is, I suppose, necessary for me to disassociate myself from that tradition.

I take it that interests, motives, wants, wishes, hopes, cravings, longings, likings, hankerings, and so on are all different, cannot be identified. I would not wish to say (which is not to say 'I am not interested in saying') that what is common to all of these is "an interest." That is not true in the (or an) ordinary sense of the word 'interest'; e.g. it does not follow from the fact that one hopes for something that therefore one is interested in that which one hopes for. One may be, but it need not be the case. If a man desperately hopes and prays for a stay of execution, should we say 'He is interested in a stay of execution.'? A man who hopes for a stay of execution could be, or could also be, interested in a stay of execution: but then he would be a queerly calm sort of person.

The fact that by 'interest' oddly enough I mean interest may seem to cast doubt on the adequacy of the hypothesis formulated above, viz. that 'good' has associated with it the condition of answering to certain interests. In particular, the appositeness of 'interests' in connection with an utterance like (85), 'It is good that she is dead.', may be questioned.

For suppose I am passionately concerned in the matter, that I am tormented by the sight of her suffering. It would then be absurd to say that the matter of her death was of interest to me. The matter of her death may be said to be of interest to some relatively dispassionate observer of the scene, but not to me. (Which is not, of course, to say that I am not interested in the matter: the words 'interest', 'interested', and so on simply will not do here.) But all this is, or would be, something of a confusion.

If I am passionately concerned in the matter, it would be odd for me to utter (85). Let it be that she has this moment died: 'Thank God she's dead.', or some such fervent utterance would be in order, not the relatively dispassionate (or, if you like, compassionate) 'It is good that she is dead.'.

221. Further confirmation of the hypothesis above is to be found in what might be called the "feeling" of the word 'good'.

For example, compare 'Her eyes glow.' with 'Her eyes glitter.': 'glow' has a warm feeling to it whereas 'glitter' has a distinctly cold feeling. Such feelings cannot sensibly be said to be somehow part of the meaning of these words, but neither can they be said to be merely associated with the words. They are associated with the words but not merely associated. 'Glow' has a warm feeling to it owing to the meaning of the word. A thing that glows emits light, whereas a thing that glitters reflects light: hot coals glow while cold polished chromium glitters. The feeling of a word is not to be identified with the meaning of the word but it is a remarkably good clue to the meaning of the word.

I take it that 'good' has a relatively dispassionate feeling: a painting that sends me into ecstasy is not one that I would pronounce to be good, neither would I say of it 'That is a good painting.'; e.g. I would not say (86)

(86)   *Guernica* is a good painting.

That would be an understatement. (Whether I am wrong in so maintaining is irrelevant here: given that I feel as I do about *Guernica*, it would be somewhat odd for me to utter (86).) *Guernica* is a superb painting. There are a great many good paintings, but *Guernica* is not one painting among many. Notice that there are a great many adjectives that are available in connection with paintings: 'excellent', 'splendid', 'beautiful', 'handsome', 'lovely', 'elegant', 'exquisite', 'magnificent', 'grand', 'gorgeous'. 'Magnificent', 'grand', 'superb', all make sense in connection with *Guernica:* but it would be odd for me to use 'good' here, and odd for anyone to use 'lovely', 'elegant'.

The fact that 'good' has a relatively dispassionate feeling is further testified to by all sorts of things, e.g. that one can say (87)

(87)   Cucumber sandwiches are good.

Cucumber sandwiches are not ordinarily a matter of passionate concern. Again, it is quite natural to speak of standards in connection with an utterance like (72), 'That is a good painting.'. One might query (72) with 'According to what standards?'. The query may occasion difficulty but the utterance is not odd or deviant. However, if one were to say 'That is an absolutely magnificent painting.', the query 'According to what standards?' would be odd, to say the least.

That 'good' has a relatively dispassionate feeling is owing to the meaning of the word: it is owing to the connection with interests.

222.   It may be said that rather than associate the condition of answering to certain interests with the word 'good' one should associate the condition of answering to certain wants, or needs, or desires, with the word. This would be a mistake: such a hypothesis is not confirmed and indeed is disconfirmed by the evidence already presented.

For example, consider (53), 'That is a good brick.'. If one is laying a brick wall, if one needs a brick, and if one is picking and choosing among a pile of old discarded bricks, one may well utter (53) in reference to a particular brick without oddity or deviation of any sort. Here it may seem as though the utterance (53) could have associated with it the condition of answering to a certain need and that it have this condition associated with it may seem to be attributable to the occurrence of the word 'good' in the utterance. But that is simply not the case. There is no reason to suppose that the utterance does in fact have such a condition associated with it. Thus even though one may not be laying brick at the time and have no need of a brick one may utter (53) by way of pointing out that some of the discarded bricks are perhaps worth preserving in that they are still sufficiently intact to answer to certain interests in connection with bricks.

More generally, if (53) is uttered then either the condition of answering to certain interests is invoked or else the utterance is deviant. But it is not the case that if (53) is uttered then either the condition of answering to a certain need is invoked or else the utterance is deviant. Since the same sort of example can be given in connection with any utterance of the distributive set for 'good' in E and since the same type of example can be given in connection with the conditions of answering to certain wants, or needs, or desires, there is no reason whatsoever to adopt and every reason not to adopt the hypothesis that the word 'good' has associated with it the condition of answering to certain wants, or needs, or desires. (One can of course say trivially that since 'good' has associated with it the condition of answering to certain interests, it has associated with it the condition of answering to certain interests, or wants, or needs, or desires, this being a simple tautology.)

223.   The relation between 'good' and 'approve' is worth considering here for it is an important source of confusion. It has been said that to say (22), 'George is good.', is to say 'I approve of George.'. This must be mistaken. There is nothing odd about (88)

(88)   George is a good father but I don't approve of him.

and neither is there anything odd about (89)

(89)   George is good but I don't approve of him.

Thus (89) might be uttered in a situation in which it is perfectly clear that what is in question is George's ability as a mathematician: George may well be an excellent mathematician even though he is an unsavory person. We approach oddity in (90)

(90)   George is a good person but I don't approve of him.

for this might suggest that one is saying *(91)

*(91)   George is a good person but I don't approve of him as a person.

Utterance *(91) is odd. Just so, even though (88) is not odd, *(92)

*(92)   George is a good father but I don't approve of him as a father.

is odd.

It is important to realize that the oddity of *(91) and *(92) does not suffice to establish that the assertion of (93)

(93)   George is a good father.

commits one to the approval of George as a father. On the contrary, the most that one could hope to infer from the oddity of *(91) and *(92) is that the honest assertion of (93) indicates that it is unlikely that I disapprove of George as a father. Thus if I assert (93), you can then infer, on the basis of the oddity of *(91) and *(92), that it is not likely to be the case that I disapprove of George as a father. But from the fact that it is not likely to be the case that I disapprove of George as a father it certainly does not follow that I approve of George as a father or even that I do not in fact disapprove of George as a father. For consider (94)

(94)   George is said to be a good father, and I suppose it's true; even so, I don't approve of him as a father.

There is, I take it, nothing odd about (94). Furthermore, even though (94) certainly suggests something like (95)

(95)   George is a good father according to ordinary standards but he is not a good father according to my standards.

(94) and (95) are quite different statements. I may be prepared to assert (94) and yet not be prepared to assert (95): I may be dissatisfied with the ordinary standards without having alternative standards of my own. Consequently I may not be prepared to say George is not a good father, and I may even go so far as to admit that he can properly be said to be a good father and yet not approve of him as a father.

Consequently, there so far appears to be no reason to say that the assertion of (93) commits one to the approval of anything at all.

224.   The thesis that there is some intimate relation between 'good' and 'approve' is a peculiarly elusive one, for it is not at all clear what the relation is supposed to be. Is it that if 'good' modifies an element then the speaker is supposed to approve of something associated with that element?

Presumably the thesis is that if one asserts (22), 'George is good.', it is George one is supposed to approve of. But if one asserts (93), 'George is a good father.', one is supposed to approve of George as a father. But what if one says (96)?

(96)   That is a good potato.

Is one supposed to approve of the thing in question as a potato? What if one says (85), 'It is good that she is dead.'? Is one supposed to approve of her being dead? 'I approve of her being dead,' would be a very odd utterance. One might approve of her being put to death, but hardly of her being dead. Again, what if one says (97)?

(97)   That is good news.

Is one supposed to approve of the news? One may, as a censor, approve or disapprove of the news being published, circulated: but to say 'I approve of the news.' would be odd.

225.   The *Shorter Oxford English Dictionary* may appear to support the thesis that there is some intimate relation between 'good' and 'approve'. Under 'approve' it has "5. To pronounce to be good, commend." But the *Dictionary*, like Holy Writ, must be read with care.

'Approve' is a word of Latin derivation that entered English via Old French 'approver'. The latter is from the Latin 'approbare', to approve. 'Approbare' is derived from 'ap' (for 'ad'), to, and 'probare', to test, try the goodness of, prove, esteem as good. The fact that the English word is from Latin via French is important. English words of French derivation tend, quite often, to be restricted in their use to relatively formal matters. Consequently, although one might plausibly construe (93), 'George is a good father.', as 'I approve of George as a father.', it would be wholly implausible to construe (98)

(98)   George is a good fellow.

as 'I approve of George as a fellow.'. This would be a very odd utterance.

I think there can be no doubt that the etymological meaning of 'approve' as to test, to try, is still to be heard in the use of the word and its cognates. We speak of something "meeting with our approval," where the suggestion is that something has been brought to a test. It is, I believe, not unnatural to say 'This strawberry meets with my approval.', but only under rather formal conditions, e.g. one is some sort of judge or inspector. Consequently, if one pronounces something to be good, one can, indeed, in many cases, be said to approve of it as the *Dictionary* listing under 'approve' indicates. Thus if one pronounces (7), 'This is a good strawberry.', one can be said to approve of the strawberry. But pronouncing that something is a good strawberry is not to be confused with saying that it is a good strawberry. A judge pronounces sentences on the accused, but I am not a judge. I can of course take it upon myself to act as a judge, yet I need not do so. If seated at my host's table I say (99)

(99)   This is a very good dish.

I am perhaps expressing my appreciation of the dish: it would be presumptuous and even rude of me to pronounce judgment on the dish. Just so, if I say (100)

(100)   George, you have been a good friend to me.

I am expressing my appreciation of George's friendship: I do not set myself up as a judge of my friend's behavior.

The formality of 'approve' and the fact that it has something to do with putting to a test are, of course, closely related factors, the former probably stemming from the latter. A further derivative factor has to do with the possibility of alteration. Presumably we put something to a test with a view to remedial action. Thus, as has been said, there is something silly in the remark 'I approve of the universe.': what difference could it make? For the same reason, there is something odd about 'I approve of the news.' and 'I approve of her being dead.', for neither the news nor her being dead are in any way subject to alteration. (But imagine that we are in the process of writing a novel: 'I approve of her being dead.', said with respect to a character in the story, would not be odd for we can alter the story as we wish.)

226. The relation between 'good' and 'approve' appears to be as follows: if someone says that something is good in a situation having a relatively formal character owing to the fact that it has something to do with putting that which is in question to a test, and if that which is in question is envisaged as subject to alteration, and if there are no indications to the contrary, the person who utters the utterance can be taken to approve of whatever is in question.

That there should be this relation between 'good' and 'approve' is not at all surprising if my hypothesis about the meaning of 'good' is correct. For if 'good' has to do with answering to certain interests as I contend, then if in a relatively formal situation one judges that a certain thing does answer to these interests, and if one gives no indication that one does not share these interests, it is quite natural to infer that one approves of the thing in question. But how one could seriously maintain that to say 'This is good.' is to say, and means the same as saying, 'I approve of this.' I find difficult to understand.

227. Another serious confusion over the word 'good' is found in the attempt to correlate a use of the word with a particular act.

A great deal of contemporary philosophy has been concerned with the fruitless task of attempting to correlate single words with types of situations, or with episodes, events, occurrences, actions, and so forth, that occur either in the context of utterance or elsewhere in the world. This has resulted in the classification of words as "evaluative," "descriptive," "prescriptive," "performative," etc. All of these classifications are of doubtful value. Words and the world do not connect in any such direct fashion.

(My remarks here are not intended to apply to such syntactic classifications as Ryle's "achievement" and "task" verbs.[3] This classification is of some interest and is more or less tenable. It is, however, simply an approximation to the verb aspects of Slavic grammar: such aspects as momentaneous, durative, continuative, inceptive, cessative, iterative, resultative, durative-inceptive.)

[3] See his *Concept of Mind.*

228.   It may be supposed that there is a correlation between the
uttering of the word 'good' and a performance of the act of commending. Just so, it may be supposed that there is a correlation
between the uttering of the word 'red' and a performance of the
act of describing. Thus it has been said that 'good' is a "term
of commendation," that 'red' is a "descriptive term" and I suppose that this is a way of saying that there is a significant correlation between the uttering of 'good' and the act of commending, between the uttering of 'red' and the act of describing. But
such correlations are not in fact to be found.

If one asks (101)

(101)   Is that a good red pigment?

one is uttering the words 'red' and 'good' yet one is neither
commending nor describing: on the contrary, one is performing
the act of asking a question. Consequently to say that whenever
one utters the word 'good' one is performing the act of commending would be to say something obviously false. Possibly
what is intended is this: if one utters the word 'good' in an utterance of English then generally (though not invariably) one
is performing the act of commending. This could be true but I
can see not the slightest reason to suppose that it is true and I
am quite certain that it is not true.

229.   There are some few expressions of English that do connect with the world in just this way. An expression like 'Tsk, tsk.'
does in fact connect with the acts of expressing either disapproval or sympathy. If someone utters the utterance 'Tsk, tsk.'
then generally (though not invariably) he is expressing either
disapproval or sympathy. Again, the phrase 'go to hell' has a
fairly high correlation with the act of speaking profanely. Even
here, however, the correlation is far from perfect: if one says 'An
evil man will go to hell.' one is not speaking profanely. The
correlation improves if we shift from 'go to hell' to 'go to
hell.' and it is well nigh perfect if we shift to 'You can go to
hell!'

Generally speaking, the utility of a word or phrase varies in-

versely with the strength of its correlation with a particular
social situation, action, event, and so forth; e.g. compare the
utility of 'good' with that of 'commendable', that of 'the' with
'go to hell'.

Generally speaking, it is evidently easier to correlate long
elements, or a sequence of short elements, of English with a
particular type of situation than it is to correlate short elements
of English directly with a particular type of situation. Thus such
correlations can be found with virtually all syntactically nondeviant whole utterances of English.

230.   But 'good' or almost any other word is a good example
of a word that cannot be dealt with as simply as the expression
'tsk tsk'. And one can see this simply by considering the various
utterances of its distributive set in E. If one were to say (102)

(102)   His account of 'good' is not good enough.

one would not be performing the act of commending: if anything one would be disparaging his view. Here one may be
tempted to patch up the view by saying that 'good' is connected
not simply with the act of commending but with the acts of
commending or discommending. This won't help.

Is it a good thing to patch up a bad theory that is better
scrapped? I have just used the word 'good' yet I have performed
neither the act of commending nor the act of discommending: I
did perform the act of asking a rhetorical question. Again, if
one says (103)

(103)   Be sure to do a good job!

one has not performed the act of commending or discommending: rather one performed the act of, say, urging. All this indicates that if there is a connection between the uttering of
'good' in English and the acts of commending or discommending possibly it is to be found only in connection with utterances
in declarative form.

But when we consider declarative utterances things are no
simpler than before. If one says (97), 'That is good news.', is one
commending the news? Or what if one says (104)?

(104)   No news is good news.

Or suppose on hearing that a sufferer from an incurable and painful cancer has died one says (85), 'It is good that she is dead.': is one commending anything? Or what of (105–110)?

(105)   We shall have good weather tomorrow.

(106)   I want a good cup of coffee.

(107)   I had a good time.

(108)   George has a good opinion of himself.

(109)   The good seats are all reserved.

(110)   A good tennis racket unfortunately costs twenty dollars.

What is one commending when one utters such utterances as these?

231.   Since the *Shorter Oxford English Dictionary* has lent its authority to the view that there is some important connection between the uttering of the word 'good' and the act of commending by saying that 'good' is "the most general adjective of commendation," it is perhaps worth while to note that the *Dictionary* can be shown to be in error on the basis of its own account of 'commendation'.

The only relevant listing under 'commendation' is "1. The action of commending." Under 'commend' there are only two relevant listings: "2. To present as worthy of acceptance or regard; to direct attention to as worthy of notice; to recommend. 3. *gen.* To praise."

If in discussing wines with a connoiseur of wines one says (111)

(111)   *Le Montrachet* is a good white wine.

one could be said to be commending this white Burgundy wine. One could be said to be directing his attention to it as worthy of notice. One could also be said to be praising the wine. But if one says to him (105), 'We shall have good weather tomorrow.', one could hardly be said to be directing his attention to the weather

as worthy of notice, nor could one reasonably be said to be praising the weather. (Note that even 'We shall have commendable
weather tomorrow.' would be somewhat absurd.)

'Commend' is a word of Latin derivation; it is from 'com'
('cum'), together, and 'mandare', to put into the hands of,
entrust to, command. Thus it connects, etymologically, with
'mandate'. The etymological meaning of 'commend' is preserved
in the current use of the word: the first listing in the *Dictionary*
is "1. To give in trust or charge: to commit." 'Commande' in
English originally had the sense of both 'commend' and 'command'. But in the course of the fourteenth century the form
'commend' was taken from the Latin 'commendare' in the original Latin sense and 'commande' in this sense gradually went
out of use. However, the etymological connection with 'command' and 'mandate' is still to be heard in the word: directing
attention has some connection with issuing a directive. It is not
altogether implausible to suppose one to be issuing a directive
to the connoiseur of wines directing him to attend to the white
wine of Burgundy as worthy of notice: it is ridiculous to suppose
one to be issuing a directive about the weather.

The word 'commend' is not worth bothering with here. (It
has little use and I daresay will soon disappear from the language.) What is interesting here, however, is the nature of the
mistake involved in saying that 'good' is a term of "commendation." It is not that the *Dictionary* has hit upon the wrong word:
there is no right word here.

232. Consider (68), 'That is good.'. Assume, what is not the
case, that generally when one utters this utterance one is commending something or someone, that such an utterance regularly
occurs only in a situation in which the speaker is performing the
act of commending. Even so: what has this to do with the word
'good'? (See 44 above.)

The utterance of the word 'good' is not necessary for the performance of the act of commending, e.g. one says 'That is fine.',
'That is splendid.', 'That is commendable.'. But neither is it
sufficient, e.g. one asks (112)

(112)   Is that good?

or one says (108), 'George has a good opinion of himself.'.

Even if we assume that 'That is good.' is generally uttered only in a situation in which the act of commending is being performed, why attribute that to the word 'good'? The word 'that' clearly has something to do with the fact that in uttering the utterance 'That is good.' the speaker may be performing the act of commending. If we were to substitute 'what' for 'that' in 'That is good.' the resultant utterance, viz. (113)

(113)   What is good.

would not connect with the act of commending: why not say that 'that' is a "term of commendation"?

The confusion here is the same as that exemplified in a remark of the form 'The word 'tiger' refers to such-and-such an animal.'. If one says 'The tiger is in the field.', not the word 'tiger' but the phrase 'the tiger' refers to the tiger in the field. To say that in saying 'That is good.' it is the word 'good' that, as it were, does the commending, or that in saying 'The tiger is in the field.' it is the word 'tiger' that refers, is to make the following mistake.

Consider a man looking at a pointillist painting: he sees a green expanse in the painting but this green expanse is in fact constituted of large blue and small yellow bits of pigment placed alongside one another. To say that 'good' is the word that, as it were, does the commending, or that 'tiger' is the word that refers, is like pointing out the blue bits of pigment in the painting and saying that they are what make the painting green.

233.   The hypothesis under consideration is this: that 'good' has associated with it the condition of answering to certain interests, which interests are in question being indicated either by the element modifying or the element modified by 'good' or by certain features of the context of utterance. An obvious question here is this: whose interests are in question? (But I am not going to try to answer it right away.)

One traditional sort of answer to this question is: no one's.

Thus it has been said that to say (72), 'That is a good painting.', is to attribute to the painting a certain characteristic, or a certain "property," or a certain "nonnatural property," or a certain "quality." That this is a confusion has already been established here: it is not possible on such hypotheses to account for the distribution of 'good' in *E*, to account for the odd sound of (39–48), (59), to account for the fact that 'good' is a high-ranking adjective, and so on. But the confusion is worth considering: it is not a total confusion, it embodies an important insight.

The *prima facie* implausibility of an analysis of (72) as 'I approve of that painting.' (or 'I approve of that as a painting.'?) is owing to the fact that, unlike 'I approve of that painting.', (72) has the form of an impersonal remark. In saying (72) one is presumably talking about the painting, whereas in saying 'I approve of that painting.' one is clearly telling someone something about oneself. Furthermore, the impersonal aspect of (72) can be stressed. Thus one says (114)

(114)   That is a good painting but I don't like it.

Again, there is nothing odd or even deviant about (115–116)

(115)   That is a good potato but I detest potatoes.

(116)   That is a good screwdriver but I have no interest in screwdrivers.

There is in general no reason at all to suppose that interests or the interests of the speaker must be in question. If I say (117)

(117)   George had a good nap.

it is ludicrous to suppose that George's nap must somehow have answered to certain of my interests: whether George naps or not need make no difference to me. What sort of nap he had need not interest me at all. Yet if you want to know and I know, I may tell you by uttering (117).

But the impersonal character of an utterance like (72), 'That is a good painting.', can easily be and traditionally has been both exaggerated and misunderstood. I don't say it is easy to understand. It isn't.

234.   If someone wanted to show, what is not the case, that an utterance of the form 'That is a good such-and-such.' is analyzable simply as 'I like that such-an-such.', the best case to consider would be one in which it was difficult for the speaker to point out any facts about the such-and-such in virtue of which it does answer to the relevant interests, in virtue of which it is a good such-and-such. Thus if a man knows nothing about roses and he says (118)

(118)   That rose over there, the one with two colors, is a good one.

the inference that he rather likes the rose is fairly safe. To say (119)

(119)   The Condessa de Sastago is a very good hybrid tea rose.

is in a standard sort of case to make an impersonal remark. But it is not always easy to leave one's self out of the picture. The man who knows nothing about roses and yet says (118) is in a difficult position. One could look at the case in the following way: he wants to talk impersonally, to keep himself out of the picture, to say something about the rose; but since he knows nothing about roses, he can find no fact about the rose to take hold of to lift himself out of himself. Consequently he lifts himself by his own bootstraps.

One wants to leave one's self out of the picture in saying (72), (119), but this is not to say that one wants to leave out all questions of interests. If on the basis of various facts about a painting I say (72) even though I dislike the painting, I am not simply leaving myself out of the picture: here, instead of lifting myself out of myself, I let myself be pulled out of myself by the pull of standards that I am foolish enough or agreeable enough or indifferent enough to give way to.

That not all question of interests can be left out in saying (72) can be seen in two ways. First, even though one can say (114), 'That is a good painting but I don't like it.', one can hardly say (120)

(120)   That is a good painting and I don't like it.

apart from a fairly special context, e.g. one in which someone has been telling me that I do in fact like all good paintings. The use of the word 'but' in (120) indicates that what follows is relevant though not essential to what preceded. Secondly, runaway standards can always be controlled: (121)

(121)   It is true enough that the painting meets those standards but is it good?

is often a sensible question. If it were not, it would be necessary to make it so. But this is true of many adjectives: 'It is true enough that it weighs fifty pounds but is it heavy?', 'It is true enough that it looks red to an ordinary person under white light but is it red?'—this is what Moore's "open question" comes to, and in a sense it makes sense.

'Good' has associated with it the condition of answering to certain interests but saying that something is good is not the same as saying that it has certain characteristics even if it is in virtue of these characteristics that it does in fact answer to the relevant interests. If we weld something's being good to its having certain characteristics, certain specific characteristics in each case, then the word 'good' is likely to be replaced by something like 'Grade A' or 'Premium grade'. But if we like, we can always use Moore's lever to prise it loose.

235.   Ordinarily, to say (72), 'That is a good painting.', or to say (122)

(122)   It is good to lie on a hot sandy beach and bask in the sun.

is to make an impersonal remark. In the latter case it is to say that lying on a hot sandy beach and basking in the sun answers to certain interests, e.g. an interest in being fit, sun tanned, and the like. These interests are interests that one has. They are not necessarily interests of the speaker or of the hearer. It is necessary only that someone have the interests in question. For though one can say (123)

(123)   That would be a good gila monster to make a pet of if
anyone were interested in making a pet of a gila
monster.

referring, say, to a particularly fine specimen, in so saying one
is not saying that the gila monster in question is a good one to
make a pet of but saying that it would be a good one on the condition that someone had the relevant interests. (Notice that (123)
would be utterly incomprehensible on the hypothesis that 'good'
has associated with it some "property" or "quality": for how
could my becoming interested in making a pet of a gila monster
result in a gila monster's having the "property of being good"?)

On the hypothesis under consideration, 'good' has associated
with it the condition of answering to certain interests, which
interests are in question being indicated either by the element
modifying or the element modified by 'good' or by certain
features of the context of utterance. The interests in question
are the interests one has. The answer to the question 'Whose
interests?' is this: whichever one has the interests in question.
Thus the question is essentially irrelevant. The relevant question is whether what is in question does or does not answer to
the indicated interests.

But all this undergoes a sea change when one turns to certain
utterances that have traditionally been of interest to philosophers.

236.   Consider the following utterances:

(124)   A charitable deed is something that is intrinsically
good.

(125)   An act of destruction is something that is intrinsically
good.

(126)   Lying on a hot sandy beach and basking in the sun is
something good in itself.

(127)   Drinking a heavy port while eating oysters on the half-
shell is a good thing in itself.

(128)   Sitting atop a flag pole is a good thing in itself.

It is sometimes said that 'good' has an "instrinic and an extrinsic sense" and thus has an "intrinsic sense" in (124–128). That is simply a silly view: one might just as well say that 'house' has a "red sense" for we sometimes speak of "a red house." In (124–128) 'good' is explicitly modified (in what we shall see to be a curious way) by the word 'intrinsically' or by the phrase 'in itself'. But such a modification may be implicit in a context of utterance.

The important point here is this: (124–128) and related utterances (types or tokens) are all deviant.

237.   Consider utterances (23), 'It is good that it is raining.', (85), 'It is good that she is dead.', and (72), 'That is a good painting.': in cases in which such utterances are uttered without deviation it is generally possible to query them with (129)

   (129)   What is good about that?

There is not likely to be anything odd about (129), neither is the query apt to occasion any difficulty in connection with (23) or (85) though (72) may prove more troublesome. More generally, the query (129) or some variant thereof is generally though not invariably appropriate in connection with declarative utterances of the distributive set for 'good' in E. (Note that (129) or variants thereof would be somewhat odd in connection with (108), 'George has a good opinion of himself.'.) That it is possible to query utterances like (23), (85), (72), with (129) (or some variant thereof) is of course to be expected on the hypothesis about the meaning of 'good' under consideration. For if 'good' has associated with it the condition of answering to certain interests then, in cases in which something is said to be good, it should be possible to ask what there is about whatever is in question in virtue of which it does in fact answer to the relevant interests.

It is possible, however, to introduce a fairly simple (-minded) variation on the theme of answering to the relevant interests. In a relatively straightforward utterance of the distributive set for 'good' in E, say (72), 'That is a good painting.', the element modified by 'good', viz. 'a painting', serves to characterize the referent of 'that' and in so doing indicates the relevant interests. Suppose, however, that 'good' is modified in such a way that an element modified by 'good' in an utterance serves to indicate the relevant interest by characterizing something that constitutes the satisfaction of that interest: one would then have an utterance concerned with what philosophers have spoken of as something "intrinsically good."

Consider (124), 'A charitable deed is something that is intrinsically good.', and (130)

(130)   It is good to be charitable.

Ordinarily if someone utters (130) one can query it with (129), 'What is good about that?'. But such a query is apt to be frowned upon by morally minded men. So I am inclined to suppose that morally minded men must have invented the following ploy, a way of blocking the question 'What is good about that?'. Suppose that on a particular occasion, thus in connection with a particular token of the type (130), the relevant interest in connection with (130) is supposed to be an interest in being charitable. If so, the element modified by 'good' in (130) serves to indicate the relevant interest by characterizing something that constitutes the satisfaction of that interest. Consequently a query like (129) becomes inappropriate. Thus a morally minded man might argue as follows: "I say (130), 'It is good to be charitable.', (or (125)?) by way of specifying something that is intrinsically good. Consequently I can point out no fact about it in virtue of which it is something good. For it itself is what I take to be good, not something about it. Being charitable answers to the relevant interest and cannot fail to do so in that it itself constitutes the satisfaction of that interest, viz. an interest in being charitable."

So if one is to query (130) in such a case, or (124–128) in any case, one cannot do so by asking what is good about it or by asking whether or not it does in fact answer to the relevant interest. And so one is led to the question, not 'Does it answer to the relevant interest?', but rather 'Whose interest does it answer to?' and with such a question the impersonal aspect of these utterances is called into question. There is nothing else relevant that can be questioned. This is one reason for supposing that such utterances must be somewhat deviant.

238.   A striking fact about the use of the word 'good' in English is that whether or not something is good can be and frequently is a matter of controversy and dispute in a way that whether or not something is yellow is not. An analysis of 'good' that failed to account for and to explicate this fact would to that extent be inadequate and unilluminating. The adequacy of the present hypothesis receives confirmation from the fact that it points to (at least) two fundamentally different types of difficulty each of which can give rise to disputes over whether or not something is good. The first is a difficulty over the interests in question; the second is a difficulty over the facts about whatever is in question.

239.   One easy explanation of some disputes over whether or not something is good can be found in the lack of a specification of the relevant interests.

Suppose someone says (131)

(131)   That is a good apple.

referring to a particular apple. Suppose the apple is extremely tart. I may be inclined to deny (131). In such a case, a simple explanation of the dispute might be that the person who said (131) was in fact maintaining an equivalent of (132)

(132)   That is a good baking apple.

whereas I took him to be maintaining an equivalent of (133)

(133)   That is a good eating apple.

Thus a dispute over (131) might be owing simply to the fact that the relevant interests were insufficiently specified: the element modified by 'good' in (131), viz, 'an apple', failed in the context of utterance to indicate unambiguously what interests were in question. An apple can answer to many different and diverse interests. Relative to certain interests, the apple may be held to be a very good apple indeed; relative to certain other interests, the apple may be held to be not good at all.

The resolution of such simple disputes is a simple matter. Instead of uttering (131) one can be more specific and utter (132) or (133). There are, in fact, two distinct ways of more clearly specifying the relevant interests: first, one can modify the element modified by 'good', as in (132) or (133), or as in (2), (9), (15), (16), (18); secondly, one can directly modify 'good' as in (4), (5), (74), (80–84).

A dispute over whether or not something is a good apple is not likely to be particularly interesting in so far as it is attributable to the lack of specification of the relevant interests. For it is easy enough in such cases to indicate what interests are or are not relevant. One can be as specific as one likes. Thus (134–138):

(134)   That is a good apple to dress a goose with.

(135)   That is a good apple for garnishing a roast.

(136)   That is a good taffy apple.

(137)   That is a good apple to photograph.

(138)   That is a good apple to grow.

240.   More interesting disputes may arise in cases in which there is a greater difficulty not in indicating the relevant interests but in appreciating what has been indicated. Thus instead of uttering (72), 'That is a good painting.', in a given context one might utter (139–148)

(139)   That is a good landscape.

(140)   That is a good oil painting.

(141)   That is a good watercolor.

(142)   That is a good cubistic painting.

(143)   That is a good Venetian painting.

(144)   That is a good genre painting.

(145)   That is a good Rembrandt.

(146)   That is a good mural.

(147)   That is a good painting for your study.

(148)   That is a good painting to study.

If someone cannot see the difference between a Venetian and a Florentine painting then of course (143) may give rise to foolish disputes. But even if one can see such a difference, if one fails to appreciate the difference or fails to appreciate the fact that the difference is indicative of and perhaps a function of a difference in interests, that Venetian and Florentine paintings do not answer to the same interests, then a dispute may arise. For example, if I say (149)

(149)   Tintoretto's *Miracle of the Loaves and Fishes* is a very good painting indeed.

someone may complain about the lack of carefully articulated contours in the work. But if one is interested in articulated contours then it is simply silly to look to the Venetians for them. (Titian is not Botticelli: Botticelli is not Titian.)[4]

241. The second fundamental type of difficulty that can give rise to disputes concerns the facts about whatever is in question. An easy explanation of some relatively uninteresting disputes over whether or not something is good can be found in the specification of the facts about what is in question in virtue of which it does or does not answer to the relevant interests.

If I say (7), 'This is a good strawberry.', and you deny it, it may be that we agree about the relevant interests, e.g. for eating as a dessert after a meal, or eating with a glass of wine, and we both agree that in order to answer to these interests the strawberry must be sweet. But I may believe that the strawberry is sweet whereas you may think it isn't. Thus a dispute over whether or not something is good may be owing to a simple disagreement over what are or are not the facts about the matter.

[4] See my "Reasons in Art Criticism," *Philosophy and Education,* pp. 219–236.

242.   Ignorance of the facts can cause difficulty but a failure to appreciate the facts is likely to be a more serious matter.

The word 'good' is sometimes said to be an "evaluative term" or a "term of evaluation." It isn't. But the suggestion is interesting. 'Evaluate' cannot be taken seriously in connection with 'good': this is indicated by such utterances as (99), (105), (97), and it is also indicated by the word 'evaluate' itself. The only relevant listing under 'evaluate' in the *Shorter Oxford English Dictionary* is "b. *gen.* To reckon up, ascertain the amount of; to express in terms of the known." The *Dictionary* account is somewhat obscure. 'Evaluate' is from the French 'évaluer'; the English word has a use rather like that of the French word. As the structure of the word suggests, 'évaluer' has to do with the notion of drawing or extracting the value from something; thus 'évaluer' connects with 'apprécier', 'fixer la valeur', 'estimer'; thus one can say 'évaluer la valeur d'un terrain'. Similarly, in English 'evaluate' has to do with the notion of drawing or extracting the value from something, but not of course in the sense of deriving value from it: 'evaluate' connects with 'appreciate', but in that sense of 'appreciate' that has to do with sizing up (undoubtedly the primary sense of that interesting word), e.g. 'appreciate the facts', 'an appreciation of the Battle of Jutland'. 'Evaluate' also connects with 'determining the value', 'estimating'.

The relevant and important word here is not 'evaluate' but 'appreciate'. If two military officers are disputing over the claim (150)

(150)   That is a good plan of attack.

the dispute may be but is not likely to be attributable to an insufficient specification of the relevant interests. Neither is it likely to be attributable to a dispute over what are or are not the facts about the matter. For each officer may base his claim on precisely the same data. The difference is likely to be attributable to a difference in their appreciation of the facts. To take a very simple example, if a friend of George hears George say 'That is an interesting theory.', he may infer that henceforth

George will pay no attention whatever to the theory. Someone else might arrive at an opposite conclusion. But if so, he would have failed to appreciate the situation. Knowing the facts about the matter, e.g. knowing that George said 'That is an interesting theory.', that he said it in a serious tone, and so forth is one thing: appreciating these facts is quite another. An interesting dispute over (72), 'That is a good painting.', is likely to be attributable to a failure of or anyway a problem in appreciation. The man who doesn't see what is good about a Fouquet may see what another sees but he may not appreciate what he sees. (Art appreciation is a matter of appreciation, though few aestheticians seem to realize it.)

243.   There are ways of dealing with, of resolving, the various kinds of disputes so far noted. These are indicated by the hypothesis about the meaning of 'good' under consideration.

First, there may be a misapprehension of some sort either about the relevant interests or about the facts of the matter. Thus a dispute may occur owing to what is essentially an ambiguity. Such a dispute can be resolved by eliminating the ambiguity. Or the dispute may arise owing to a difference of opinion about the facts. The resolution of such a dispute clearly calls for some sort of factual discussion, or investigation, or the like. If the person is laboring under a misapprehension about the facts, it is necessary to remove that misapprehension. This may be a simple matter of providing him with information, evidence, and so forth or it may be necessary to re-educate or even educate the person. If he is incorrigibly stupid, it may be impossible to resolve the dispute to the satisfaction of both parties.

Secondly, a dispute may arise owing to a failure of or a problem in appreciation. If the person fails to appreciate the interests involved, the situation, the painting, the characteristics of the object, or whatever is in question, the dispute cannot be resolved in any simple way. Education of some sort is most likely called for; e.g. if he fails to appreciate what is essentially a strategical situation, a course in logistics may be called for; if he fails to appreciate certain facts about a contract, a lesson in law may be desirable. Presumably so-called "juvenile delinquents" fail to appreciate and possibly are incapable of appreciating the facts of essentially moral situations; in such cases some sort of moral education or moral training is called for.

A difference between disputes of the second and disputes of the first type is this: if George and Josef are disputing whether or not something is good and their dispute is of the first type then I am inclined to say that one or both of them may be right or that one or both of them may be wrong. (Both may be wrong in the following sort of case: George says of a certain apple that it is a good apple, meaning that it is a good cooking apple; Josef says it isn't, meaning that it isn't a good eating apple. Suppose it is in fact a good eating apple but not a good cooking apple. Then both are wrong.) Whether one or both are right or wrong, in this sort of case I am inclined to say that there is in fact a right or wrong about the matter. I am also somewhat inclined to say this if George and Josef are disputing whether or not something is good and their dispute is of the second type. But I am then less strongly inclined to say it. To speak of right and wrong somehow seems less appropriate in connection with matters of appreciation. And when one turns to deviant utterances concerned with what is "intrinsically good" all talk of who is right and who is wrong is wholly out of place, which is another reason why such utterances are deviant.

244.   Consider an utterance token of the type (151)

(151)   It is good to destroy one's fellow man.

or an utterance of the type (125), 'An act of destruction is something that is intrinsically good.', or of the type (152)

(152)   Destroying one's fellow man is in itself something good.

Let it be that in uttering (151) the speaker is concerned only to specify something that is "intrinsically good," thus the modification of 'good' by 'in itself', or by 'intrinsically', is implicit in the context of utterance; thus in that context the speaker would accept (152) or perhaps even (125) as an equivalent or virtual equivalent of (151). Obviously (151) can serve and (125) and (152) do serve to express a monstrous view, one that can only appall any sane and civilized man. Thus I am not inclined to utter (153)

(153)   It is not good to destroy one's fellow man.

for (153) is somewhat absurd: it is not a question of whether destroying one's fellow man does or does not answer to certain interests. This is not a matter of interests but of something monstrous. Thus I am rather inclined to utter (154)

(154)   It is monstrous to hold that it is good to destroy one's
        fellow man.

As far as I am concerned, someone who held a view expressed by (125), (151), or (152) would be something of a monster, for the view is monstrous. But this is not to say that it is mistaken, or in error, or incorrect, or the like. One can rightly say that the view is monstrous, evil, but not that it is mistaken. What mistake is being made?

Again, consider the following sort of case. I say (155)

(155)   This is a good wine.

and someone denies it. It may be that we agree or anyway seem to agree about the relevant interests, e.g. for drinking while eating some blue-point oysters on the half shell. Thus instead of (155) I might say (156)

(156)   This is a good wine to drink with oysters on the half
        shell.

We may both agree that the wine in question is relatively dry, e.g. a light dry sauterne. But he may maintain that in order to be a good wine to drink while eating oysters on the half shell the wine must be quite sweet, e.g. a port, whereas I maintain that in such a case it must be relatively dry.

Here the dispute is over whether the fact that the wine is relatively dry indicates that it does or does not answer to the relevant interests. But there are obviously at least three different views that might be held: first, that the fact that it is relatively dry indicates that it does answer to the relevant interest; secondly, that that fact is simply irrelevant and indicates nothing at all; and thirdly, that that fact indicates that it does not answer to the relevant interests.

If someone denies my claim that a light dry sauterne is a good wine to drink while eating oysters on the half shell and insists that in such a case a heavy port is good, the difference between us can be said to be a matter of taste, for we quite obviously have different tastes in the matter. As far as I am concerned, he has no taste. (He of course may say the same of me.) But this is not to say that he would be mistaken in saying (155) or (156) in reference to a heavy port.

245. Disputes of the type in question, over the "intrinsically good," are essentially rooted in a difference in persons, a difference of sensibility, of interests. For an informed difference of opinion over the relevance of certain facts here simply reflects a difference of sensibility or of interests.

Instead of saying (155) or (156) in reference to a heavy port, the person might say (157)

(157)   A heavy port is a good wine to drink with oysters on the half shell.

I say it isn't. He says it is. So he tries it and says 'Just as I thought: a heavy port is just the thing with oysters.'. I point out to him that this may kill his taste in other matters. He replies that that may be so but says (127), 'Drinking a heavy port while eating oysters on the half shell is a good thing in itself.'. I try it and find it loathesome. Again, someone says (126), 'Lying on a hot sandy beach and basking in the sun is something good in itself.'. I point out to him that doing so may be conducive to skin cancer. He replies that he did not mean to say that it was "extrinsically good." He meant to say and did say that it was something good in itself, "intrinsically good." And he argues: 'Perhaps you don't find it so. I do.'.

Disputes over (126–128) are likely to differ from disputes over (124–125) in only one respect: the latter are important, the

former are not. Important or not, there is no resolution of disputes over the "intrinsically good." But there are ways of putting
an end to them, e.g. rubber truncheons, actual or socialized, the
critic's sneer, education, moral training, and the like—all the
pressures that can be brought to bear on individuals to put an
end to their individuality when as often happens it becomes intolerable. And one way of putting pressure on the person one is
disputing with is to insist in no uncertain terms and tones that
he is "mistaken," a familiar misuse of 'mistaken'. One can put
an end to such disputes. But not everything that puts an end
to a question counts as an answer.

246.   The main hypothesis that has been under consideration
is this: that 'good' has associated with it the condition of answering to certain interests. I take it that the hypothesis has been
well confirmed by the evidence presented. I conclude that apart
from certain minor, derivative, or deviant cases, 'good' in
English means answering to certain interests.

As evidence in support of this contention one can offer utterances (1–157). The adequacy of the analysis is manifested in the
fact that on the basis of the analysis it is possible to account for,
to explain, the distribution of 'good' in *E*.

As against this contention one can cite such utterances as
(158–160)

(158)   It is a good two miles off.

(159)   He played a good hour on the cello.

(160)   He's looking pretty good in there today.

One has to strain a bit, I would not deny it, to make the analysis
fit. But that doesn't matter. That the analysis will not easily fit
this or that case, what does that prove? For it does fit the other
cases cited and so one can always construe the cases that don't
fit as special cases. Only one thing will upset the analysis presented here: a better one.

There are variations on the theme, but this is what 'good'
means: answering to certain interests.

BIBLIOGRAPHY

(OF WORKS REFERRED TO)

Aquinas, T. *Summa Theologica*. London: Washbourne, 1911–1922.
Bentham, J. *Works*. London: Simkin, Marshall & Co., 1843.
Bloomfield, L. *Language*. New York: Henry Holt and Co., 1933.
Chao, Y. R. "The Non-Uniqueness of Phonemic Solutions of Pho-
netic Systems," *Bulletin of the Institute of History and Philology*
(Shangai: Academia Sinica, 1934), IV, 363–397.
Chomsky, N. *Syntactic Structures*. 's Gravenhage: Mouton & Co.,
1957.
——, with M. Halle and F. Lukoff. "On Accent and Juncture in
English," in *For Roman Jakobson* ('s Gravenhage: Mouton & Co.,
1956), pp. 65–80.
Frege, G. *Die Grundlagen der Arithmetik*. Breslau: W. Koebner,
1884.
Fries, C. C. *The Structure of English*. New York: Harcourt, Brace
and Co., 1952.
Harris, Z. "Distributional Structure," in A. Martinet and U. Wein-
reich (eds.), *Linguistics Today* (New York: Linguistic Circle of
New York, 1954), pp. 26–42.
——. *Methods in Structural Linguistics*. Chicago: University of
Chicago Press, 1951.
Hockett, C. F. *A Course in Modern Linguistics*. New York: Mac-
millan Co., 1958.
Jakobson, R. "Two Aspects of Language and Two Types of Aphasic
Disturbance," pt. II of R. Jakobson and M. Halle, *Fundamentals
of Language* ('s Gravenhage: Mouton & Co., 1956).

Kittredge, G. L., and F. E. Farley. *An Advanced English Grammar.* New York: Ginn and Co., 1913.

Leopold, W. F. *Speech Development of a Bilingual Child.* Evanston: Northwestern University Press, 1947.

Masserman, J. H. *Principles of Dynamic Psychiatry.* London: W. B. Saunders Co., 1946.

Nida, E. A. *Morphology.* 2d ed.; Ann Arbor: University of Michigan Press, 1949.

Pike, K. L. *The Intonation of American English.* Ann Arbor: University of Michigan Press, 1945.

Ryle, G. *The Concept of Mind.* London: Hutchinson University Library, 1949.

de Saussure, F. *Cours de linguistique générale.* 2d ed.; Paris: Payot, 1949.

Strawson, P. F. "Truth," *Analysis,* IX (1949), 83–97.

Weinreich, U. "Is a Structural Dialectology Possible?" in A. Martinet and U. Weinreich (eds.), *Linguistics Today* (New York: Linguistic Circle of New York, 1954), pp. 268–280.

Wells, R. "The Pitch Phonemes of English," *Language,* XXI (1945), 27–39.

Wittgenstein, L. *Philosophical Investigations.* Oxford: Basil Blackwell, 1953.

——. *Tractatus Logico-Philosophicus.* New York: Harcourt, Brace and Co., and London: Kegan Paul, 1922.

Ziff, P. "Reasons in Art Criticism," in I. Scheffler (ed.), *Philosophy and Education* (Boston: Allyn and Bacon, Inc., 1958), pp. 219–236.

Index of Names and Subjects

(Reference is to page numbers)

251

Index of Special Signs and Symbols